ETHICAL CONSUMPTION

ETHICAL CONSUMPTION

Social Value and Economic Practice

Edited by
James G. Carrier and **Peter G. Luetchford**

berghahn
NEW YORK • OXFORD
www.berghahnbooks.com

Published in 2012 by

Berghahn Books

www.berghahnbooks.com

Library of Congress Cataloging-in-Publication Data

Ethical consumption : social value and economic practice / edited by James G.
   Carrier and Peter G. Luetchford.
      p. cm. Includes bibliographical references and index.
ISBN 978-0-85745-342-6 (hardback) – ISBN 978-1-78238-676-6 (paperback) –
ISBN 978-0-85745-343-3 (ebook)
   1. Consumption (Economics)--Moral and ethical aspects. 2. Social values.
   3. Social ethics.
   I. Carrier, James G. II. Luetchford, Peter G.
   HB835.E843 2012
   174'.4--dc23   2011039295

British Library Cataloguing in Publication Data

A catalogue record for this book is available from
the British Library.

Printed on acid-free paper

ISBN: 978-0-85745-342-6 hardback
ISBN: 978-1-78238-676-6 paperback
ISBN: 978-0-85745-343-4 ebook

CONTENTS

PREFACE

The origins of this collection lie in a workshop held at the University of Sussex in April 2007, 'Hidden hands in the market', organised by Geert De Neve, Jeff Pratt and Peter G. Luetchford (see De Neve *et al.* 2008). The topics of the fifteen papers presented there varied widely, but many of those present were concerned with ethical consumption in one or another form. Certainly this was true of the two of us: Carrier was concerned with the logical nature of ethical consumption and Luetchford was concerned with the practices and images of ethical coffee production.

We were sufficiently intrigued by ethical consumption that we took the opportunity of the 2008 meeting of the European Association of Social Anthropologists, held in Ljubljana, to put together a panel on the topic. To our surprise and delight, after the panel was over the members, joined by some from the audience, ended up talking at sidewalk cafes and restaurants in a warm and sunny city for two days, trying to figure out what we had and what sort of approach might encompass it all. The result is the Introduction and the papers in this volume.

This volume reflects another history as well, the intellectual history of the two of us. For James Carrier, that history is a long concern with the nature of economic values, relations and institutions, especially as they exist in Western societies. For Peter Luetchford, the long concern has been with agriculturalists, particularly in an area in north-west Costa Rica where people grow coffee that is certified Fairtrade. These two concerns complemented each other in a way that is particularly pertinent for this volume, for Carrier was concerned with life at the receiving end of ethical consumption, while Luetchford was concerned with life at the producing end. Both of those concerns are reflected in the thinking that underlies this volume.

More than many collections of papers, this one is a collaborative effort. During those two days of talk by the river in Ljubljana, trying to make sense of what we had, we informed and encouraged each other, and focused each other's thinking. Unfortunately, Deborah Gewertz and Fred Errington, who were involved with the panel, were unable to contribute to the volume because of the press of other commitments. While this volume is poorer by their absence, it is richer for their participation in that talk. The volume is richer as well for the participation of Richard Wilk, who was not in the panel but agreed to contribute to the Conclusion.

James G. Carrier and
Peter G. Luetchford
January 2011

Bibiliography

De Neve, Geert, Peter G. Luetchford, Jeff Pratt and Donald C. Wood (eds) 2008. *Hidden hands in the market: ethnographies of fair trade, ethical consumption and corporate social responsibility. Research in Economic Anthropology* 28 (special issue).

INTRODUCTION

James G. Carrier

Ethical consumption has attracted increasing attention in Europe and North America over the past few years. As it has become more popular, the label has been applied to more and more different things, which makes it important to identify what it means. The words themselves are an obvious place to start. They indicate that it means taking into account the moral nature of objects when deciding whether or not to consume them. That moral nature could, in principle, spring from almost anywhere; in contemporary ethical consumption commonly it springs from the objects' social, economic, environmental and political context. Ethical consumers, then, are those whose decisions about what to consume (the 'consumption' part) are shaped by their assessment of the moral nature of that context (the 'ethical' part).

This encompasses a range of activities. Those who go to an ecotourism resort for a holiday rather than a conventional one, who bring their purchases home in their own bags rather than those provided by the shop, who refuse to buy cosmetics that have been tested on animals, who prefer the products of a company with a programme of corporate social responsibility, who take a train rather than a plane, all are basing their decisions on their assessment of the context of the objects on offer. Those who refused South African wine under the old apartheid regime, like those who refused Nestlé's products around 1980, rejected objects because they found aspects of their context to be wrong. The same is true of those who refused sugar produced with slave labour in the 1820s, as it is of Whites in the American South in the 1940s who refused to drink from a glass that a Black had used, and of those in 1930s Germany who refused to buy things sold by Jews.

My examples started with the uncontentious and ended with things that few people would recognise as ethical consumption. This breadth suggests that, if we want to make sense of ethical consumption, we need to go beyond the words. This Introduction will lay the analytical ground for the chapters that follow by going beyond those words, by locating ethical consumption in various of its social contexts to see what insights they generate. This, of course, requires approaching ethical consumption as a social phenomenon. The easiest way to do this is to start with its most obvious form.

Identifying Ethical Consumption

The sort of ethical consumption that attracts the greatest public attention is the growing preference for objects that are produced in ways that are seen to be socially and environmentally good; or, at least, better than the alternatives on offer. The most obvious examples of this are objects that satisfy the requirements of one or another certifying organisation, such as the Forest Stewardship Council, the Soil Association or the Fairtrade Foundation. Of these, perhaps the most visible and most talked about is Fairtrade.

Certification by the Fairtrade Foundation is available only for objects produced and transacted in ways that meet particular standards. Coffee, for instance, can be sold as Fairtrade only if the merchant behaves in particular ways in relation to the producers and only if the producers are people who are organised and act in specific sorts of ways (Fairtrade Labelling Organizations International 2006). Although certification requirements vary for different items, broadly they enjoin a degree of social and economic cooperation and equality, and a loose, general concern to protect the natural environment. The most important Fairtrade products are foodstuffs produced in tropical regions: coffee, tea, cocoa and bananas. These come from places far from those who buy them, which gives some ethical consumption an air of 'nimbyism': a morality sensitive to what goes on elsewhere, but 'not in my back yard'.

The rising demand for these products indicates the growing popularity of ethical consumption. In Britain, for instance, sales of Fairtrade products increased by 49 per cent from 2005 to 2006, and rose about 80 per cent in the following year, to £493 million (Hickman and Attwood 2008); the 2009 sales were £800 million (Treanor 2010). Sales increased markedly thereafter, as Cadbury's decided to make their very popular Dairy Milk chocolate bar with Fairtrade cocoa starting in the summer of 2009, which was expected to increase UK sales of Fairtrade cocoa by about £180 million a year (Bowers 2009), and the large UK sugar company Tate & Lyle decided to shift all their commercial and industrial sugar to Fairtrade (Wearden 2008).

The moral values that concern ethical consumers vary widely. The decision to start consuming ethically can be taken with reference only to oneself or it can reflect a desire to become part of a social movement. It can be intended to bring about a better household or a better world. The goal can be to reduce global warming, secure a better life for farmers in Central America or protect fish stocks in the North Atlantic. But while their values and goals are diverse, ethical consumers have an activity in common, which they use to achieve their disparate ends. That activity is the first of the contexts in which I place ethical consumption, the practice of deciding what to buy and what to avoid: shopping.

Viewed by an individual in a supermarket, shopping may be the way to secure the objects one needs or wants for one's life. When viewed from a distance, however, it is the point where the economic, commercial world of production and retail trade meets the social world of household, family and friends. The relationship between these two realms of life, which I call economy and society, is a context that is important for understanding ethical consumption. It is so because it places ethical consumption in terms of broader social values and practices, making it easier to consider it not as a unique contemporary phenomenon but as, perhaps, one instance of a set of related social movements and practices.

The economy and society at issue, though, are not what would be revealed to a dispassionate observer, for this is not likely to be what motivates ethical consumers, or most other people. Rather, that motivation will come from what people think these realms are like and what they think the relationship between them is and ought to be. Ethical consumption, then, is a collective commentary on these realms and their relationship. As such, it is inherently, if not always overtly, political. Being concerned with economy, society and their relationship, it is about collective ideas, values, processes and institutions; being concerned to affect aspects of these realms and their relationship, it is necessarily a critique and an effort to bring about change. This political dimension does not preclude more private motives for ethical consumption. People can, for instance, decide to buy organic food because they think it will benefit their health. However, if personal desire is the only reason to do so, it lacks the collective or public dimension that makes ethical consumption not an idiosyncrasy, but a social practice.

Economy and Society

If we are to place ethical consumption in this context, it is necessary to consider the ways that people understand the realms of economy and society. With that foundation laid, we can see how ethical consumption relates to those two realms. In Europe and North America people of course see economy and society in many different ways. However, some understandings are fairly widespread and seem useful for thinking about ethical consumption.

For instance, a number of scholars, especially in the United States, have identified a basic cultural distinction between areas of life that look very much like economy and society. That distinction is not, moreover, something that resides only in people's minds. Rather, as Constance Perin (1977) shows, it is realised in the separation of residential areas from commercial and industrial ones, and so is manifest in land use and urban layout. Equally, Chaya Piotrkowski (1979: 87–98) shows that many people organise their day in ways that maintain, and even exaggerate, the difference between the social and economic sides of their lives. They change their identities at the end of the working day, shrug off their jobs and refuse to let them impinge on their domestic lives.

More generally, David Schneider says that this distinction underlies central elements of people's understanding of kinship in the US, by which he means the ways that people understand themselves and their relationships with others. Furthermore, he argues that people do not see the two realms only as distinct. In important ways, they also see them as opposed:

> The family as a symbol is a pattern for how kinship relations should be conducted; the opposition between 'home' and 'work' defines these meanings quite clearly and states them in terms of the features which are distinctive to each and opposed to the other. (Schneider 1980 [1968]: 45)

Echoing Schneider, Steve Barnett and Martin Silverman (1979: 51) argue that people see these realms as engaging different aspects of their beings. In the economic realm, the world of work, an insubstantial aspect of one's being is engaged, for that is the realm of 'individuals (more or less) freely entering into agreements to do certain things in accordance with certain standards and rules.' Earlier, Talcott Parsons (1959: 261) anticipated these points, and echoed the still earlier view of Weber (1978 [c. 1914]: 956–69), when he said that, at work:

> roles are organized about standards of competence or effectiveness in performing a definite function. That means that criteria of effective performance … must be predominantly universalistic and must be attached to impersonally and objectively defined abilities and competence through training.

The result is that the self that is engaged in the economic realm is not what people take to be their real self: 'at work, it is what one does and how he does it that counts. Who he is is not supposed to really matter' (Schneider 1980 [1968]: 47).

On the other hand, in the social realm people see their selves and relationships in terms of 'things which people believe to be real things, which are in an important sense thought to be internal to the individual or continuous with the individual as a concrete being' (Barnett and Silverman 1979: 51). Here, it is your being and your personal relationships with others that are important, not how well you perform your assigned tasks. As Schneider (1980 [1968]: 47) puts it:

> even if a spouse rates low on every measure of competence or productivity which can be applied, from the output of clean shirts per week to the number of fond endearments issued per month, this in itself is not proper or sufficient grounds for terminating a marriage.

Although concern with people's core being in the social realm is clearest in the family, it is important as well in friendship. This is illustrated in Helen Gouldner and Mary Symons Strong's description of middle-class American women. For instance, they report the way that one woman distinguished between her neighbours, with whom she was linked only by the accident of residence and the routines of keeping house, and her friends.

> Even though you meet the same mothers and children over and over again and spend hours on end talking, you don't necessarily meet with people you want to become friends with. … The relationship between the mothers is not based on who you are, but on how close you live to each other and whether the kids get along. It's a matter of convenience more than being attracted to someone and choosing them as friends. (Gouldner and Strong 1987: 65; see generally Carrier 1999)

It is worth repeating that these two realms are not simply distinct. Rather, they oppose each other, as do the elements that motivate people in the two realms and that symbolise each: love and money. Schneider (1980 [1968]: 46) points to the depth of this opposition when he says:

> Home is not kept for money and, of those things related to home and family, it is said that there are some things that money can't buy! The formula in regard to work is exactly reversed at home: What is done is done for love, not for money! And it is love, of course, that money can't buy.

And again, Talcott Parsons (1959: 262) said pretty much the same thing earlier: 'Broadly speaking, there is no sector of our society where the dominant patterns stand in sharper contrast to those of the occupational world than in the family.'

I have said that the economy and society described here, an important part of the context of ethical consumption, are cultural entities. That is, they are not objective summaries of different aspects of people's daily round, but instead are symbols of different types of existence. And those are idealised types. Doubtless people experience friendship and self-sacrifice at work and rational calculation and self-seeking at home. That is not, however, the point. Rather, what these writers describe is a collective cultural summary of different kinds of values and different aspects of people, their lives and relationships. Further, because these realms are opposed to each other, the understanding of each feeds off that of the other, for they define each other negatively, as people fasten on, even celebrate, the differences between them. Maybe not one's own home and family, but certainly home and family in general is a realm of durable, affective relationships characterised by generosity and mutual concern. Perhaps not one's own workplace or local shops, but certainly economic life in general is a realm of transient impersonality full of people concerned only with profit and loss, who know the price of everything and the value of nothing.

Although distinct, these two realms are not independent of each other, with no way for the operations of one to affect people in the other or with no way for the motivations of one to be expressed in the other. In fact, ethical consumption is just such an expression, for it involves assessing the context of objects offered for sale in the economic realm in terms of values like personality, mutuality and equity, which are part of the social realm. In using these assessments to shape their market transactions, ethical consumers inject social values into the economic realm. In this they are using the economy as a signalling system. This is a familiar part of economic thought (e.g., Spence 1976), which holds that when people buy one thing rather than another, their purchase signals their preference, a signal that passes up the chain from shop to wholesaler to manufacturer. Companies that want to stay in business will attend to those signals and adjust their operations accordingly. Thus, although the label directs our attention to the social world of consumption, ethical consumption relies on the market and the economic realm to achieve its goals.

In the preceding paragraphs I have considered ethical consumption in terms of the cultural distinction between economy and society. Approaching ethical consumption in terms of that context indicates that, whatever its particularities, it is one instance of a more general set of processes and concerns. That is because the distinction between economy and society appears to be important in places and times outside of the modern West, and hence outside of the home of present-day ethical consumption. This is indicated by a set of papers edited by Jonathan Parry and Maurice Bloch, *Money and the morality of exchange* (1989). Drawing on what their contributors have to say, Parry and Bloch argue that this distinction is widespread, perhaps a feature of all societies.

Parry and Bloch make their argument when they assert the common existence of two spheres of circulation, which resemble the realms that Stephen Gudeman calls 'community' and 'market' (described at length in Gudeman 2001, 2008). One of these realms entails transactions that are understood in terms of long-term goals and relationships, for they are intended to solidify and reproduce durable, collective institutions and values. Examples of this are the way that Christmas presents solidify and reproduce the family, brideprice payments do the same for kin groups and their relationships, ecclesiastical endowments do so for religious practices and foundations. The other sphere entails transactions that are understood in terms of short-term goals and relationships, for they are intended to satisfy immediate and individual desires. Examples of this are the way that trade at a village market allows a person to get food for a week, buying and selling furniture allows someone to pay the rent, hiring a labourer for half a day clears up the back garden.

As is the case with the realms of economy and society, these two spheres are associated with different norms and values (this is explored in Wilk 1996: 147–53). In the long-term sphere, people are expected to be generous and motivated by a collective good. In the short-term sphere, they are expected to be more self-serving and even competitive. Given the differences between these two spheres, commonly the boundary between them is important and crossing it is problematic and must be done carefully. For instance, converting wealth gained in the short-term realm into forms appropriate to the long-term is virtuous, but has to be guided by the proper morality, rather than be simply a way to seek fame. Likewise, as Paul Bohanan (1955) argues for the Tiv, crossing the boundary in the other direction should be a last resort, when times are so tough that the only alternative is the dissolution of the social unit. Otherwise it is immoral, because it betrays the group and its values. That was the criticism Harold Macmillan, then Lord Stockton, made of Margaret Thatcher, in 1985. When her government disposed of Britain's national industries, she was, he complained, 'selling off the family silver'.

Emerging Economy

I have presented ethical consumption as an instance of a concern that appears in many societies with the relationship between economy and society. This does not mean, however, that people in different societies all see these realms as having the same content and significance. Rather, they are likely to have different expectations, motivations and experiences in economic and social activities. Moreover, these will be shaped by, as well as shape, economic life, the ways that people carry out the production and circulation of things.

Further, these ways are not timeless features of a society. Rather, they are likely to change over time. In most Western societies, people's economic lives have changed markedly during the past three centuries. Attending to these changes and their consequences helps us to understand the distinction between economy and society, and so helps us to see how the concerns expressed in ethical consumption have been expressed in other ways in the past. Increasingly over those centuries, people's experiences of economic life have been of wage labour and retail trade (see Carrier 1995: Chaps 2–4). Increasingly also, those experiences have diverged from what people expect in the social realm. This is only another way of putting an observation that Parry (1986: 467) has made. Over that period, he said, 'the economy becomes increasingly disembedded from society, ... economic relations become increasingly differentiated from other types of social relationship'. The most famous advocate of this separation, Adam Smith (1976 [1776]: 18), put it more starkly: 'It is not from the benevolence of the butcher, the brewer, or the baker, that we expect our dinner, but from their regard to their own interest'.

This emergence and expansion of a distinct economic realm has not been an easy process. Rather, it generated tension and conflict because it reordered people's lives and threatened their values, at times radically and painfully. This is to be expected, for the emergence and development of the modern, Western realm of economy that concerns ethical consumers is the emergence and development of capitalism.

Recall that Marx, the most famous student of that emergence, argued (e.g., Marx and Engels 1948 [1848]: Part I) that the economy became a distinct realm of life in a way that, hitherto, it had not been. The European feudal societies that preceded capitalism all, of course, had an economic realm in the objective sense: people engaged in economic activity by producing and circulating objects and services. However, it was an economic realm only in that objective sense, because economic activity was ordered by and understood in terms of things other than sheer economic calculation. Religion, kinship, locality, politics and personal fealty bound economic actors to their activities and to each other in ways that do not resemble the economic realm as it is seen to operate today.

However, with the emergence of capitalism the rising bourgeoisie threw off these constraints. Increasingly they came to operate, and think, in terms of monetary profit alone. They had to. While Weber's (1958 [1904–5]) ascetic Protestants may have sought profit for religious reasons, as a sign of their election, with the passage of time the sheer existence of firms rationally pursuing profit put pressure on all firms to do the same, or go under. The economy stepped forth as a separate realm governed by a distinctive logic that, said Weber (1981 [1923]: Chap. 22), enjoined the systematic and rational pursuit of profit in the context of the private ownership of raw materials, equipment and labour; by means of a market that ignores social identities and relations; with the reduction of all aspects of economy to monetary cost; and with an impersonal and predictable system of law. Marx and Engels (1948 [1848]: 11) said the same thing differently. The emergence of capitalism:

> has pitilessly torn asunder the motley feudal ties that bound man to his 'natural superiors,' and has left no other bond between man and man than naked self-interest, than callous 'cash payment.' It has drowned the most heavenly ecstasies of religious fervour, of chivalrous enthusiasm, of philistine sentimentalism, in the icy water of egotistical calculation.

The development and expansion of such an economic system led to reaction, as people sought to protect the values and relationships that they saw being threatened, such as E.P. Thompson (1968) described in *The making of the English working class*. While their notion of what was being threatened may have been shaped by the emerging economic system (see Kahn 1990), the values and relationships at issue were part of the social realm and the threat was real. So, for instance, early in the nineteenth century English textile workers protested, often violently, against the introduction of machines that imposed an alien logic that made their economic activities more distant from pre-existing social values. 'Machinery was at issue because it was used in ways which specifically interfered with these values' (Calhoun 1982: 65). The English Luddites were not alone, for much of Europe experienced the Revolutions of 1848.

Another famous student of the emergence of capitalism is Karl Polanyi, though the historical period that he describes in *The great transformation* (1957 [1944]) and the issues that concern him are different from those that concerned Marx. The period ranges from late in the eighteenth century to the middle of the twentieth; the issue is the spread of the market. The pertinent aspect of this spread was the growing self-regulation of markets, their increasing freedom from government or other collective constraint, so that economic logic could operate unhindered by the values of the social realm. Polanyi argued that this led to massive social and political disruption, culminating in what Winston Churchill (1948) called the 'second thirty years war', the two great wars in Europe in the first half of the twentieth century. Reaction set in and constraints were imposed: Keynesian economic policies protected individuals and households from the market; the Bretton Woods system protected currencies and the countries that issued them from the market.

Polanyi (1957 [1944]: 130) describes that expansion, disruption and reaction as 'a double movement: the market expanded continuously but this movement was met by a countermovement checking the expansion in definite directions'. In this the market, the economic realm, first is disembedded from society. That is to say, increasingly it operated independently of social regulation or constraint. However, market excess led to disruption, reaction and a re-embedding of the economy.

Time has, of course, moved on since Polanyi wrote, and what he appeared to see as a fairly permanent constraint on the economic realm turns out to look more like a moment in a cycle. Keynesian economic policy and the Bretton Woods system decayed in the 1960s and 1970s; the final three decades of the twentieth century saw the ascendance once more of the ideology of the free market (Carrier 1997), trumpeted in books with titles like *The end of history* (Fukuyama 1992) and often given the name 'neoliberalism'. However, these decades also saw a succession of disruptive speculative excesses. Increasing public protest against the expansion of market values and relations at the expense of social ones, perhaps most visible in the form of the World Trade Organisation, coupled with increasing official concern about those market excesses, appear to mark the onset of another re-embedding, the second stage of another double movement.

Marx, Polanyi and the other great analysts of the rise and spread of the impersonal, rational economic system that is capitalism drew our attention to big changes in the relationship between economy and society. Theirs is a picture of powerful forces striding, in capital letters, across the pages of history. These are difficult to relate to anything so mundane as the shopping that is at the heart of ethical consumption. However, the changes that those analysts describe have seen reactions and accommodations that appear in more private realms, and that begin to resemble the shopper's decision to buy Fairtrade coffee rather than a different sort.

An almost invisible example of this is the way working-class families treated money in parts of the United States around 1900, described by Viviana Zelizer (1989). She says that people took their impersonal wages and physically divided them into different containers. The money placed in each was dedicated to a different household need, and so expressed the social relations and obligations of the people within it. Certainly there was more to this than just the family policing the boundary between economy and society by socialising the product of the economic realm when it entered the household. However, equally certainly, the practices Zelizer describes effected that socialising. This tale of working-class American families and their money jars points to something important for understanding ethical consumption. The more mundane areas of life, more private than the political-economic structures that concerned Marx, Polanyi and the rest, bear the mark of the tensions between economy and society, and particularly of people's efforts to maintain a social sphere in the face of an expanding economic sphere and its products.

One anthropologist who has considered these more mundane areas is Daniel Miller, in his work on consumption (e.g., 1987) and shopping (e.g., 1998). Miller argues that people in modern societies confront a world of material objects that is alienated from them. In saying this, he echoes Marx's observation that the development of capitalism means that those who make things increasingly do so at the direction of others, who own the material they work on and the tools they use. As a consequence, the things people make increasingly are separated from the intentions and social situations of those who make them. In our terms, though not in Miller's, people increasingly see production and its fruits as part of economy, increasingly distinct from society. In Marx's terms, people increasingly are, and see themselves as being, alienated from their labour, from what they make through that labour and from the products of capitalist enterprise generally.

Miller says that people react negatively to this. I have already mentioned the more visible and violent forms of this reaction, the Luddite riots and the Revolutions of 1848, in which workers sought to reclaim control of production. Miller points to a less obvious reaction, the rise of mass consumption and shopping, as people invest less of their selves in the world of work, and instead see purchasing and consumption as the more meaningful economic activity. In it they seek to use alienated commodities, the unpromising products of the economic realm, to create personal, affective lives in the social realm. They do so through the selection of objects that, they think, will fit and reflect the social relations in which they will use those objects.

Building on the arguments that Miller made, as well as the ideas of Marx and Marcel Mauss (1990 [1925]), I have looked at one aspect of the emergence of this sort of shopping in Britain and the United States: the rise of modern Christmas in the middle third of the nineteenth century (Carrier 1995: Chap. 8), characterised by the massive, collective purchase of commodities in retail establishments, and their conversion into gifts given in social relationships, especially in the family. Taken together, the shopping and the giving reflect both the separation of economy and society and people's ability to recreate society in the face of economy, by wresting recalcitrant commodities from the economic realm and converting them into objects suitable for giving in, and reproducing, close and durable personal relationships. As Miller suggests, people do this all year. However, at Christmas they all do so at once in a stylised, exaggerated way that celebrates and reaffirms their ability to make this transformation, and so their ability to maintain society in the face of an intrusive economy.

The Luddite riots, the Revolutions of 1848, American families apportioning their weekly pay packet and the emergence of mass consumption and of modern Christmas point to ways that people have been concerned about the same thing that, I argued, is the concern of ethical consumption: economy, society and their relationship. They also illustrate an important point. In different times and places, people experience and think about economy and society differently; the relationship between the two realms differs and people seek to affect that distinction in different ways. Put in other words, a recurring set of relations and concerns can take different forms in different circumstances. This has implications for those who are interested in understanding ethical consumption. It means that they can find cases that may look nothing like ethical consumption but that are concerned with the same issues and relationships, like Zelizer's working-class money jars and the Luddites. However, it also means that cases that may look like ethical consumption at first glance turn out to be concerned with different issues and relationships.

An example of the latter is that of the Quakers, who, since the start of their religion, have advocated what looks like ethical consumption. However, Peter Collins (this volume) shows us how the moral basis of the Quaker consumption ethic reflects things other than a concern about economy and society, in their case Biblical injunction. Moreover, in their commercial activities they appeared happy to see the objects they transacted as commodities free of their context. This is illustrated by an eminent Quaker mill owner in the first half of the nineteenth century, Henry Ashworth, who said that 'cotton spinners would buy cotton from anywhere and "they asked no questions as to whether it was slave-grown or not"' (Boyson 1970: 233). The danger of assuming that what appears to be ethical consumption really is an instance of it is illustrated as well by those English people who refused to buy slave-grown sugar early in the nineteenth century. They may look like present-day ethical consumers: their buying decisions reflected their evaluation of the context of the sugar. However, without further investigation it is not clear where those people thought the wrong in slavery lay and what assumptions were at work. Were they objecting to slavery because it denied a humanity of both slave and master, because it denied religious salvation to slaves, because it denied to slaves the chance to be independent transactors selling their labour freely on the market?

Equally, I said, we need to be careful not to dismiss a practice as being unrelated to ethical consumption simply because it does not resemble it on the surface. For instance, ethical consumption does not look much like modern Christmas, with its mass buying. However, as I described, that buying is central to a collective affirmation of the ability to maintain the family as a haven in a heartless economic world. The same is true with the Luddites, whose rejection of mechanisation looks nothing like ethical consumption. However, if those machines embodied an attack on desired social values and relations by an encroaching impersonal, economic realm, then Luddites,

Christmas shoppers and ethical consumers all are concerned with the relationship between economy and society.

The different attempts to protect the social realm from the incursions of the economic are all about the same basic issue but, as I have observed, those incursions take different forms at different times and people respond to them differently. With ethical consumption, the incursion appears to be the intensification and geographical expansion of economy, whether in reality or in people's perceptions. The intensification appears as the increasing rationalisation of economic activity of all sorts, from agricultural production to the staffing of shops, in the pursuit of greater profit; the expansion appears as the increasing reliance on manufacture and agriculture carried out elsewhere, intruding economic values in places where they are assumed to be alien and to have undesirable effects. The response is an effort to slow or even reverse this process through the preference for objects that embody the values threatened by that incursion, a preference manifest in shopping and passed up the chain through the signalling system.

Comparative Issues

In the preceding paragraphs I approached ethical consumption in terms of an important part of its context, which is the cultural distinction between society and economy. As I said, doing so is rewarding, for it allows us to see ethical consumption as one of a number of ways that people have sought to protect the social realm from what they see as an encroaching and threatening economic realm.

Seeing ethical consumption in terms of that cultural distinction, and particularly as a collective commentary on the relationship between economy and society, raises questions. The first of these concerns goals: what is the proper relationship between economy and society that is sought? The second concerns means: what ought to be done to achieve that goal? The third is agents: who are the people who can work to achieve that goal, and how ought they to be related to each other and to the realm that they seek to affect? I turn to these now.

I will address these questions by placing ethical consumption in a different context, that of other social movements and bodies of thought concerned with the relationship between economy and society. Doing so helps illuminate the set of decisions, whether conscious or not, that ethical consumption involves, decisions about what people want, how they ought to achieve it and who or what ought to do the achieving.

Goals

Ethical consumption contains an image of what economic activity ought to be like and how the economic realm ought to reflect or differ from the social realm. Also, though perhaps less obviously, it contains an image of what the social realm is like. Part of understanding ethical consumption is understanding these images, and placing it in a comparative framework allows us to see other views of economy, society and their relationship, and how ethical consumption resembles or differs from them.

People can, for instance, prefer that their relations with the economic realm be distant and impersonal. These are the sort of relations implicit in organisations such as the Consumers' Association (now 'Which?') in the UK and the Consumers Union in the US, which encourage people to see objects for sale dispassionately, in terms of value for money. In this they construe objects as bundles of utilities or use value, bereft of personality or sociability in either their production or their sale (see Carrier 1995: 120–2). There are many reasons to want this impersonality.

To begin with, if people want, as Miller agues, to create social worlds with the commodities at hand, they may find it easier to do so if the commodity and the purchase are impersonal, are blank slates on which the purchaser's identity and social relationships can be written easily. Impersonality in economic relations has a further attraction, particularly apparent to those obliged to live without it. Often enough, poor householders have wanted to be free of personal relationships with shopkeepers on whom they rely for credit and who can break them when times are bad. Equally, many people have been attracted by impersonality of the sort illustrated by Montgomery Ward, a mail-order firm in the US. They proclaimed that they cared only about the impersonal transaction of object for cash. As they said in their 1876 catalogue, 'We sell our goods to any person of whatever occupation, color or race' (in Hendrickson 1978: 222).

My examples suggest that sociality in economic interchange may be desirable only to those who routinely conduct their economic lives free of it. The social realm may look rather different to those for whom economic transactions necessarily occur in the context of social relations, such as the poor family needing credit from the local shopkeeper or the Black man confronting merchants who are more concerned with the colour of his skin than with the colour of his money. Such people may see virtues in an impersonal economic realm that are not apparent to ethical consumers, with their different experiences of economy. If so, they are in good company. Their view, that the economic realm ought to be independent of the social, flourished in Western thought at the time when the economic and the social were not so separated as they are for the social strata where ethical consumption flourishes (e.g., Hirschman 1977; Silver 1990). So, the attraction that a more socialised economy has for ethical consumers may reflect the fact that, for them, sociality in economic activity is optional rather than necessary.

In contrast to those who prefer anonymity in economic activity, ethical consumers think that at least some of their economic relationships ought to be personal. This appears in the old Fairtrade slogan about 'cutting out the middleman'. For people with this view, producers and consumers ought to deal directly with each other, which accounts for some of the attraction of buying directly from local producers such as farmers. Again, the Fairtrade organisation illustrates this, with its images of producers of Fairtrade-certified products, whether on their website (www.fairtrade.net) or on the bags of coffee on the supermarket shelf, such as is described by Peter Luetchford (this volume). The Fairtrade organisation is not alone in this. A growing number of companies are introducing schemes that allow purchasers to go on a website, enter a code and locate the farmer who grew what they bought. These companies include producers like Dole, for the organic bananas they sell in the US, and retailers like Waitrose and Tesco in the UK (Stone and Richtel 2009).

Direct trade between producers and consumers is not new, but has been the experience of most people for most of human history. Furthermore, direct, local trade has long been valued. In many parts of England it was enshrined in regulations that made it difficult for outsiders to trade and that required producers to offer their wares to local householders before seeking to sell elsewhere (Carrier 1995: 64–5). This valuation, however, often reflected an assessment of the more economic advantages of direct trade, rather than the more social ones. So, many would have agreed with the criticism of intermediaries expressed by one American pamphleteer early in the nineteenth century: 'their meer *handing of Goods one to another*, no more increases any Wealth in the Province, than Persons *at a Fire* increase the *Water in a Pail*, by passing it thro' Twenty or Forty hands' (in Crowley 1974: 88). Even Adam Smith, that symbol of impersonal economic rationality, had little time for intermediaries in trade, arguing that, compared to farmers and manufacturers, they did little to increase the wealth of the nation (Lubasz 1992: 49).

Of course, the disparaging of intermediaries in ethical consumption is associated with economic value: those who grow Fairtrade-certified products have a financial inducement to do so. However, for ethical consumers the appeal of direct trade is not economic: that inducement, after all, increases the wealth of the producers' nations, not the consumers'. Rather, it seems to spring from the distinctly social desire for equity, fair dealing between maker and buyer, of the sort that was common in colonial America. 'It was the traditional view that exchange ... was a social matter involving reciprocity and redistribution: competition, in the sense of one man's gaining at the expense of another, was a violation of this traditional ethic' (Crowley 1974: 6). A different value arising from the social realm also seems to make direct trade appealing. Items acquired directly from the producer carry that producer's identity. One wheat farmer, who sells to a milling company that allows purchasers to identify the farm that grew the wheat in the bag of flour that they bought, put it this way: 'The person who puts that scone in their mouth can now say, "Oh my God, there's a real person behind this." ... They are going to bite into that bread or pastry and know whose hands were on the product' (Stone and Richtel 2009). This reduces the impersonality of objects, and so can make them better suited for use in social relationships (see Carrier 1995: Chap. 6).

The value that ethical consumers put on personality and direct trade is relatively easy for them to realise. Unlike the household confronting an overbearing butcher or baker, most ethical consumers do not confront real makers of what they buy. This allows them to construct these producers as congenial people who share their values. The farmers who grow the organic crops can be construed as doing so not for impersonal commercial reasons, but for reasons that are more deep-seated, 'thought to be internal to the individual' (Barnett and Silverman 1979: 51). They can be construed as living the organic life that, as Audrey Vankeerberghen (this volume) describes, many ethical consumers value. Similarly, the smiling smallholders who grow the coffee can be imagined as producing for Fairtrade because they embrace the values, rather than because, as Luetchford (this volume) describes, they want a better position in the international coffee market. And, of course, those who buy ethical fabrics made by Bangladeshi women can assume that those women are grateful for paid work that empowers them, rather than, as Lill Vramo (this volume) describes, seeing that work as a shameful public recognition that their households do not have the resources to be self-reliant.

It appears, then, that ethical consumers preferring direct trade and other consumers preferring impersonal trade may well want the same thing, that the objects in their lives not be impersonal commodities. However, their approaches differ. Ethical consumers seek objects that already carry identity, that of their makers. The others seek impersonal objects that they can stamp with the identities and social relationships with which they will be associated. Both, however, differ from those for whom personality in economic relations signals subordination, whether poor families confronting merchants on whom they rely for credit or merchants confronting rich customers on whom they depend for trade (McKendrick, Brewer and Plumb 1982: 198).

It is worth noting that the preference for direct trade helps explain why buying locally overwhelmingly means buying food grown locally and why Fairtrade sales overwhelmingly are of foodstuffs. Unlike trousers, books and hard-drives for computers, these are things that can be imagined and presented as having been produced by a person, whether the local farmer who delivers vegetables to your door, the smallholder pictured on the bag of ethical coffee or the farmer you see on a web page. This preference also helps explain one aspect of the nimbyism in ethical consumption mentioned earlier: the fact that ethical consumers generally do not seem very concerned about the conditions of work of the clerks who stock the store shelves or the drivers who deliver the crate- and pallet-loads from warehouse to shop; that they appear unconcerned that Starbucks, which advertises its ethical concerns, violates United States labour law to prevent its staff joining a union (Greenhouse 2008). Those people are parts of the web of intermediaries that stands between producer and consumer.

Means

In different circumstances, those with different views of the two realms can deal with the relationship between economy and society in different ways. As I have described already, people wanting to protect the social sphere from the encroachments of the economic could socialise money in the way of Zelizer's working-class families with their money jars, or celebrate their ability to impose social meanings and relationships on impersonal commodities through modern Christmas. Such activities protect the social realm by socialising the products of the economic. They do so, however, in different ways. Unlike Zelizer's money jars, Christmas stresses the importance of shopping, and so resembles ethical consumption.

I have already pointed to another way that shopping can be used to tame the economy, which is the approach to objects illustrated by the Consumers Union and the Consumers' Association. That approach polices the boundary between economy and society by treating objects as impersonal material utilities. In doing so it helps strip objects of the social images that advertisers, creatures of the economic realm, seek to impose on them. This is a more subtle form of policing, because those images are themselves part of the social realm, rather than the economic: when advertisements associate a commodity with affection and a happy household, they are appropriating social values for economic ends. Those who read these words may see that appropriation as an unexceptionable part of life. However, not that long ago it caused dismay, visible in works like Vance Packard's (1957) *The hidden persuaders*. That book was an extended complaint about the use of 'motivational research' in advertising. Packard's concern, translated into my terminology, was that advertisers were taking values that emerged in the social realm and using them to manipulate people in ways that reflected values in the economic realm (as in, e.g., Sunderland and Denny 2007).

There are, then, different ways in which purchaser choice can be used to affect the relationship between economy and society. Those who urge the dispassionate approach are as concerned with that relationship as are those who want to find just the right gifts in their Christmas shopping, and they are just as concerned as those who buy ethically. However, there is one important matter on which they differ. Only ethical consumption is overtly concerned to inject into the economic realm values that spring from the social. To do so, it makes use of two central elements of the economic realm: the desire of companies for the greatest profit; the relationship between sales and profit. The result is a fusion of economic and social values, revealed in the words of Penny Newman, at the time head of Cafédirect, a British company that sells Fairtrade-certified coffee: 'If you want to change the trading system you've got to be on the same terms as the conventional system. You need to make a profit' (in Martinson 2007).

In effect, Cafédirect is part of the signalling system that I mentioned previously, and the profit that it makes is part of the signal. Remember that when buyers select one object over another, they emit a signal about their preferences among the objects that they confront. So, for instance, when buyers select Fairtrade-certified coffee at £2.40 for a half-pound bag over other coffees on offer that are priced between £1.85 and £2.20, those buyers are emitting a signal that says that they will pay more for coffee produced in a particular way than they will for coffee that is not, a signal realised in the profit of companies like Cafédirect. This can be put in more formal terms. Firstly, the morals of ethical consumers, which arise in the social realm, shape the value that those people put on the different objects that are for sale. Secondly, those values affect the price that those consumers are willing to pay for those objects. Thirdly, this affects which of the objects they buy, and which they do not. Fourthly, those purchases convey the signal that goes up the chain from shop to wholesaler to manufacturer. When manufacturing firms attend to this signal and shape their practices accordingly, the values of ethical consumers are injected into the economic realm. At least, that is the assumption. As I show later on, in practice things are not so straightforward.

Agents

I said that the third of the issues I would describe is the agents who work to achieve the proper relationship between economy and society: how they ought to be related to each other and to the realm that they seek to affect. And again, different sets of people, with their different concerns with the relationship between economy and society, have stressed different sorts of agents and of relationships among them.

One early, modern view of such agents and their relationship emerged in the cooperative movement. This began to flourish in Britain in the middle of the nineteenth century: by the 1880s there were over a thousand cooperative societies with more than half a million members (Jefferys 1954: 17). The power of this movement to affect the economic realm and its relation to the social did not rest on individuals choosing freely in their personal economic transactions, any more than the power of the labour movement rested on individuals choosing freely in their personal negotiations with their employers. Rather, like the labour movement, it rested on organisation, in this case the cooperative societies, which were (and remain) corporate bodies that set up cooperative retail stores linked, eventually, to cooperative wholesale organisations. The cooperatives relied on the people who belonged to them and who bought in their stores. However, their power sprang from the organisations that united those people: it was those organisations that acquired premises, located sources of supply and purchased, transported and sold things.

Moreover, the cooperatives did not seek to affect the economic realm by modifying one or another company or commercial practice. Rather, they created economic institutions to serve their own purposes. This makes them unusual, for most other efforts to address the relationship between economy and society have sought to influence the operation of existing institutions, rather than create new ones. I have already mentioned one such effort, the Keynesian economic policies that were designed to affect companies and markets in order to restrict what were seen as their harmful effects. With few exceptions, they did so without creating novel economic institutions. While the advocates of Keynesian policies differed from the cooperative movement in this way, they resembled it in another. They saw institutions rather than individuals as the appropriate agent, though for Keynesians it was governments representing citizens, rather than cooperative societies representing members.

Like most Keynesians, then, and unlike the cooperative movement, ethical consumption does not seek to shape the relationship between economy and society by creating new economic institutions. There are, of course, organisations associated with ethical consumption, such as the Fairtrade Foundation and the Soil Association. However, they set standards and certify companies and objects that meet them; they do not trade. In this, they are perhaps best seen as part of the signalling system, for their standards and certifications make more visible the signals generated when ethical consumers make their purchases. Or, as the chair of the Environmental Information subcommittee of the House of Commons put it, 'An effective environmental labelling regime will … generate the kind of market signal needed to trigger a transformation in business activities all the way down the supply chain of a particular product' (in Watt 2009).

While ethical consumption differs from the cooperative movement and resembles the Keynesians in its reliance on existing economic institutions, it stands opposed to both in another way. Unlike them, it sees individuals, not institutions, as the source of efficacy in shaping the relationship between economy and society. This efficacy springs into being when an individual chooses to buy one thing rather than another, and it is expressed through the aggregate of market transactions, rather than through meetings of the local cooperative society or national elections. The sort of individual who has this efficacy has been called a 'citizen-consumer', and this name captures nicely the mixture of public (citizen) and private (consumer) elements in ethical consumption. Citizen-consumers deploy their personal resources, their money, in ways that, they think, will help them achieve their more public, social goals and their more personal, material satisfaction.

Comparing Goals, Means and Agents

I have sketched the goals, means and agents of different sets of people and bodies of thought concerned with the relationship between the realms of economy and society. As I said, my purpose was to help reveal what is contained in ethical consumption by putting it in the context of other ways that people have sought to address the relationship between those realms. My comparisons have touched on many issues, but what I have said indicates that ethical consumption appears both to reject and embrace the economic realm.

The rejection lies in the goal. Ethical consumption seeks to replace the impersonal calculation and task orientation that is part of the economy with personality: objects that are made not by machines or robot-like wage labour in companies seeking the greatest profit, but by people who invest themselves and their values in what they produce. People link themselves with those producers when they purchase and consume their products, so complementing personality with sociality. The personality is, as I have indicated, only an image, for it relies on third-party representations (see below) or, at best, on brief, commercial interactions. The people portrayed on the bag of Fairtrade coffee are likely to live a very long way from the purchaser and their lives are likely to cross in no discernible way. Even the farmer who sells local produce is likely to have no other link to the purchaser than those sales. It is, thus, only an image, but perhaps imagination is the closest to the real thing that people can get in a system with extensive division of labour and long-distance trade.

Although ethical consumption rejects the economic realm in its goals, it appears to embrace economy in its means, as in the Norwegian embrace of 'trade, not aid' that Vramo (this volume) describes. That is because the better lives and worlds that ethical consumers want are to be achieved through the existing institutions and practices of the economy. In adopting, even stressing, purchasing decision as the key to achieving its goals, ethical consumption necessarily accepts the market as the vehicle for the expression of morality, whether in the form of the transaction between purchaser and retailer or the transactions further up the chain that extends back to the producer.

Ethical consumption does not embrace economy only in its means. In addition, it embraces, or at least does not challenge, economy in its agents. In stressing individual purchasers and their decisions, ethical consumption echoes the idea that in the economic realm people are not linked to each other in any substantial or durable way, but only temporarily in terms of the task at hand. That stress also reflects a central element in the dominant, public ideology of the market, the individual choosing freely, described by Carrier and Wilk (this volume). It reflects as well, of course, a central element in neoliberal thinking, that is, that risks should fall on individuals who buy, who are able to reduce those risks by choosing wisely, rather than falling on companies that make and sell, which are able to reduce them by conforming to public regulation (this is elaborated in Moberg and Lyon 2010). There is, then, nothing substantial in ethical consumption that would encourage the organisation and collective action to achieve common goals that is alien to the economic realm. Moreover, the potency of these agents does not spring from things that are important in the social realm, like their personal identities and relationships. Rather, it springs from their command of that most powerful symbol of the economic realm, money.

Practical Context

Thus far I have considered aspects of the context of ethical consumption that can help us to understand the common factors that drive ethical consumption generally as a social phenomenon. However, ethical consumption is more than just an expression of those common factors, because it is more than just a general social phenomenon. That is because that general phenomenon is manifest by concrete sets of ethical consumers who are influenced by their concrete, practical, social context, and who engage in practical actions that shape and are shaped by that context. These practical contexts are the concern of the balance of this Introduction.

Ethical consumers do not float in some undifferentiated space, but exist in particular places and times. This means that even if they all share a concern with the relationship between economy and society, the concerns of any particular set of ethical consumers and the ways that those concerns are expressed will be influenced by factors that may not influence other sets. Similarly, ethical consumption involves engaging in practical actions that are at the intersection of people's values and the context in which they purchase and consume objects of different sorts. Attending to these practical contexts illuminates ethical consumption in terms of a question different from those addressed thus far: in what ways do these contexts shape the appearance of ethical consumption and its effects?

Specificity

I have said that understanding specific sets of ethical consumers requires attending to features of their time and place that influence their general concern with the relationship between economy and society. Because these are specific to concrete sets of people, they resist ready, systematic summary, a resistance apparent in the diverse Hungarian ethical consumers that Tamás Dombos describes in his chapter in this volume. Here, then, I will only illustrate the sorts of things that can be important, drawing on some of the material in different chapters in this volume.

The first is the way that historical experience can affect how people think about the relationship between economy and society and express those thoughts in ethical consumption. The significance of that experience is illustrated by Lill Vramo's chapter on ethical consumption in Norway. As she notes, that country has had an enviable international reputation and a history of significant aid to poorer countries. However, over time and for reasons partly beyond Norway's control, Norwegians decreasingly have seen themselves as generous donors aiding grateful recipients. Instead, more and more they see themselves as foolish givers confronting crafty takers. While this change is not unique to Norway, it is especially significant there because of the country's earlier commitment to aid. This historical circumstance finds expression in ethical consumption, the embrace of 'trade not aid'. Superficially, that embrace appears to entail a strengthening of the economic, in the form of international commerce, at the expense of the social, in the form of assistance to the poor. However, as Vramo shows, for many Norwegians that embrace reflects a desire to make economy more moral.

National history has a different sort of effect for some of the ethical consumers in Hungary that Dombos describes. Perhaps because of the shock of the collapse of the old Communist system, its reverberations and the betrayal of dreams that followed it, some Hungarians embrace ethical consumption as a criticism of public life. One form this takes is as an assertion of personal morality in a society increasingly seen as populated by amoral opportunists. Another form is the adoption of ethical consumption as a criticism of the alliance of government and business that many see as running and ruining the country. In extreme form, as Dombos describes, this results in an ethical consumption that is intensely nationalistic, intended to restore national pride and spirit in a country seen as permeated by and subservient to foreign interests.

Distinctive historical effects, albeit on a smaller scale, appear in what Giovanni Orlando says in his chapter on a group of ethical consumers in Palermo, in Sicily. For them, the significant experiences revolve around the growth of the city in the second half of the twentieth century. This was not, however, desired urban development. Rather, it was seen as driven by greedy, corrupt speculators who were happy to take control of public land without permission and build on it without approval, and who were associated with Mafia and Christian Democratic party interests on the island. In all this, city, provincial and even national governments were unwilling or unable to intervene. These experiences led the people Orlando describes to want to protect the social realm from the predations of economic interests, but also led them to think that conventional political activity was pointless. Instead, they turned to ethical consumption as an expression of their values, and to the passing of ethical goods on to others as a way of spreading those values. Here, then, as with the national case Vramo describes and some of the Hungarians that Dombos describes, the vagaries of historical circumstance help us to understand the different ways that ethical consumption reflects a concern with economy and society.

A different sort of factor appears in Amanda Berlan's chapter, one more purely cultural than historical. She is concerned with public perceptions of the ethical status of cocoa, especially claims that much of the chocolate that people buy is tainted with child labour and something akin to slavery. She illustrates this with the position of Cadbury's, a large British chocolate company. She notes that Cadbury's is often included in the list of ruthless and exploitative firms, even though they have a history of fairly responsible, even ethical, policies. That inclusion points to the importance of a common assumption, that large companies are unethical. This ascription has some validity, but remains problematic because large companies are hostage to their very size. They are more likely than small ones to attract public scrutiny and be visited by government inspectors, and if they are caught in illegal or unethical practice, they find it hard to do what small companies can, change the name on the letterhead and resume trading. In pointing to this and other cultural assumptions, Berlan shows how expressions of people's concern with the relationship of economy and society are shaped not only by their cultural understandings of these two realms. Those expressions can be shaped as well by presuppositions of other sorts that are part of ethical consumers' context.

A factor of yet a different sort deserves consideration, one that springs from the importance attached to consumption in modern Western societies. That is the social costs that can be associated with various types of ethical consumption and that can influence the actions of ethical consumers. Two chapters in this volume address somewhat different aspects of this, Peter Collins's, concerned with Quakers, and Cindy Isenhour's, concerned with Swedes.

I said that Quakers probably should not be considered ethical consumers of the sort that has been discussed in this Introduction. Even so, some of what Collins describes is pertinent, particularly the position of prosperous Quaker merchants and manufacturers in England around the middle of the nineteenth century. That position illustrates the social pressures that people can experience when their consumption is unusual. Put briefly, the economic position of these Quakers should have led to their incorporation into the upper reaches of the middle class. However, their plain Quaker consumption meant that they did not appear or act in ways that would allow them to mix easily with many of their economic equals. They found it hard, then, to claim the social rank that their prosperity justified, with the result that many of them abandoned their Quaker faith and its plain consumption.

What Collins describes points to the importance of consumption, ethical or otherwise, in social life. This is illustrated by some of the Swedish ethical consumers that Isenhour describes. They approached ethical consumption in different ways than did Quakers, with different social effects. Many of the more committed among them, however, confronted the problem of Collins's prosperous Quakers: their consumption cut them off from many of the people with whom they normally would expect to interact. As Isenhour explains, in Sweden there is strong pressure to consume at a fairly high level, which makes the position of ethical consumers there more difficult than that in many other countries. However, contextual factors of the sort that Collins and Isenhour describe are likely to shape ethical consumers' practices everywhere to some degree. This is illustrated by some of the Hungarians that Dombos describes. A recurrent theme in their talk is the resistance they encounter when they argue for ethical consumption among family and friends, and the fear of some that such argument would produce rejection and the weakening of valued social relationships.

The points that I have made here complicate the way that I rendered ethical consumption in the previous parts of this Introduction. This complication is an extension of a point made earlier, that a concern with economy, society and their relationship will take different forms in different settings. What concerned me previously in this Introduction was settings that differed in terms of the predominant forms of economy and society. The preceding paragraphs, on the other hand, were concerned with settings of another sort, historical and cultural factors that are not overtly about economy and society but that can influence the ways that people understand the relationship between those two realms and the ways that they act to affect it.

I turn now to a different set of contextual factors. These are not important because of how they can influence the orientation of ethical consumers. Rather, they are consequences of the practice of ethical consumption, especially once it has become a recognisable social and economic activity. Not only are these factors of a different sort than those considered previously in this section, their effects are different as well. They are worth attention because they help show how complicated and problematic ethical consumption is.

Signalling Ethical Consumption

Those who favour ethical consumption seek to communicate their preferences. I have already noted how their purchases communicate by means of the economic signalling system. In addition, when they communicate their preferences to others through their consumption practices, they are also part of a social signalling system. This complicates ethical consumption, because much of it is not immediately visible, and hence does not signal very clearly. A cup of coffee looks like a cup of coffee, and does not proclaim itself as Fairtrade or not. To make matters worse, much ethical consumption, especially that intended to protect the environment, involves foregoing consumption: the flight not taken, the old car not replaced, the new clothes not bought. As Collins's chapter reminds us, of course, contemporary ethical consumers are hardly the only people to confront this problem, nor are they the first.

One way of dealing with this complication is straightforward: people can become conspicuous ethical consumers. This is obvious with things that blatantly announce their morality, such as the bag that proclaims, in large letters, 'I am not a plastic bag'. Somewhat more subtle is a product sold by the Scotmid Co-operative stores where I live, which advertise their commitment to ethical products. It is an inexpensive cotton bag that is advertised as Fairtrade. It is recognisably ethical because of the small trademarks it bears and because it looks like undyed, coarse-woven cloth, the sort of thing that characterises simplicity. There are, of course, other products that attest to the ethics of the purchaser. The social activist Bono established a charitable scheme called 'Product (RED)' (Ponte, Richey and Baab 2008). Companies that join it can label their wares accordingly, without actually changing their commercial practices, and purchasers can signal their morality by displaying them.

There are yet more subtle ways that ethical consumers pass messages through the social signalling system. For instance, an increasing number of people and companies in the US are installing small wind-turbines to generate electricity and so reduce their use of fossil fuels. These are less efficient than solar panels, whether used to generate electricity or to produce heat, and appear to produce less energy than advertised (Jowit 2009). However, they do have an advantage. 'Perched high above a building, wind turbines serve as a far more visible clean-energy credential than solar panels, which are often hard to see' (Galbraith 2008). Their visibility makes them attractive. A senior administrator of Harvard University said that the turbines that his institution is installing are 'outward symbols of our commitment to renewable energy and sustainability here on campus' (in Galbraith 2008).

Forms of consumption less visible from the street can signal ethical concerns in other ways. In her discussion of Swedish ethical consumers Isenhour describes one, protecting the environment by buying old objects instead of new. People who do this for ethical reasons and who want to signal their morality will, of course, need to distinguish themselves from those who buy second-hand simply because it is cheap. Some of the Swedes Isenhour describes do this by the careful selection of old objects that are not yet antiques. In doing so, they select objects of high quality that are aesthetically pleasing, but that are not genuinely old and rare. A similar quiet signalling is the purchase of 'authentic' foodstuffs, most visible in the Slow Food movement. Those are certified as produced in the locality with which they are associated historically and in ways that are traditional and artisanal rather than rationalised and capitalised (Pratt 2007). As Cristina Grasseni (this volume) describes, such produce rejects the economic realm in favour of the social in two ways: it is free from the taint of industrial agriculture; its purchase supports traditional rural ways. The consumer's commitment to the values associated with authentic foods can be made visible through involvement in things like the Slow Food movement: buying in the right shops, cooking with the right recipes, attending the right festivals (Severson 2008).

Isenhour's and Grasseni's descriptions of ethical consumption show how ethical consumers' signals convey information about class and taste, as well as ethics. This is not the conspicuous consumption of the leisure class that Veblen (1927: 87) describes, which is a sign of wealth, the 'unremitting demonstration of the ability to pay'. Rather, it resembles Weber's view of status groups, distinguished by 'the principle of their consumption of goods as represented by special "styles of life"' (Weber 1978 [c. 1914]: 937, emphasis omitted). This is the approach that Bourdieu (1984) elaborated in *Distinction*.

For Bourdieu, taste entails two kinds of distinction. The first is distinction among the different things available for consumption: *coquilles St Jacques à la Provençale*, as opposed to tinned spaghetti loops. The second is distinction among people with different consumption preferences: those who know the difference and care, as opposed to the ignorant and indifferent. As this suggests, for Bourdieu taste is social.

To begin with, it is only when people's preferences are recognised by others that they cease to be idiosyncrasies and become tastes. This social recognition is facilitated by the fact that people's preferences are not random. Rather, they are primarily the result of cultural transmission from their social milieu, initially when they are growing up and learning the distinctions that make for taste. Because learning these distinctions takes time, and because acquiring items to be consumed takes money, those from milieux higher up the socioeconomic scale will acquire tastes different from those lower down. Put crudely, taste is a function of class, and the power of the dominant classes means that theirs are the dominant tastes. However, the common assumption that taste is a personal matter masks this, and people's preferences often are seen to reflect their better or worse taste, rather than their different class locations. As this suggests, the preferences of those in lower strata are denied legitimacy, just as some of the Swedes that Isenhour describes thought that their modest consumption led others to deny their legitimacy. Their taste is seen to be impoverished or inadequate, rather than different.

Because consuming ethically is a preference, like taste, what Bourdieu says in *Distinction* may apply to ethical consumption. When people signal their ethical preferences, they are expressing a set of values that is shaped by their social milieu. However, the importance of milieu, what Josée Johnston (2008) calls the political economy of ethical consumption, will be masked by the claim that ethical preferences are an individual matter. At the simplest level, ethical products tend to cost more than others, so that ethical consumption is easiest for the rich, which echoes what Bourdieu says about tasteful consumption. Moreover, because of their social influence, it is their ethical preferences, expressed through their consumption, that will be recognised as ethical. The consumption of the rest, like some of the Hungarians that Dombos describes, will be seen to be devoid of ethics rather than being seen to express different ethics that reflect different social locations and resources. This is echoed in what Orlando says of ethical consumers in Palermo in his chapter. They saw the consumption of the poor as not being ethical, which they explained as the result of ignorance or of a lack of money. By seeing divergence as the result of ignorance or poverty, rather than as dissent, these explanations serve to solidify the values of ethical consumers and make them legitimate.

In this, Orlando's ethical consumers echo what seems to recur in ethical consumption. People's ethical preferences are a function of their milieu, and especially their class, as I illustrated in my discussion of why people of different class positions would place different values on sociality in economic transactions. Indeed, sociality and other values associated with ethical consumption look rather like what Bourdieu (1984: 77) calls 'the tastes of luxury … the tastes of individuals who are the product of material conditions of existence defined by distance from necessity'. However, the ethical values involved often are presented as being self-evident and beyond debate. How, after all, can one oppose helping impoverished farmers in the Third World or saving the environment? In being constructed in this way, ethical consumption leads to what Bourdieu calls 'misrecognition', treating tastes that reflect people's social locations as instead reflections of natural moral sensibility. In this, ethical consumption 'tends to produce … the naturalisation of its own arbitrariness' (Bourdieu 1977: 164).

Ethical Consumption Commerce

The second consequence of ethical consumption that I consider revolves around what happens when it is sufficiently common that companies take notice of it and it becomes an element of commerce. This touches on central elements of ethical consumption. For one thing, if companies take notice it means that the economic signalling system is working, which would justify seeing individuals transacting in the market as the appropriate agents to affect the relationship between the economic and social realms. Further, if those companies bring their commercial practices into line with the values of ethical consumers, this would justify seeing existing economic institutions and values, especially the profit motive in a competitive market, as the appropriate means for affecting that relationship. Some might, of course, argue that companies need to change because their values change, rather than merely to maintain their profit. However, it seems difficult for a movement that embraces the capitalist market as its main means, to complain when companies in that market are motivated by profit.

More fundamentally, however, it is not clear that the appearance of ethical consumption commerce will produce results that accord with the values of ethical consumers, a disjunction between ethical ends and market means considered in Moberg and Lyon (2010). Of particular concern here is the assumptions concerning the signalling system and the individual purchaser as agent which underlie ethical consumption. These rest on a further assumption, that purchasers are reasonably able to assess objects in terms of their ethical criteria. That assumption is uncertain for a number of reasons, including the preconceptions of consumers that Berlan describes in her chapter. Here, I am concerned with a particular set of reasons, the processes at work within the very market that ethical consumption embraces, processes that reduce the likelihood that purchasers will be able to make reasonable assessments of the ethical nature of what is for sale. These range from the straightforward to the complex.

At the simplest level, companies that want to engage in ethical consumption commerce, that want to sell to ethical consumers, can describe their products accordingly, without regard for how much such a description is justified. Commercial deception is nothing new and remains fairly common. Two cases will illustrate this. Firstly, the Advertising Standards Agency, in Britain, ruled that it was misleading to advertise the Renault Twingo as an 'eco' car with low CO_2 emissions because it is, in fact, one of the most polluting cars of its size (Pearce 2008). Secondly, the Securities and Exchange Commission, in the

United States, charged Pax World, one of the leading American companies running ethical mutual funds (unit trusts), with violating its advertised ethical investment standards; the company paid a $500,000 fine and loosened the standards (Lieber 2008).

This desire of companies to appear more ethical to consumers than they are in fact is not reducible simply to greed and chicanery. It also has a systemic cause, the economic signalling system. This does not link companies only to customers. It links them to investors as well, and they appear to send rather different signals. A study released early in 2008 found that when US companies announce their corporate commitment to 'sustainability' their share prices fall. One of the authors of the study said: 'The pattern was clear — the more aggressive the goal, the more the stock price fell' (Deutsch 2008). Thus, while ethical consumers may want 'sustainability' as a company strategy, the investors who drive share prices do not, and those prices are taken as the key indicator of company performance and affect the pay of senior management.

Ethical consumers who are aware of such commercial practices and, hence, distrust claims that companies make about what they sell, are likely to find themselves in the position of some of the Swedes that Isenhour describes in her chapter. They were concerned especially about their impact on the natural environment, and the conscientious among them spent a lot of time trying to discover the likely consequences of different sorts of purchases. In doing so, they confronted what some call 'green noise' (Williams 2008), a host of urgent and often contradictory messages about the environmental effects of different products and practices (see, e.g., Bhanoo 2009; Navarro 2009; Vidal 2009). In economists' parlance, ethical consumers trying to decide what to buy confront very high information costs.

In such situations it is reasonable for ethical consumers to seek some organisation that they can trust. In her chapter, Vramo points to this trust in her description of an ethical shop in Norway and the people who buy there. The shop sold products that had been designed in Norway and produced in Bangladesh under ethical conditions. In their public statements, the shop adhered to the notion of 'trade not aid', and said that the products were sufficiently attractive to compete with normal commodities. Shop customers appeared to see things differently. They told Vramo that they were relieved to buy there: they had an organisation that they could trust to make the ethical judgements. While this tactic is understandable, it has pitfalls. Just like Renault and Pax World, indeed like every business, Vramo's shop needs customers, and that need can lead companies to focus more on ethical image than on ethical practice. This seems to be the case with the Whole Foods supermarket company in the United States (Johnston 2008) and, as I have noted already, with Starbucks, whose ethical image is contradicted by their efforts to deny their employees the right of free association. Once again, then, commercial practices make the ability of consumers to assess the ethical status of objects uncertain.

Those who want to simplify deciding what to buy can, of course, fall back on certification schemes, such as that of the Fairtrade Foundation, the Soil Association or Slow Food International. However, not all certification systems are alike, and it can be hard to discover which ones are trustworthy. This is illustrated by the Ethical Trading Initiative (www.ethicaltrade.org), an attractively-named certification scheme that has a number of large companies as adherents. The scheme's standards are reasonably high, but it is not clear how much they are enforced: as of late in 2006, when the scheme had been running for some time, no company had been denied certification for failure to conform (van der Zee 2006; see also Smithers and Smith 2009). Similarly, the US Department of Agriculture is, under 1990 legislation, supposed to inspect foods labelled organic on a random basis to assure that they meet the legal definition of 'organic'. However, according to a report by the Department's Inspector General, no such inspections were carried about between 2006 and 2008, and enforcement of standards was lax to the point of being nonexistent (Neuman 2010).

To compound the problem, some certification schemes allow manufacturers themselves to decide if their products meet the criteria. This seems to be the case with the EnergyStar system in the US, run jointly by the Department of Energy and the Environmental Protection Agency (Wald 2010). Apparently, 'companies that make refrigerators, washing machines, dishwashers, water heaters and room air-conditioners ... can certify those appliances themselves' (Wald 2009). Independent certification, however, does not necessarily solve this problem, because firms often rely on private companies to inspect them. Those companies are subject to, and may succumb to, commercial pressure to keep their fees low and their rate of favourable inspection reports high (see, e.g., Moss and Martin 2009; Seversen and Martin 2009).

The existence of schemes like the Ethical Trading Initiative and EnergyStar does not mean that there are no reliable certification systems with reliable inspection systems that offer reasonable protection against chicanery. However, even the existence of honest and honourable systems does not resolve the problems that ethical consumers face. For one thing, the criteria of certification can change without being noticed. In her chapter on organic agriculture in Belgium, Vankeerberghen describes a change in 2007 in the EU criteria for certification of food as organic. Many Belgian organic farmers objected to the change, arguing that it relaxed the standards and weakened the distinctiveness of the category. They argued also that the relaxation came about because the growing demand for organic food had attracted large-scale food companies, and that they were the driving force behind the new criteria. While these changes attracted some public interest, they were likely to be invisible to most ethical consumers, who, understandably, focus on the label rather than the details of what it means.

To make matters even more difficult, reasons to relax certification standards may in fact accord with the values of many ethical consumers. This possibility is presented in Cristina Grasseni's chapter in this volume, on ethical consumption in Italy. She describes the case of Bitto, a cheese distinctive to an alpine area in Lombardy. This cheese had been assigned a Protected Designation of Origin by the EU. Demand for the cheese increased and the body that oversaw the designation allowed the gradual expansion of the area in which it could be produced, as well as a change in its composition. These changes, invisible to someone facing the cheese in a supermarket, altered the nature of what Bitto cheese is. However, those advocating the changes put forward arguments that would make sense to many ethical consumers. The cheese is produced in a depressed, mountainous region. Expanding the authorised area would allow more people to produce it, and so help secure their economic position. The change in its composition allowed for a greater substitution of cow's milk for goat's milk, benefiting local dairies, which were in decline. Both of these changes, thus, would sacrifice authenticity, but would improve the economic prospects of a region that had been becoming poorer for decades.

In their different ways, however, both of these chapters remind us that to focus on changes in certification criteria that are relatively invisible to consumers is to miss a larger point. That is, certification itself can impose a rational impersonality that ethical consumers often reject. Vankeerberghen, for instance, describes the ways that those who have long produced organic food see it as reflecting a way of life and a set of understandings and values concerning the relationship among food, nature and people. For them, the formal criteria of certification are a betrayal, for they ignore these values and relationships, being concerned instead only with the technical aspects of agriculture. Under them, the decision to produce organic lettuce, for instance, becomes simply a commercial judgement guided by market rationality. Grasseni makes a similar point in her chapter. She says that local food, a reflection of producer and place that is expressed in the Fairtrade picture of the smallholder on the package, has changed in ways that reflect the expansion of ethical consumption commerce, and has done so in ways that many ethical consumers would reject. With the spread of certification schemes and growing demand, food that is produced locally in a way that reflects local people's resources and needs becomes displaced by a global category, 'local food', that encourages uniformity and market appeal.

The certification systems that Vankeerberghen and Grasseni describe raise yet another, and more subtle, challenge to the ability of ethical consumers to assess products for sale adequately. Although they involve much more than the fundamentals of competitive commercial practice, such systems rest on them: like the firms that inspect a processing plant to see if it qualifies as organic, companies that produce and sell Fairtrade-certified commodities want the profit, as the head of Cafédirect said. To get it they need sales, and to get sales they need to do more than be ethical: they need to appeal to customers. That need points to a further complication in ethical consumer commerce, and involves something I call 'ethicality' (Carrier 2010).

Ethical consumers want to buy things that satisfy their values. Those values are, of course, abstract. An ethical coffee drinker, for instance, might want coffee that is non-exploitative, produced in a way that does not exploit the growers. 'Non-exploitative', however, is not something that exists concretely in the world. Rather, it is an abstraction that is applied to practices in the world. Because it is an abstraction, it needs to be made 'legible' (Scott 1998), visible and recognisable to those concerned with it. A simple example of this legibility is found in something that Peter Luetchford describes in his chapter, the pictures of growers, typically smiling people of markedly ethnic aspect, that appear on bags of Fairtrade coffee and on the Fairtrade Foundation website (www.fairtrade.net).

These images may, to continue the example, be selected by people in the Fairtrade organisation or the companies that roast the coffee to represent non-exploitative coffee production. However, their selection is shaped by more than how well they represent that production in any objective sense. For one thing, the images need to be recognisable to potential purchasers as representations of concepts like 'non-exploitative', which is another way of saying that they need to make 'non-exploitative' legible. This means that those who select the images need to take into account people's preexisting assumptions, even if dispassionate analysis shows that those assumptions are not particularly valid. So, if people believe, as Berlan's chapter indicates, that small is likely to be more ethical than large, or that the presence of working children is immoral, then the images selected for the coffee bag need to reflect those beliefs if they are to be recognisable to potential purchasers.

Moreover, these recognisable images have to be attractive: they have to portray things with which the potential purchaser would be happy to be associated. So, for example, someone who looks like a self-reliant smallholder likely would be preferable to someone who looks like a migrant labourer or wage worker, even though all are part of producing Fairtrade-certified coffee (e.g., Luetchford 2008; Lyon 2009). The selection of these images, then, is shaped by what the selectors think are the values and assumptions of potential customers, and by what they think will be attractive enough to generate sales. And if those selectors are wrong, their coffee will not sell: they will have to pick other images or go out of business.

These images, then, are intended to make 'non-exploitative coffee production' legible in an appealing way. However, they end up being more than that. Very few of the people who see the picture on the bag know much about growing and processing coffee, about patterns of social and economic relations in places where coffee is grown or about the operation of roasters and certifying organisations, the sorts of things that Luetchford describes in his chapter. So, while they may have a sense of what 'non-exploitative' means in the abstract, they are unlikely to have an independent way of deciding whether or not a particular instance of coffee production is non-exploitative. In this circumstance, it is reasonable to expect that people's assumptions of ethicality, of the moral nature of coffee production in this case, will be defined by the numerous images that they see, especially when those images are associated with reputable bodies like the Fairtrade organisation. So it is that our ethical consumers come to define ethicality in terms of the things that make it legible, the repeated photographs of smiling smallholders that they see on bags of Fairtrade-certified coffee, photographs themselves shaped by the economic pressures that affect coffee companies.

There is nothing very mysterious about this process, by which representations of ethicality become the basis of its definition, nor does it require that those consumers are especially gullible. It is, after all, no different from figuring out what 'cat' means by seeing a hundred things that people call cats. The result, though, is that social values that appear to be opposed to the values and practices of the economic realm end up being shaped by them and so reflect them. At the same time, the images and the associated texts assure purchasers that the makers of the things that they buy share their values. Those recognisable and attractive makers are portrayed as wanting the same personal link between maker and consumer as do ethical consumers, as wanting the same sorts of things in their lives, and as seeing economy, society and their relationship in the same way. In the process of this sort of representation, and for good commercial reasons, the local beliefs and values of ethical consumers in Europe and North America are transmuted into something found among right-thinking folk everywhere.

Conclusion

Every analytical approach to social life is an act of naming, and every name is partial. To call what I am writing with 'a pencil' is partial, for it points to some things and ignores others. However, the point of analytical approaches, like the point of names, is not to be complete, which is not possible in any event. Rather, it is to be useful.

The analytical approach to ethical consumption that I have used in this Introduction certainly is partial. Among other things, it ignores the effects of ethical consumption on retail sales and CO_2 emissions; it ignores the effects of ethical consumption on the domestic lives of consumers; it ignores the ways that ethical consumption can echo old colonial views of the world; it ignores the range of political engagements of those who buy Fairtrade coffee or organic vegetables. I have ignored these things because they do not seem very helpful in achieving the goal that I have sought in this Introduction. That is to consider ethical consumption not in its uniqueness, but in terms of its commonality with other social processes, movements and sets of beliefs.

I have pursued this by placing ethical consumption in an important feature of its social context, the cultural understanding of economy and society as distinct realms of people's lives and of society more generally. As I have noted, this sort of understanding is not purely cultural, purely contemporary or purely Western. It is not purely cultural: I have noted how it also reflects the organisation and practices of the production and circulation of things, as it also reflects people's experiences of these. It is not purely contemporary: I have shown how it is a recurring feature of public life since the rise of capitalism, attested in the intellectual realm by writings of Marx and Weber and in the social realm by the Luddite riots and the Revolutions of 1848. It is not purely Western: as Parry and Bloch argue, it is a feature of many societies around the world.

Approaching ethical consumption in this way does not only help us to understand it by seeing it in terms of larger, long-standing issues and processes. It also helps us to approach it critically. One way it does this is by letting us relate it to other efforts to address the relationship between economy and society. This makes possible what I have only sketched in this Introduction, consideration of the ways that the goals, means and agents of ethical consumption compare with the goals, means and agents of those other efforts. With this comparison we can begin to see not only what ethical consumption embraces, but also what it foregoes.

Seeing ethical consumption in terms of the relationship between economy and society facilitates a second critical approach illustrated in this Introduction. That is to see it in terms of the social and economic practices in which it exists and which it seeks to affect. As I have shown, those practices can create problems as ethical consumers seek to signal their morality to others. As I have also shown, they can raise questions about the assumption that market transactions are an effective way to bring about the changes in the economic realm that ethical consumers want.

As I indicated in this Introduction, and as the chapters that follow indicate in their different ways, ethical consumption is not just buying morally. In spite of its stress on individuals making ethical choices, it is not understandable in terms of the choices that they make in supermarket aisles. Rather, it is a complex and problematic activity, not least because the abstract idea of buying morally will be realised in different ways in different contexts. It is only by exploring those contexts and that complexity and considering the ways that it is problematic, by looking at what it ignores as well as what concerns it, by understanding not just its core actions but also its unintended associations and effects – it is only by exploring all these things that we can begin to consider what ethical consumption is, what it tells us about ourselves and the world, what it can and can not do.

Acknowledgement

A version of this paper was presented at the Seminar on Politics, Society, the Environment and Development at Barnard College, of Columbia University, and at the Anthropology Department seminar at the University of Sussex. I am grateful for the stimulating questions and comments of those who attended.

Bibliography

Barnett, Steve and Martin Silverman 1979. Separations in capitalist societies: persons, things, units and relations. In *Ideology and everyday life*, S. Barnett and M. Silverman, pp. 39–81. Ann Arbor: University of Michigan Press.

Bhanoo, Sindyan 2009. Calculating emissions is problematic. *The New York Times* (22 October). www.nytimes.com/2009/10/23/science/earth/23biofuel.html?_r=1&scp=1&sq=Calculating%20Emissions%20Is%20Problematic%20&st=cse

Bohannan, Paul 1955. Some principles of exchange and investment among the Tiv. *American Anthropologist* 57: 60–70.

Bourdieu, Pierre 1977. *Outline of a theory of practice*. Cambridge: Cambridge University Press.

———— 1984. *Distinction: a social critique of the judgement of taste*. London: Routledge & Kegan Paul.

Bowers, Simon 2009. Sweet deal: Dairy Milk to carry Fairtrade badge. *The Guardian* (4 March). www.guardian.co.uk/environment/2009/mar/04/cadbury-fair-trade-dairy-milk

Boyson, Rhodes 1970. *The Ashworth cotton enterprise: the rise and fall of a family firm, 1818–1880*. Oxford: Clarendon Press.

Calhoun, Craig 1982. *The question of class struggle*. Chicago: University of Chicago Press.

Carrier, James G. 1995. *Gifts and commodities: exchange and Western capitalism since 1700*. London: Routledge.

———— 1997. Introduction. In *Meanings of the market: the free market in Western culture* (ed) J. Carrier, pp. 1–67. Oxford: Berg.

———— 1999. People who can be friends: notions of the self and of social relationships. In *Only connect: the anthropology of friendship* (eds) Sandra Bell and Simon Coleman, pp. 21–38. Oxford: Berg.

———— 2010. Protecting the environment the natural way: ethical consumption and commodity fetishism. In *Conservation and capitalism* (eds) Dan Brockington and Rosaleen Duffy. *Antipode* 42 (special issue): 668–85.

Churchill, Winston 1948. Untitled speech at the Hague, 7 May. http://ukinnl.fco.gov.uk/resources/en/pdf/pdf1/postnl_relationschurchill

Crowley, J.E. 1974. *This Sheba, self: the conceptualization of economic life in eighteenth century America*. Baltimore: Johns Hopkins University Press.

Deutsch, Claudia H. 2008. Saving the planet? Not with my money. *The New York Times* (26 March). www.nytimes.com/2008/03/26/business/businessspecial2/26price.html?ref=businessspecial2

Fairtrade Labelling Organizations International 2006. Generic standards. www.fairtrade.net/generic_standards.html

Fukuyama, Francis 1992. *The end of history and the last man*. New York: The Free Press.

Galbraith, Kate 2008. Assessing the value of small wind turbines. *The New York Times* (3 September). www.nytimes.com/2008/09/04/business/04wind.html?ref=business&pagewanted=all

Gouldner, Helen and Mary Symons Strong 1987. *Speaking of friendship: middle-class women and their friends*. Westport, Conn.: Greenwood Press.

Greenhouse, Steven 2008. Starbucks loses round in battle over union. *The New York Times* (23 December). www.nytimes.com/2008/12/24/nyregion/24starbucks.html?_r=1&ref=business

Gudeman, Stephen 2001. *The anthropology of economy*. Oxford: Blackwell Publishers.

——— 2008. *Economy's tension: the dialectics of community and market*. New York: Berghahn Books.

Hendrickson, Robert 1978. *The grand emporiums*. New York: Stein & Day.

Hickman, Martin and Karen Attwood 2008. Fairtrade sales double to £500m as supermarkets join trend. *The Independent* (25 February). www.independent.co.uk/news/business/news/fairtrade-sales-double-to-163500m-as-supermarkets-join-trend-786931.html

Hirschman, Albert O. 1977. *The passions and the interests*. Princeton: Princeton University Press.

Jefferys, James B. 1954. *Retail trading in Britain: 1850–1950*. Cambridge: Cambridge University Press.

Johnston, Josée 2008. The citizen-consumer hybrid: ideological tensions and the case of Whole Foods Market. *Theory and Society* 37: 229–70.

Jowit, Juliette 2009. Many home turbines fall short of claims, warns study. *The Guardian* (13 January). www.guardian.co.uk/technology/2009/jan/13/wind-turbine-efficiency-postlethwaite-cameron

Kahn, Joel S. 1990. Towards a history of the critique of economism: the nineteenth century German origins of the ethnographer's dilemma. *Man* (N.S.) 25: 230–49.

Lieber, Ron 2008. Socially responsible, with egg on its face. *The New York Times* (22 August). www.nytimes.com/2008/08/23/business/yourmoney/23money.html?_r=1&ref=business&pagewanted=all

Lubasz, Heinz 1992. Adam Smith and the invisible hand — of the market? In *Contesting markets: analyses of ideology, discourse and practice* (ed) Roy Dilley, pp. 37–56. Edinburgh: Edinburgh University Press.

Luetchford, Peter G. 2008. The hands that pick fair trade coffee: beyond the charms of the family farm. In *Hidden hands in the market: ethnographies of fair trade, ethical consumption and corporate social responsibility* (eds) Geert De Neve, P.G. Luetchford, Jeff Pratt and Donald C. Wood. *Research in Economic Anthropology* 28 (Special Issue): 143–70.

Lyon, Sarah 2009. 'What good will two more trees do?' The political economy of sustainable coffee certification, local livelihoods and identities. In *Surroundings, selves and others: the political economy of environment and identity* (eds) James G. Carrier and Paige West. *Landscape Research* 34 (special issue): 223–40.

McKendrick, Neil, John Brewer and J.H. Plumb 1982. *The birth of a consumer society*. Bloomington: Indiana University Press.

Martinson, Jane 2007. The ethical coffee chief turning a fair profit. *Guardian Unlimited* (9 March). www.guardian.co.uk/environment/2007/mar/09/food.business

Marx, Karl, and Frederick Engels 1948 [1848]. *Manifesto of the Communist Party*. New York: International Publishers.

Mauss, Marcel 1990 [1925]. *The gift*. London: Routledge.

Miller, Daniel 1987. *Material culture and mass consumption*. Oxford: Basil Blackwell.

——— 1998. *A theory of shopping*. Cambridge: Polity Press.

Moberg, Mark and Sarah Lyon 2010. What's fair? The paradox of seeking justice through markets. In *Fair trade and social justice: global ethnographies* (eds) S. Lyon and M. Moberg, pp. 1–24. New York: NYU Press.

Moss, Michael and Andrew Martin 2009. Food problems elude private inspectors. *The New York Times* (5 March). www.nytimes.com/2009/03/06/business/06food. html?th=&emc=th&pagewanted=all

Navarro, Mireya 2009. Environmental groups spar over certifications of wood and paper products. *The New York Times* (11 September). www.nytimes.com/2009/09/ 12/science/earth/12timber.html?_r=1&scp=1&sq=Environmental%20Groups%20 Spar%20Over%20Certifications%20of%20Wood%20and%20Paper%20 Products%20&st=cse

Neuman, William 2010. U.S. plans spot tests of organic products. *The New York Times* (19 March). www.nytimes.com/2010/03/20/business/20organic.html?ref=us

Packard, Vance 1957. *The hidden persuaders*. New York: David McKay Company.

Parry, Jonathan 1986. The gift, the Indian gift and the 'Indian gift'. *Man* 21 (N.S.): 453–73.

——— and Maurice Bloch (eds) 1989. *Money and the morality of exchange*. Cambridge: Cambridge University Press.

Parsons, Talcott 1959. The social structure of the family. In *The family* (ed) Ruth Nanda Anshen, pp. 241–74. New York: Harper and Row.

Pearce, Fred 2008. The great green swindle. *The Guardian* (23 October). www.guardian.co.uk/environment/2008/oct/23/ethicalbusiness-consumeraffairs

Perin, Constance 1977. *Everything in its place: social order and land use in America*. Princeton: Princeton University Press.

Piotrkowski, Chaya 1979. *Work and the family system*. New York: The Free Press.

Polanyi, Karl 1957 [1944]. *The great transformation: the political and economic origins of our time*. Boston: Beacon Press.

Ponte, Stefano, Lisa Ann Richey and Mike Baab 2008. *Bono's Product (RED) initiative: wedding hard commerce and corporate social responsibility*. Copenhagen: Danish Institute for International Studies. www.diis.dk/graphics/Publications/WP2008/ WP08-13_Bono%92s_Product_%28Red%29_Initiative_Wedding_Hard_ Commerce_and_Corporate_Social_Responsibility.pdf

Pratt, Jeff 2007. Food values: the local and the authentic. *Critique of Anthropology* 27: 285–300.

Schneider, David 1980 [1968]. *American kinship: a cultural account* (Second edition). Chicago: University of Chicago Press.

Scott, James C. 1998. *Seeing like a state*. New Haven: Yale University Press.

Severson, Kim 2008. Slow Food savors its big moment. *The New York Times* (23 July). www.nytimes.com/2008/07/23/dining/23slow.html?th=&emc=th&pagewanted=all

——— and Andrew Martin 2009. It's organic, but does that mean it's safer? *The New York Times* (3 March). www.nytimes.com/2009/03/04/dining/04cert.html?_ r=1&sq=Organic%20safer&st=cse&scp=1&pagewanted=all

Silver, Allan 1990. Friendship in commercial society: eighteenth-century social theory and modern sociology. *American Journal of Sociology* 95: 1474–504.

Smith, Adam 1976 [1776]. *An inquiry into the nature and causes of the wealth of nations*. Chicago: University of Chicago Press.

Smithers, Rebecca and David Smith 2009. Tesco 'breaking promise' to South African fruit pickers. *The Guardian* (15 May). www.guardian.co.uk/business/2009/may/15/ tesco-south-africa-workers-conditions

Spence, Michael 1976. Informational aspects of market structure: an introduction. *The Quarterly Journal of Economics* 90: 591–97.

Stone, Brad and Matt Richtel 2009. Forging a hot link to the farmer who grows the food. *The New York Times* (27 March). www.nytimes.com/2009/03/28/technology/internet/28farmer.html?ref=technology

Sunderland, Patricia L. and Rita M. Denny 2007. *Doing anthropology in consumer research*. Walnut Creek, Cal.: Left Coast Press.

Thompson, E.P. 1968. *The making of the English working class*. Harmondsworth: Penguin.

Treanor, Jill 2010. Fair trade sales rise 12% despite 'difficult year'. *The Guardian* (22 February). www.guardian.co.uk/business/2010/feb/22/sales-of-fair-trade-products-rises-12-percent

Veblen, Thorstein 1927. *The theory of the leisure class*. New York: Vanguard Press.

Vidal, John 2009. UN's forest protection scheme at risk from organised crime, experts warn. *The Guardian* (5 October). www.guardian.co.uk/environment/2009/oct/05/un-forest-protection

Wald, Matthew L. 2009. EnergyStar appliances may not all be efficient, audit finds. *The New York Times* (18 October). www.nytimes.com/2009/10/19/business/energy-environment/19star.html?_r=1&scp=1&sq=Energy%20Star%20Appliances%20May%20Not%20All%20Be%20Efficient,%20Audit%20&st=cse

————2010. Audit finds vulnerability of EnergyStar program. *The New York Times* (25 March), www.nytimes.com/2010/03/26/science/earth/26star.html?ref=us

Watt, Nicholas 2009. Shoppers need clear labels to put a stop to 'greenwash'. *The Guardian* (23 March). www.guardian.co.uk/politics/2009/mar/23/greenwash-advertising

Wearden, Graeme 2008. Tate & Lyle hopes Fairtrade will sweeten results. *The Guardian* (23 May). www.guardian.co.uk/business/2008/may/23/tateandlyle.fooddrinks

Weber, Max 1958 [1904–5]. *The Protestant ethic and the spirit of capitalism*. New York: Charles Scribner's Sons.

———— 1978 [c. 1914]. *Economy and society*. (Guenther Roth and Claus Wittich, eds), Berkeley: University of California Press.

———— 1981 [1923]. *General economic history*. New Brunswick, NJ: Transaction Books.

Wilk, Richard 1996. *Economies and cultures: foundations of economic anthropology*. Boulder, Col.: Westview Press.

Williams, Alex 2008. That buzz in your ear may be green noise. *The New York Times* (15 June). www.nytimes.com/2008/06/15/fashion/15green.html?_r=1&sq=Green%20noise&st=nyt&oref=slogin&scp=1&pagewanted=all

van der Zee, Bibi 2006. They sweat, you shop. *The Guardian* (14 December). www.guardian.co.uk/business/2006/dec/14/retail.ethicalliving

Zelizer, Viviana A. 1989. The social meaning of money: 'special monies'. *American Journal of Sociology* 95: 342–77.

Section I

PRODUCERS AND CONSUMERS

As indicated by their invocation in the Introduction, the chapters in this volume describe people in a variety of places to make a variety of points. However, the four that form the first section of this volume are concerned especially with an important element of ethical consumption: the relationship between producers and consumers.

In their attempt to counter the increasing subordination of life to impersonal economic calculation, many ethical consumers seek to socialise what they buy. They seek to link the object to the people who grow or make it and, often, they seek to assure that those producers are treated equitably. As was noted in the Introduction, however, those producers commonly live a very long way away from the people who buy those products, and the techniques and relations in which those things are produced are unknown to the purchaser. One consequence of this is that the relationship between producer and consumer is defined by something other than the intersection of their lives and practices.

That relationship, then, is likely to exist primarily in the purchaser's mind rather than in the experiences of daily life. And what is in that purchaser's mind is shaped in important ways by the information about and images of the producer that the purchaser confronts, as well as by the values and assumptions that affect the purchaser's interpretation of that information and those images. As one might imagine, the results of this mediated relationship are problematic, in a number of ways and for a number of reasons.

One way in which that relationship is problematic is described in the first chapter in this section, Amanda Berlan's 'Good Chocolate? An Examination of Ethical Consumption in Cocoa'. As she argues, the images of and information about cocoa producers presented to chocolate purchasers can be radically simplified to the point of being wrong-headed. This, at least, seems to be the case with the campaign against abusive practices in cocoa production that she describes. She agrees that there may be such practices, but as she notes, the campaigners did more than assert abuse and argue against it. Rather, in their efforts to attract support they portrayed a highly stylised, purified and stereotyped world of cocoa production, a sort of reverse ethicality. On the one hand are large, heedless or immoral companies and tainted cocoa; on the other are small, ethical companies and fair-trade cocoa.

How did this portrayal come about and why did it get the reception that it did? To answer these questions we have to look at the values and assumptions common among the people those campaigners were addressing. Berlan observes that, in the form of chocolate, cocoa has a special cultural value, associated strongly with close social relations, the family and friends who give, receive and share chocolate. Thus, more than other common foods, immoral chocolate is alarming. Allied with this is something else, the assumption that big organisations are prone to be bad, whether Big Business or Big Government. These values and assumptions might have been fairly unimportant if people knew how cocoa was grown and processed, how things like Fairtrade certification operated and how the cocoa market worked. However, for many people these are opaque, technical matters, which leaves the field open for those values and assumptions to operate unchallenged. The result is that the claims of the campaigners become plausible and even compelling.

The point we can draw from Berlan's chapter, then, is that people's perceptions of the social, economic and other contexts of the things that they confront in a shop may be more a consequence of their values and assumptions than they are of the relations and practices of production and trade. Moreover, to recall a point made in the Introduction, those who want to appeal to Western consumers, whether to boycott large chocolate companies or to buy ethical products, need to cater to those values and assumptions in their publicity. The next chapter in this section provides another example of this, concerned not with tainted cocoa but with ethical coffee. It is Peter Luetchford's 'Consuming Producers: Fair Trade and Small Farmers'.

Much of the work done by anthropologists on ethical consumption has been concerned with how things look from the perspective of producers and growers (e.g., Luetchford 2008; Lyon 2009; Moberg 2008). In his chapter, Luetchford also uses that perspective. However, his concern is with the relationship between what those producers and growers experience on the one hand, and on the other the images and information presented to ethical consumers. As is the case with Berlan's cocoa, with Luetchford's coffee that relationship is problematic.

Luetchford sets the stage for his description of coffee production by considering those images and that information. As he demonstrates, ethical coffee, particularly specialist coffee sold as Fairtrade-certified and the like, differs from conventional coffee by socialising what is in the bag. The potential purchaser is presented with growers, their villages and their children, all committed to a durable relationship with the ethical roaster who buys their coffee. For this socialising to be attractive, it needs to invoke things that are both legible and appealing. The images and information do this by indicating that the coffee is produced by a community of independent smallholders, the faces printed on the back of the bag. It is also worth noting that commonly the text on the bag distinguishes Fairtrade from regular coffee, which is described a being produced under more onerous conditions.

Like the ethical cocoa that Berlan describes, however, the operation of the coffee market means that this distinction is not that clear. The coffee in the regular bag may well be as ethical as that in the Fairtrade bag, produced by the same growers in the same way but sold to a different roaster-buyer.

The cooperatives in Costa Rica that Luetchford describes, producing Fairtrade-certified coffee, did include independent smallholders. However, as his chapter explains, such people were hardly typical, or even all that common. Some growers owned substantial holdings, only a small part of which was in coffee. Some growers were landless, working someone else's land in return for a share of the proceeds. Moreover, many of the hands that worked the crop were the hands of casual workers, some from the locality but many migrant workers from Nicaragua. The cooperatives he describes sold coffee to roasters as Fairtrade-certified, but were willing to sell the same coffee to conventional roasters if they thought it was beneficial and were, at times, in a relationship with the Fairtrade organisation that was almost adversarial.

Of course none of what Luetchford describes detracts from the fact that those cooperatives produced coffee that met the Fairtrade criteria, from the fact that they willingly sold coffee regularly to Fairtrade roasters or from the fact that they benefited from these sales. What Luetchford describes does, however, point to the problematic nature of the relationship between the information and images on the bag of ethical coffee and the lives and practices of the growers. Just as few people in a supermarket in Europe or North America know how cocoa is produced, few know how coffee is produced. A manifestation of this is a large sign above the display of coffee in a Whole Foods supermarket in suburban Washington that I saw in February 2009. It had a picture of the branches of a coffee tree with a pair of hands holding some of the berries. The caption said that the coffee sold in the supermarket was picked by hand. This sign makes sense only if people who shop there are ignorant of the fact that, except in extraordinary circumstances, all coffee is picked by hand, from the most industrial and chemical-ridden to the most ethical and shade-grown.

This ignorance means that coffee companies face few constraints other than the commercial in their selection of the information and images that they present. And that commercial constraint encourages them to select things that are recognisable and appealing. This means that what they select is more likely to be a reflection of the ideas and assumptions of potential purchasers than it is to be a dispassionate reflection of coffee production. The result, as Luetchford argues, is that ethical consumers confront a simple world that looks rather like their own, or like what they wish for in their more nostalgic moments. The coffee is grown by independent smallholders, the sturdy yeomanry of English history and the settlers of the American West. Not only independent but also self-reliant, they manage and harvest the crop themselves. And in their long-term alliance with their roaster-buyers, they embrace the values enshrined in Fairtrade certification and expressed by ethical consumers.

In their chapters, both Berlan and Luetchford look at agricultural producers in tropical regions and at Fairtrade certification as the mark of ethical production. Ethical consumption, of course, involves things other than those producers and that certification. These other things are considered in the next chapter in this section, '"Trade, not aid": Imagining Ethical Economy', by Lill Vramo. The Norwegian store that she describes, Fair Shop, sells housewares and similar items rather than foodstuffs. However, they too socialise what they sell: these things are designed by Fair Shop but are made by impoverished women in Bangladesh, who are employed in an ethical way. As Vramo describes, the socialising is coy. Customers are not told about the women being helped until after they make their purchases, but everyone seems to know what is going on and it is unlikely that many people are surprised.

Because this socialising is coy, items in the shop have no photographs of the people who make them and no descriptions of their work. Instead, people are free to imagine them, and Vramo describes that imagining in terms of a tale of the empowerment of disadvantaged Bangladeshi women through paid work outside the home. This tale is not, of course, peculiar to thoughts about women in Bangladesh, for it is a staple of those who have been concerned with women's position in Western society for much of the last century. Women should not be restricted to the domestic sphere; they should be able to achieve the dignity that comes from being productive; the money they earn makes them less dependent on others, especially the men around them.

This is not just a common Western tale. In addition, it is the tale that those who work at Fair Shop tell each other, a tale that makes being a shop clerk something worthwhile, rather than being a fairly low-status job. Of course those Bangladeshi producers are a long way from Norway, Fair Shop, its workers and customers, so that it is easy to imagine this tale in relation to those women. Unfortunately, however, its relationship to the lives and thoughts of the Bangladeshi workers is as problematic as the portrayals of cocoa and coffee production that Berlan and Luetchford describe.

Vramo points to two main reasons for this. The first and simplest is material. Work producing for Fair Shop is irregular and even though the pay rate is moderately generous, the amount of money earned is too small to make a material difference to the women who produce what Fair Shop sells. The second reason is more complex. This tale of women being empowered through paid work outside the household may be a staple of Western thought, but it is not the tale that these women tell, except, of course, when a member of Fair Shop flies to Bangladesh to visit. Then, the visitor hears the standard gratitude for empowering these women through that work. The Bangladeshi women's own tale, however, is not one of progress and empowerment, but of decay. To work outside the home for money in the way that these women do is a matter of shame rather than hope. That is because such work marks them as being so poor that they can not stay at home, managing the family resources and relationships.

The first three chapters in this section describe ways that ethical consumers are presented with images of producers as part of the socialising of the ethical objects on offer, whether to make them attractive (Luetchford, Vramo) or to make them fit subjects of boycott (Berlan). In all these cases, producers and consumers are far apart, so that socialisation can and does contain a large dose of imagination. However, there are times when producers and consumers are not so far apart. Then, the desire for personality and socialisation that seems to motivate many ethical consumers can be realised in a way not possible with Ghanaian chocolate, Costa Rican coffee or Bangladeshi fabrics. That situation is described in the last chapter in this section, Audrey Vankeerberghen's '"Today, one can farm organic without living organic": Belgian Farmers and Recent Changes in Organic Farming'.

In Belgium, and in much of Europe, organic farming has not been simply a set of agricultural techniques. Rather, it has been the expression of a set of understandings and values that link farmers, nature, food and the people who eat it. This is the 'living organic' of Vankerbeerghen's title. For those who practised it or who sought organic food, it meant farming in a way that respected the processes and cycles of nature. Farms generally were small and farmers commonly sold their produce directly to consumers, either at farm shops or in local markets. This way of selling was good for the environment, because it entailed little transportation, and it meant that the food was fresh. Moreover, it meant that farmers were able to do what they had to do in the absence of formal certification, develop durable relations with consumers based on trust. In all, then, organic agriculture looked like what ethical consumers want.

This situation began to change in the 1990s. In that decade ethical consumption started to become popular and, more narrowly, reports of the emergence of BSE and of the appearance of salmonella and dioxin in their food made many people unhappy about its safety. For both reasons, the demand for organic food increased and a form of what the Introduction calls 'ethical consumption commerce' began to emerge. An important part of the foundations that allowed that emergence was laid by an EEC regulation of 1991, which defined organic agriculture. It did so in purely technical terms, focusing on the sorts of agricultural inputs farmers had to use if their produce were to be classed as organic. The values and relationships were ignored.

The result of all this, as Vankeerberghen explains, is that since the middle of the 1990s the nature of organic farming has been changing, though the image of the older form of organic agriculture has remained important in people's minds. Small farmers who live organic confronted a growing number of large corporations that were producing certified organic food. These corporations were happy to follow the technical requirements of EU regulations in order to secure the higher prices that organic certification allows, and they were happy to stock supermarket shelves with impersonal produce rather than establish durable relationships with consumers. Those who work for these corporations are, to invoke Vankeerberghen's title once more, the people who 'can farm organic without living organic'. Those who farm in the older organic way are still there, but find themselves losing their ability to influence new national and EU regulations, as they find themselves losing sales to consumers who increasingly find their organic food in the supermarket aisles more easily and cheaply than at the farm shop.

Vankeerberghen's description of the way that organic farming in Belgium has changed in the last couple of decades does not only provide an instance of the emergence of ethical consumption commerce. In addition, what she has to say reinforces the points I have drawn from the three previous chapters: the relationship between the consumers' image of producers and their actual lives and practices is problematic. In this case it is not because producers are at a great distance from consumers. Rather, it is because producers who are not that far away become invisible to consumers, who increasingly see only the produce on the shelves and in the bins of their supermarkets.

There is a further point that we can draw from Vankeerberghen's chapter. As Luetchford explains in his chapter, ethical consumption often is said to be attractive because it breaks down the barrier between producers and consumers. However, the willingness of Belgian consumers to abandon the local market and the farm shop for the supermarket suggests that this attraction may be of a peculiar sort. It may well be that most people are happier with the image of the producer than with the reality, with the idea of sociality than with the complex, recurring interactions that create it. This should, in retrospect, be no surprise, for images can be comforting and congenial in a way that is unlikely with real cocoa and coffee growers, Bangladeshi textile workers and Belgian chicken farmers.

To make this point is to raise the question of why and how people become ethical consumers and how that consumption affects them in different ways. That question is the focus of the second section of this volume.

Bibliography

Luetchford, Peter G. 2008. *Fair trade and a global commodity: coffee in Costa Rica*. London: Pluto Press.

Lyon, Sarah 2009. 'What good will two more trees do?' The political economy of sustainable coffee certification, local livelihoods and identities. In *Surroundings, selves and others: the political economy of environment and identity* (eds) James G. Carrier and Paige West. *Landscape Research* 34 (special issue): 223–40.

Moberg, Mark 2008. *Slipping away: banana politics and fair trade in the Eastern Caribbean*. Oxford: Berghahn.

Chapter 1

GOOD CHOCOLATE? AN EXAMINATION OF ETHICAL CONSUMPTION IN COCOA

Amanda Berlan

This chapter investigates some of the current meanings attached to a particular commodity, cocoa, and the way in which it is constructed as ethical or unethical. The question of how different parties create, build and sustain the ethical qualities of a product is especially significant in relation to cocoa. As a key ingredient in chocolate, it has achieved quasi-celebrity status in the developed world and it amply illustrates Arjun Appadurai's (1986: 6) claim that 'a commodity is a thoroughly socialised thing'. Chocolate is both adored and boycotted, and has made front-page headlines for being healthy, fattening, comforting, ethical, exploitative and even been the subject of a 'revolution'.[1] These headlines show the polarisation of assessments of cocoa, and the way these focus on the rights and wrongs of some of the ingredients in chocolate.

In this chapter my aim is to deconstruct the ethicality of cocoa in order to understand some of the current ideas that are attached to it and why cocoa is often described using labels such as ethical or exploitative. I am interested to unpick these labels based not on producer experiences but on the basis of anthropological theory. To anticipate a point I develop later in this chapter, the work of Mary Douglas is used to suggest that the representations of ethical consumption in binary and oppositional terms is over-simplistic and problematic because it does not necessarily guide consumers to make the most informed ethical choices. In this respect, what I present about the ethicality of cocoa draws attention to the role of social anthropology in understanding ethical consumption more broadly and in helping make sense of the moral maze confronting consumers in their daily lives.

Ethical Consumption Past and Present

Ethical consumption has become a widely recognised concept in the UK, and many ethically sourced products are now found on the shelves of supermarkets.

Fairtrade products, those certified by the Fairtrade Labelling Organization (FLO), are probably the most visible sign of ethical consumption. In recent years, they have achieved a greater market penetration in the UK than in other European countries. Confirmation of the importance of the ethical-consumption market was provided in 2006 by the Ethical Consumerism Report, a survey produced by the Co-operative Bank in the UK. The report (Co-operative Bank 2006) stated that the total value of ethical consumerism had overtaken retail sales of alcohol and tobacco for the first time, a change which was seen as something of a landmark in the broader landscape of consumption in the UK. However, although the growth in ethical consumption is rightly hailed as a significant achievement, the process of ascribing moral qualities to goods and services is less of an innovation, and more complex, than it may initially seem.

As outlined in the Introduction to this volume, ethical consumption has historical antecedents, such as the campaign to boycott slave-grown sugar early in the nineteenth century (see also Collins, this volume). Other early examples of ethical products include the 1885 initiative to identify cigars made by unionised workforces with a blue ribbon, allowing consumers to support the free organisation of labour (New 2004: 17); and the ethically traded products sold in the US, France and Germany early in the twentieth century through buyers' associations. In these associations (*ligues sociales d'acheteurs* in France, *Käuferbund* in Germany), 'every act of consumption was regarded as linked to every act of production, everybody being responsible … [for] the well being of producers by their consumption choices' (De Ferran and Grunert 2007: 219). These associations organised the first conference on socially responsible consumption in Geneva in 1908, which was attended by delegates from many European countries and the US. These delegates belonged to a network of reformers from Protestant and Catholic backgrounds who wanted to improve working conditions. They saw themselves, and consumers more generally, as having responsibilities for the welfare of producers.

There is also evidence of trade for the ethical purpose of redistributing wealth in preindustrial societies. For instance, Marshall Sahlins describes the way the Busana of New Guinea paid 10–12 shillings for Tami Islander bowls, and then exchanged them for pots made by villagers to the south, which were worth only 8 shillings. When asked about this practice, the Busana said of the southern potters: 'They live in such hungry country. Besides we want pots for ourselves and to exchange for mats and things' (Sahlins 1972: 290, quoting Hogbin 1951: 92). More broadly, even as early as the fourth century BC, Aristotle distinguished between the domestic economy, which is exchange on the basis of mutual needs; and exchange for profit, which served only to accrue wealth. He stated: 'The former is indispensable and laudable; whereas the latter … is justly disparaged as being contrary to Nature and enriching one party at the expense of the other' (Aristotle 1923: 27).

These examples indicate that attributing moral significance to a product and to the economic exchange of which it is a part is not exclusive to socially minded consumers in the modern era. They also point to a universality of attributing moral significance to everyday goods. This supports the view, based on the interpretations of different cross-cultural examples provided by Parry and Bloch (1989), that 'Fair trade may well touch on a cross-culturally engrained moral sensitivity' (De Neve, Luetchford and Pratt 2008: 6). The universality of ethical consumption, and the categorisation it involves, is investigated in greater depth later in this chapter.

However, although earlier examples are indicative of trade going beyond economic rationality, the meanings and values that underlie those examples may differ vastly from those of modern ethical consumption. As stated in the Introduction to this volume, we should not assume they have common roots and understandings. In the examples cited, 'ethical' was perceived to be synonymous with socially responsible, but there are clearly other possible interpretations of the word. Though the labelling of different acts of consumption may give rise to expectations of commonality, these acts are imbedded in a complex and highly variable social matrix of personal and collective understandings of morality, poverty and wealth, trade, social conscience, consumption, socioeconomic status and many other things. In order to demonstrate this, the present chapter considers the specific associations attached to cocoa and what they reveal about consumption more broadly.

From a personal perspective, my thinking relating to ethicality in cocoa has shifted considerably since I was first involved in research on cocoa and Fairtrade ten years ago. While my sympathy for ethical consumption remains unchallenged (both as it relates to Fairtrade and to ethical trade more broadly), field work with cocoa producers in different countries and involvement with different stakeholders in the world of chocolate has challenged me to consider new perspectives, which I now think are worthy of anthropological attention. Having received research funding from the Cadbury Cocoa Partnership in 2009–10, I have become more familiar with some of their operations than with those of other companies, and this chapter discusses some of their initiatives which can be said to relate to ethical consumption. However, as will be apparent, this is not with a view to promoting or defending Cadbury or any large chocolate company. Rather, it is an attempt to unpack and bring to the surface some of the assumptions that appear to be implicit in ethical consumption, both about chocolate and more generally.

'Ethical' and 'Exploitative' Cocoa

Following allegations of labour abuses in the production of cocoa in West Africa, demands for ethically sourced cocoa abounded in the UK and North America. These demands revolved primarily around two key issues, the first of which was labour. This followed reports in the media such as the following, from *The Guardian*:

No one knows how many children die as they are shipped to the cocoa plantations of West Africa. What is known are the appalling conditions on many of the boats. Those who have lived to tell of such things say they were left with a tiny amount of food and only filthy drinking water for a journey that lasts days. (McGreal 2001)

Other reports said that 'more than half the world's chocolate' was produced in abusive conditions and that children were 'working 12-hour days carrying heavy sacks of cocoa beans' (Jones 2001). This issue also received coverage in the US media. For example, the Knight Ridder News Service stated:

There may be a hidden ingredient in the chocolate cake you baked, the candy bars your children sold for their school fund-raiser or that fudge ripple ice-cream cone you enjoyed on Saturday afternoon. Slave labor. … The lucky slaves live on corn paste and bananas. The unlucky ones are whipped, beaten and broken like horses to harvest the almond-sized beans that are made into chocolate treats for more fortunate children in Europe and America. (Raghavan and Chatterjee 2001)

Understandably, such reporting affected the buying behaviour of many consumers. However debatable some of the allegations on this subject might have been (a point I return to below), they resulted in a meteoric rise in demand for 'ethical' cocoa, defined as cocoa produced without any abusive labour practices. At the time, the only cocoa produced under identified labour standards was cocoa certified by FLO, and the Fairtrade mark quickly became the hallmark of acceptable labour conditions. In the words of a campaigner for trade justice who wrote to me in 2007:

[A]bout 6 years or so ago I happened to see a Blue Peter report on the use of child labour on cocoa plantations, and felt so strongly about the issue I immediately stopped eating chocolate! Since then I've only eaten Fairtrade.

The second issue around which conceptualisations of ethicality in cocoa crystallised was whether the cocoa was sourced, manufactured into chocolate and sold by multinational corporations. This was pertinent for many people, who saw such corporations as ethically weak. For example, consumers wrote to newspapers asking:

If Cadbury Schweppes is a responsible and ethical business … with honest motives for the health and wellbeing of ordinary children, what is it doing to 'touch the millions' of poor, exploited cocoa producers and child labourers farming and processing cocoa in West African plantations? (Ayres 2003)

Many sources blamed abusive labour practices on low prices in the world cocoa market, on irresponsible chocolate manufacturers and on imbalanced supply-chain dynamics. Without doubt, all of these can influence labour practices. However, the same could be said of other things that were not included in debates of ethicality in cocoa: in the countries involved, sound governance, national trade and labour policies, law enforcement, broader sociocultural factors and household decision making also shape labour issues. However, instead of seeing Third World farmers, governments and institutions as central to addressing the perceived depravity of the cocoa trade, most of those concerned with the issue focused on the purchasing decisions of Western consumers.

Following these media stories, the simple act of buying a bar of chocolate came to acquire heavy moral implications. Ethicality in cocoa became increasingly polarised according to binary classifications: labour practices were described as fair or unfair, ethical or exploitative; the cocoa was pure or tainted with abuse; the companies involved wanted to help or 'screw' the farmers. As the example of the Fairtrade campaigner given above showed, this meant that many people saw unethical cocoa as polluting, and saw themselves as being tainted or defiled if they consumed it. For instance, one source (Pellizzari 2002) distinguished between 'bondage' and 'clean' cocoa beans.

Concerns about labour violations in the chocolate supply chain gained considerable currency internationally and formed the basis of many initiatives that aimed to improve the rights of abused workers in cocoa. These include the Harkin–Engel Protocol, an international agreement signed in September 2001 by different stakeholders, including major chocolate companies, which aims to end child labour in the production of cocoa. Another example is the International Cocoa Initiative, founded in 2002. This partnership between chocolate companies, labour unions and non-governmental organisations aims to prevent child labour and hazardous labour practices in cocoa.

Beyond Labels

The ethics of cocoa, and the moral dimension of chocolate, may not appear to warrant any further discussion or explanation. If cocoa production involves labour abuses, then revulsion and the desire to eradicate such practices appear to be understandable and unproblematic responses. Furthermore, it is no surprise that the power asymmetries between multinationals and producers provide ample scope for relations between these parties to include some form of malpractice.

In the case of cocoa, however, there are a number of reasons why ethicality is not as straightforward as it may appear initially. Firstly, as already noted, some of the news reports portraying labour practices were problematic and in some cases very subjective. These issues are varied and too complex to treat adequately here (examples and further discussion can be found in Anti-Slavery 2004; Berlan 2009; Finkel 2005). However, and briefly, it is important to note that there is considerable variation in labour statistics on cocoa,[2] and some of the media coverage did not provide a representative picture of cocoa production.

Globally, the majority of cocoa, not just cocoa certified as ethical, is produced under conditions in keeping with core international labour standards. Kevin Bales (2007: 181–83), president of Free the Slaves, the US sister organisation of Britain's Anti-Slavery International, puts it this way: 'only a tiny fraction of the world's cotton or cocoa or steel has slave input … for every criminal using slaves to grow cotton or cocoa or sugar, hundreds or thousands of farmers are producing the same crops without using slaves'. Of course the fact that cocoa is mostly produced under acceptable conditions does not excuse any abuse which takes place and appropriate interventions must occur if abuse is uncovered. It does, however, mean that it is wrong to characterise the entire industry as being based on abusive practices.

The categorisation of cocoa as either Fairtrade or exploitative is also problematic because the distinction between Fairtrade and conventional cocoa is not entirely straightforward. Cocoa cooperatives have to be certified Fairtrade in their entirety in order to be certified at all. However, due to insufficient demand in the West for fairly traded cocoa, they can not always sell all their produce as Fairtrade-certified (for a similar situation concerning coffee, see Luetchford, this volume). An example of this is the Ghanaian cocoa producers' cooperative Kuapa Kokoo, which is certified as meeting Fairtrade standards. There have been periods when demand for Fairtrade-certified cocoa was so low that 97 per cent of the cooperative's cocoa was purchased by mainstream multinational buyers. It is therefore misleading to assume that cocoa certified as Fairtrade is produced under conditions different from those of non-certified cocoa. In many cases the cocoa is the same. Of course, the certification and traceability of Fairtrade cocoa (as well as the payment of a Fairtrade premium enabling community development) are crucial advantages of Fairtrade over other forms of trade. However, it should not be assumed that labour standards in non-Fairtrade production are necessarily poor. Many cocoa farmers with acceptable labour standards are not certified Fairtrade and not all cocoa produced according to Fairtrade standards is sold as such. The ethical status of the cocoa in the chocolate bar is, therefore, not always clear-cut.

Similarly, companies within the UK chocolate industry have laid claims to ethicality in different ways. For example, the company Hotel Chocolat describes its ownership of a cocoa plantation in St Lucia as a central part of its 'Engaged Ethics' policy. Their website describes how their notion of ethicality in cocoa is defined through the acts of providing a stable market, paying above market prices and setting up a cocoa estate and chocolate-making facilities in St Lucia (Hotel Chocolat n.d.). Here, ethical ends are served by a UK company becoming a central agent in the production of chocolate in a developing economy. By contrast, Divine Chocolate (in addition to being certified Fairtrade) is part-owned by Kuapa Kokoo and the cooperative receives a share of company profits and has representatives on the company's board. In this case, ethical ends are served in a different way, by having producers from a developing country be part-owners of a company that produces chocolate in a developed country. There is some commonality in these two approaches, particularly the integration of producers and their wider communities into the making and marketing of chocolate in order to secure greater returns for them. More fundamentally, these examples illustrate that there are many possible meanings of 'ethical'. This further illustrates that the notion of ethicality in cocoa is more complex that simple binary categorisations such as 'good' or 'bad'.

Hotel Chocolat and Divine Chocolate are not isolated examples of companies dealing with cocoa being explicitly ethical. Another example is the ice-cream makers Ben & Jerry's, owned by Unilever. They have a philanthropic ethos and were the first ice-cream company in the world to use Fairtrade-certified ingredients. In February 2010 they announced that they were going to be entirely Fairtrade throughout their range, which includes many cocoa-based products. This raises further questions about the validity of the common assumption that there is a clear distinction between the practices of large multinational companies using cocoa and those of small, less mainstream firms.

Cadbury and Social Responsibility

I have already noted that a concern for ethics among consumers is not a strictly modern phenomenon. Equally, corporate concerns with the well-being of employees and suppliers are not exclusive to the modern era. Indeed, the UK chocolate industry has a long history of ethical concerns and practices. Companies such as Rowntree (acquired by Nestlé in 1988), Cadbury (which became part of Kraft Foods in 2010), Fry of Bristol (purchased by Cadbury in 1919) and Terry's of York (also now part of Kraft Foods) were all steeped in philanthropic traditions linked to their Quaker origins. Hot chocolate was initially developed as a socially responsible alternative to alcoholic drinks, as was coffee (see Luetchford, this volume). The early Quaker chocolate manufacturers were concerned to provide a safe and healthy working environment for their employees, as well as education and housing for them (on the role of Quakerism in ethical consumption, see Collins, this volume).

In the case of Cadbury, concern for the working conditions of their employees extended beyond the factory floor. By the early 1900s, Cadbury, like some other chocolate companies, had built up a reputation for being ethical through their considerable emphasis on their employees' welfare. In 1901 they learnt that the cocoa beans they were buying from Portuguese plantations on the island of São Tomé had been produced using slave labour. This matter was taken very seriously by the company, but their response involved lengthy and slow-moving field investigations (excellently detailed in Satre 2005).

The British press, having reported appalling working conditions and the use of shackled slaves on plantations, openly ridiculed the company owners 'as "those virtuous people" who cared not a whit for the "grimed African hands" whose sweat was "so essential to the beneficent and lucrative operations at Bournville'", where the Cadbury chocolate was being produced (Satre 2005: 128). Incensed by such comments, Cadbury sued in October 1908, asserting that the words used by *The Standard* represented libellous claims that their officials:

> were hypocrites, who, professing to be philanthropists and to be concerned in the improvement of conditions of life and work amongst the working classes, acquiesced in a system of brutalising servitude enforced by wanton cruelty amongst the natives of Portuguese West Africa, and that they were fit objects for odium and contempt. (In Satre 2005: 128)

The outcome was that the jury decided in favour of Cadbury, although they were only awarded one farthing in damages (the smallest possible amount).

The firm remained dissatisfied with working conditions in São Tomé, so Ghana (then the Gold Coast) became their main supplier of cocoa in 1909. Changing suppliers was not, however, a straightforward operation. The cocoa from Ghana was found to be of poor quality and farmers required extensive training in fermentation practices and quality control (which Cadbury subsequently provided) in order to overcome these problems. Quality improved and Cadbury began paying a bonus for good quality cocoa in 1910. By 1940, 95 per cent of Ghana's cocoa was classed as being superior quality.

The emphasis on quality promoted by Cadbury enabled Ghana to develop its cocoa industry, which helped it to acquire a reputation for excellent cocoa and made a considerable contribution to national development. For example, the higher price for cocoa after the Second World War meant that the Ghana Cocoa Board made huge profits. By 1946, it had amassed over £20 million; by 1951, this had reached almost £200 million (Foster 1965: 179). Ghana is presently the only significant producer whose cocoa fetches premium prices for quality on the world market: their cocoa contains only about half the level of defective beans set by international standard. This premium amounts to $200–250 over the prevailing international price per metric tonne, which is currently about $3,200. For comparison, Fairtrade cocoa fetches a fixed premium of $200 per tonne[3] and, as I have noted, the demand for Fairtrade cocoa can be limited. Therefore, the Ghanaian quality premium is significant, especially as they export large volumes of cocoa.

In addition to efforts to boost the quality of production, in the first half of the twentieth century Cadbury built an agricultural training centre and infant welfare centres, and awarded scholarships to cocoa farmers' children. Since 2000 they have built hundreds of wells in cocoa-growing villages in Ghana. In 2008 the company launched the Cadbury Cocoa Partnership, which involves an investment of £45 million over ten years in different cocoa-producing countries.

It is often said that corporations become interested in social responsibility only when it is likely to affect profits, but the historical background of Cadbury suggests otherwise. However, I have not presented these examples as a promotional exercise for Cadbury or any other chocolate company mentioned. Rather, I have used these examples to illustrate that perceptions of the ethicality of chocolate are prone to particular biases. Large companies, and sometimes Cadbury explicitly, are often construed as lacking moral integrity of the sort that Fairtrade is taken to embody. For example, at the third Fairtrade International Symposium in 2008, one of the speakers stated that Cadbury had been exploiting farmers for over a hundred years in Ghana and that their current investments were only as a result of pressure from Fairtrade. When challenged, the speaker admitted that the statement was not accurate and that Cadbury had a long history of investing in communities in Ghana. Such a response raises an interesting question: why, in spite of evidence and knowledge to the contrary, do discourses of multinational greed and exploitation still dominate debates on the ethics of cocoa?

Deconstructing Categories

The process of deconstructing the Manichean dichotomies at the heart of claims about the ethics of cocoa must be preceded by a caveat. The specific policies of individual companies should not be taken to represent the company's entire operations in the developing world, the operation of the chocolate industry or of multinational corporations more broadly. Clearly, not all companies invest in producer countries to the same extent and even firms with an ethical stance are not always consistent. On many issues companies justifiably incur criticism. More fundamentally, the aim of this chapter is not to dispute the fact that many of the goods we consume daily *are* based on exploitative practices. Rather, this chapter is intended to suggest that probing popular perceptions of the cocoa industry is worthwhile because they can mask contradictory assumptions, and because they touch on deeply embedded beliefs and values. The question of how particular constructions of ethical consumption are shaped and sustained is epistemological rather than moral, though the processes it addresses touch on people's moral perceptions of particular aspects of their world. This volume's Introduction raised this question in its discussion of ethicality. That discussion pointed to some of the processes that can shape the content of such constructions. Here I want to pursue the question further.

At a basic level, the discourses of right and wrong concerning cocoa and chocolate have prevailed for what might seem obvious reasons. One of these is that communities producing cocoa for Western consumption are poor by any reasonable standards: even producers owning large tracts of land may not achieve profits if prices drop. Moreover, they are vulnerable to adversity of various kinds. For many people the reasons for this spring from the practices of chocolate manufacturers. However, this ignores the influence of the practices of national and local governments as previously explained, just as it ignores the effects of individual circumstances, unsustainable farming practices, environmental issues and a host of other pertinent factors. This focus is understandable, because chocolate companies are more visible and accessible to Western consumers than these other factors.

Ideas about the ethics of the cocoa trade have been heavily influenced by trade justice campaigns. These have rightly placed the emphasis on persuading consumers to change their buying habits rather than on providing a detailed exegesis of all the reasons underlying Third World poverty (this resembles the ethical consumers and traders described by Vramo in this volume). Realistically, UK consumers are less likely to be able to bring about changes in government policies in Ghana than they are to, for example, persuade retailers in the UK to stock more Fairtrade products. In such a situation, there is little point in campaigners drawing attention to wider issues. As a result, it is no surprise that common notions of ethicality ignore some of the factors that affect farmers. The media has also been instrumental in shaping ideas of rights and wrongs in cocoa, and reinforced the tendency to condemn rather than to contextualise. While the legal battle between Cadbury and *The Standard* shows that the press has long been involved in debates about trade justice, the advent of the internet and other new technologies has reinforced this.

It must also be said that chocolate companies themselves are partly responsible for this selective attention. While Fairtrade companies have publicised their ethical stance and their activities to help farmers widely, larger companies have been less active in this respect. As a result, many consumers simply do not know that conventional chocolate firms also invest in producer communities, and thus assume that they are not investing in them or even that they are exploiting them. The Introduction to this volume describes ethical consumption as a signalling system: when people buy one thing rather than another, their purchase signals their preference and that signal passes up the line from shop to wholesaler to manufacturer. Companies that want to stay in business will attend to those signals and adjust their operations accordingly. Signals do not, however, flow only from consumers to companies; they also flow the other way. In particular, Fairtrade companies, through their marketing, have established a brand name that emits the loudest ethical signal. Consumers, increasingly dissatisfied with reports of sweatshops and corporate greed, have responded and adjusted their buying behaviour and their expectations of companies accordingly.

Consumption and Pollution

I have described some of the things that can help us to understand the constructions of ethicality in cocoa. However, some questions remain unanswered. Why are the social investment policies of particular companies absent from the discourses of campaigners for social justice? How did the chocolate industry come to be classified in simplistic, perhaps fallacious, terms? Can large firms ever cleanse their image? Common criticisms of corporations and cocoa may seem inconsistent and even incoherent, but I suggest that they are, in fact, rational. In order to understand this, it is necessary to consider the concepts of classification and judgement in more depth.

The work of Mary Douglas, and especially *Purity and danger* (2004 [1966]), is enlightening in making sense of such issues. This work investigated the concepts of dirt, pollution and purity and the way these concepts are constructed in society. Douglas contends that they can not be understood if we see them only as being about their overt concern, health and hygiene. Rather, we need to recognise that they also are about respecting social conventions, norms and values. Famously, she argued that 'dirt is matter out of place' (2004 [1966]: 44). Much of Douglas's argument is premised on the view 'that rational behaviour involves classification, and that the activity of classifying is a human universal … and that classifying is at the basis of human coordination' (2004 [1966]: xvii). She further argues that 'the yearning for rigidity is in us all. It is part of our human condition to long for hard lines and clear concepts' (2004 [1966]: 200). The ethical debate about chocolate exemplifies these ideas in a variety of ways. At the most basic level, constructions of ethicality in cocoa manifest the human impulse to classify, which, according to Douglas, is an inherent feature of rational behaviour; hence the imposing of labels such as 'fair', 'ethical' or 'exploitative' on companies and their operations.

Furthermore, the allegations of child and slave labour that were influential in shaping discourses on the ethicality of cocoa were potent in the public arena precisely because they offended the sensitivities of consumers by bringing together irreconcilable categories. Chocolate is associated with gift giving, love, indulgence, comfort and, for some, health. Child labour and slavery conjure up images of poverty, desperation and suffering. The conjunction of these two concepts made chocolate tainted, dirty in Douglas's sense: children and slaves were clearly 'matter out of place' in the chocolate supply chain. For ethically minded consumers, eating chocolate was tantamount to eating dirt. As a result, ordinary chocolate became highly offensive and morally polluting, and the chocolate industry needed to be cleansed, purified of this pollution. In the words of one advocacy group, the International Labor Rights Forum:

> Chocolate is a sweet business with disgusting ingredients – like child slavery. … Cocoa's first consumers are chocolate companies, which could clean up the industry by refusing to buy beans produced by children. (Smith 2009)

Such discourses also occur, of course, in relation to things other than chocolate. In an article on child labour in a factory making clothing for Gap in Delhi, *The Observer* urged Western shoppers to ask themselves: 'Is this top stained with a child's sweat?' (in De Neve, Luetchford and Pratt 2008: 10). The article quoted a spokesman for Gap, who said that tens of thousands of items would be withdrawn from the market, and that the affected products would be prevented from ever being sold in their stores. De Neve, Luetchford and Pratt (2008: 10) comment that:

it is widely believed that the 'sweat' of child labour, and with it the guilt of exploitation, stains the garment and would be transferred onto the person buying it …. [This indicates how] the commodity is a sign value for a morality and a relationship that has to be restored, but also that immorality can be contained and transferred in the physical 'stains' of unacceptable labour conditions. The consumer is directly affected, both morally and physically. Why, otherwise, would these garments have to be removed from our shops?

In keeping with Douglas's analysis of pollution and dirt, the removal of these garments could be interpreted as a purification of the supply chain and the objects that pass through it, for it would restore the ethical balance that was breached by the presence of labouring children. In cocoa, the identification of moral pollution in the supply chain, the demarcation of beans as being either 'bondage' beans or 'clean' beans, the cleansing of the supply chain through Fairtrade or other initiatives, are all arguably a form of separating, classifying and cleansing.

Deconstructing Ethical Consumption

The human tendency to see pollution of the sort Douglas describes, and to act to purify the objects that we confront, may be inherent, but it is not neutral. As Ian Hacking (1992) has argued, categorisation is intrinsically evaluative and used to justify perceptions of the world. Based on Hacking's (1982) observation that each term we use carries its own 'style of reasoning' about the world, Joanna Overing (1987: 74) argues:

> Each label we apply is the centre of numerous lines or relational ties that connect it to other words, behaviours, and propositions about the world or about particular worlds. Our definitions are, necessarily, always stuck to particular understandings either of the world or of worlds of particular kinds. Think of the baggage associated with such labels as the following: tribal, pre-State, hunting and gathering, capitalist, African, South American. The very use of such a term conjures up in the mind of the reader a number of other terms and a very specific kind of existence in the world, a process of decoding which is but a statement of both the power and the danger of our labelling, especially when it is taken too seriously, i.e. thought to define the facts of the matter.

The evident tendency to categorise cocoa, its associated business practices and companies in antithetical moral terms, illustrates the idea that the process of categorising social facts entails some form of judgement. Furthermore, it appears that the labels placed on cocoa and on practices in the chocolate industry are thought to define 'the facts of the matter' without need for further questioning. As a result, people wishing to take into account the moral nature of objects when deciding whether or not to consume them have made their choices based on very specific, and very partial and situated, ideas about ethics and responsibility in the supply chain. This is problematic. Like the images that define an ethical world, described in the Introduction to this volume (see also Carrier 2010), these labels have been invoked by parties with very specific interests, such as the media or campaigning groups. Inevitably they are partial and based on particular perspectives, and so require further consideration.

Having discussed the role of classification and judgement, it remains necessary to clarify some of the apparent incongruities at the heart of ethical consumption. Once more, the work of Mary Douglas offers useful insights. She argues that the 'hard lines and clear concepts' that our tendency to categorise encourages bring their own problems. This is especially so when we seek to apply these lines and principles to the world we confront. She (2004 [1966]: 200) says:

> we have to either face the fact that some realities elude them, or else blind ourselves to the inadequacy of the concepts. The final paradox of the search for purity is that it is an attempt to force experience into logical categories of non-contradiction. But experience is not amenable and those who make the attempt find themselves led into contradiction.

This helps to explain why certain discourses about the ethicality of cocoa appear contradictory. The neat categorisations of chocolate as either 'ethical' or 'tainted', like the blanket designation of big companies as bad (especially when people acknowledge their history of concern for producers and workers), suggests something other than simple inattention. Rather, they illustrate the broader shortcomings of attempts to force our realities into neat categories. Discussions of ethics, especially in relation to trade, suffer most especially from such attempts: the ethical dimensions of trade are much too complex to fit neat categories of understanding, and attempts to force them to fit result in fundamental contradictions.[4] This can be problematic for ethically minded consumers: consuming ethically is a noble aim, but it can only be translated imperfectly into action.

Strict categorisation also can not accommodate the rapidly changing landscape of ethical consumption in the UK without risking contradiction. For example, for social justice campaigners who identified multinational companies as exploitative and Fairtrade companies as ethical, it becomes difficult to categorise companies when they bear the characteristics of both. Many Fairtrade marketing campaigns emphasise the transformative power of the Fairtrade movement (Berlan 2008) and what Caroline Wright (2004: 671) describes as 'happily ever after narratives'. What if the entire UK chocolate industry became Fairtrade? Would an entire industry go from being polluted with the sweat of slaves and children to being the saviours of the poor? This seems unlikely. Faced with the proliferation of corporate social responsibility initiatives and the prospect that all large companies could acquire Fairtrade certification, consumers may start searching for a different way of distinguishing between the companies perceived to be genuine from the companies perceived to be jumping on the ethical bandwagon.

This in turn brings to light one of the fundamental tensions within the Fairtrade movement, and the broader ethical-trade movement of which it is a part. That movement includes people who want to change the practices of large companies to make them more ethical, as well as those who believe that these companies can never be truly ethical. The result is a mixed message. Companies are encouraged to change their practices, for example by adopting the Fairtrade mark, but simultaneously are criticised for 'jumping on the ethical bandwagon' if they do so. That criticism suggests that, in the eyes of at least some ethical consumers, companies that change their practices are not doing enough. Rather, they need to embrace ethical principles. However, this seems short-sighted in a movement that embraces the capitalist market as its preferred means: firms in that market are going to continue to take profit seriously.

Conclusion

In this chapter my aim has been to unwrap the concept of ethical consumption with reference to a specific commodity. This has brought to light many issues of broader relevance. Historical and current examples of corporate responsibility in the chocolate industry have illustrated the limitations of labelling companies either as heroes or villains. The concepts of right and wrong are much more relative and complex than they may seem, although in some cases (such as if a company is found to be knowingly using slave labour) clear wrongs still, of course, exist. However, for the most part, the biases in constructions of ethicality in cocoa can result in ethical consumers making decisions on the basis of only partial knowledge. Consumers tend to conceive of the intentions of companies simplistically, and understanding and evaluating labour standards is considerably undermined if reduced to black-and-white categories.

More broadly, this chapter has shown that people have long seen objects as more than the sum of their utility and cost, and have long sought to act on that perception. It has also shown that moral ideals about trade, even though they may be presented as straightforward and readily executable, are not easily realised. Such ideas are not pure expressions of moral reasoning, but instead necessarily reflect the broader consumerist discourses of our time. In the case of cocoa, as I have noted, ideas of ethicality have been shaped by trade-justice campaigns and the media. As a result, discourses about ethicality and cocoa often reflect the moral and political imperatives of the benevolent West rather than the realities of world trade that they claim to depict. More broadly, constructions of ethicality in cocoa reflect wider anxieties about a global system of trade. This leads people to feel that they are disconnected from what they consume and to think that companies are unfairly profiting from the individuals 'behind the labels'. In turn, this prompts a desire to have a connection with producers, as Luetchford (this volume) describes for ethical coffee (see also De Neve, Luetchford and Pratt 2008; Dolan 2008; Luetchford 2008).

However, the concept of 'ethical consumption' does not reflect only the time and place, and culture and society, of ethical consumers. As I have argued, it also demonstrates enduring aspects of human existence. Anthropology is well placed to shed light on these and on the ways that they shape ethical consumption. My use of the ideas of Mary Douglas indicates that even though the moral consciousness of UK consumers may seem far removed from the Old Testament and tribal cosmologies that concern her, all construct taboos, fear and pollution in particular ways and seek to restore purity based on systems of classification. In this respect, the study of ethical consumption offers insights reaching far beyond notions of justice in international trade and raises questions at the very heart of human cognition and behaviour.

Notes

1. The chocolatier Willy Harcourt-Cooze led the campaign known as 'Willie's chocolate revolution' to market bars of chocolate containing a high cocoa content in order to try to change the taste of UK consumers away from chocolate with a high sugar and fat content.
2. For example, Bales (2007: 193) states that estimates for the use of slave labour in cocoa in the Ivory Coast vary between 1 and 90 per cent. He then says: 'Today we still do not know the truth, not even a rough guess as to the actual extent of slave labor in cocoa' (see also Anti-Slavery 2004: 50).
3. This was increased from $150 per metric tonne in October 2010, the first increase since 1997.
4. The Fairtrade discourses discussed in this chapter relate primarily to conceptualisations of organisations. For discussions of the discourses in relation to producers, see Berlan (2008), Dolan (2008), Jaffee (2007) and Luetchford (2008).

Bibliography

Anti-Slavery International 2004. *The cocoa industry in West Africa: a history of exploitation*. London: Anti-Slavery International.

Appadurai, Arjun 1986. Introduction: commodities and the politics of value. In *The social life of things: commodities in cultural perspective* (ed) A. Appadurai, pp. 3–63. Cambridge: Cambridge University Press

Aristotle 1923. *The politics*. London: Macmillan and Company.

Ayres, Natasha Nina 2003. Letter to the editor. *The Guardian* (7 May). www.guardian.co.uk/theguardian/2003/may/07/guardianletters2

Bales, Kevin 2007. *Ending slavery: how we free today's slaves*. Berkeley: University of California Press.

Berlan, Amanda 2008. Making or marketing a difference? An anthropological examination of the marketing of fair trade cocoa from southern Ghana. In *Hidden hands in the market: ethnographies of fair trade, ethical consumption and corporate social responsibility* (eds) Geert De Neve, Peter G. Luetchford, Jeff Pratt and Donald C. Wood. *Research in Economic Anthropology* 28 (Special Issue): 171–94.

——— 2009. Child labour and cocoa: whose voices prevail? In *Child work in the twenty-first century: dilemmas and challenges* (ed) Madeline Leonard. *International Journal of Sociology and Social Policy* 29 (special issue): 141–51.

Carrier, James G. 2010. Protecting the environment the natural way: ethical consumption and commodity fetishism. In *Conservation and capitalism* (eds) Dan Brockington and Rosaleen Duffy. *Antipode* 42 (special issue): 668–85.

Co-operative Bank 2006. *The ethical consumerism report 2006.* Manchester: Co-operative Bank. www.co-operativebank.co.uk/images/pdf/er_report_2006.pdf

De Ferran, Florence and Klaus G. Grunert 2007. French fair trade coffee buyers' purchasing motives: an exploratory study using means–end chains analysis. *Food Quality and Preference* 18: 218–29.

De Neve, Geert, Peter G. Luetchford and Jeff Pratt 2008. Introduction: revealing the hidden hands of global market exchange. In *Hidden hands in the market: ethnographies of fair trade, ethical consumption and corporate social responsibility* (eds) G. De Neve, P.G. Luetchford, J. Pratt and Donald C. Wood. *Research in Economic Anthropology* 28 (Special Issue): 1–30.

Dolan, Catherine 2008. Arbitrating risk through moral values: the case of Kenyan Fairtrade. In *Hidden hands in the market: ethnographies of fair trade, ethical consumption and corporate social responsibility* (eds) Geert De Neve, Peter G. Luetchford, Jeff Pratt and Donald C. Wood. *Research in Economic Anthropology* 28 (Special Issue): 271–96.

Douglas, Mary 2004 [1966]. *Purity and danger.* London: Routledge.

Finkel, Michael 2005. *True story: murder, memoir, mea culpa.* London: Random House.

Foster, Philip 1965. *Education and social change in Ghana.* London: Routledge & Kegan Paul.

Hacking, Ian 1982. Language, truth and reason. In *Rationality and relativism* (eds) Martin Hollis and Steven Lukes, pp. 48–66. Oxford: Blackwell.

——— 1992. World making by kind-making: child abuse as example. In *How classification works: Nelson Goodman among the social sciences* (eds) Mary Douglas and David Hull, pp. 180–238. Edinburgh: Edinburgh University Press.

Hogbin, Ian 1951. *Transformation scene: the changing culture of a New Guinea village.* London: Routledge & Kegan Paul.

Hotel Chocolat n.d. *Rabot Estate – A cocoa plantation story.* Royston, Herts: Hotel Chocolat. www.hotelchocolat.co.uk/Rabot-Estate--A-Cocoa-Plantation-Story-ARabot_Story/

Jaffee, Daniel 2007. *Brewing justice: fair trade coffee, sustainability, and survival.* Berkeley: University of California Press.

Jones, Barbara 2001. Concerns grow for slave ship children. *Daily Mail* (16 April) www.dailymail.co.uk/news/article-38622/Concerns-grow-slave-ship-children.html

Luetchford, Peter G. 2008. The hands that pick Fair Trade coffee: beyond the charms of the family farm. In *Hidden hands in the market: ethnographies of fair trade, ethical consumption and corporate social responsibility* (eds) Geert De Neve, P.G. Luetchford, Jeff Pratt and Donald C. Wood. *Research in Economic Anthropology* 28 (Special Issue): 143–70.

McGreal, Chris 2001. Aboard the slave ship of despair: traffickers buying up the young in west Africa. *The Guardian* (16 April). www.guardian.co.uk/world/2001/apr/16/chrismcgreal

New, Steve J. 2004. The ethical supply chain. In *Understanding supply chains: concepts, critiques and futures* (eds) S.J. New and Roy Westbrook, pp. 253–80. Oxford: Oxford University Press.

Overing, Joanna 1987. Translation as a creative process: the power of the name. In *Comparative anthropology* (ed) Ladislav Holy, pp. 70–87. Oxford: Basil Blackwell.

Parry, Jonathan and Maurice Bloch (eds) 1989. *Money and the morality of exchange.* Cambridge: Cambridge University Press.

Pellizzari, Paul 2002. Consumers force chocolate industry to take steps to stop slave production. *Toronto: The Better Directory* (10 February) www.torontothebetter. net/2tgbd-slave.htm

Raghavan, Sudarsan and Sumana Chatterjee 2001. Slave labor taints sweetness of world's chocolate. *Kansas City Star* (Knight Ridder News Service) (23 June). www. globalexchange.org/campaigns/fairtrade/cocoa/kansascitystar062301.html

Sahlins, Marshall 1972. *Stone age economics.* Chicago: Aldine-Atherton.

Satre, Lowell J. 2005. *Chocolate on trial: slavery, politics and the ethics of business.* Athens, Ohio: Ohio University Press.

Smith, Michelle 2009. Chocolate's secret ingredient – child slavery. International Labor Rights Forum. www.laborrights.org/stop-child-labor/cocoa-campaign/ news/12070

Wright, Caroline 2004. Consuming lives, consuming landscapes: interpreting advertisements for Cafédirect coffees. *Journal of International Development* 16: 665–80.

Chapter 2

CONSUMING PRODUCERS:
FAIR TRADE AND SMALL FARMERS

Peter G. Luetchford

My local supermarket stocks over one hundred kinds of coffee from a dozen different suppliers. The products range from the instant freeze-dried coffees of global companies, through specialist coffees associated with specific regions, to fair-trade goods bearing social and environmental messages. These latter, niche-market coffees attract purchasers by distinguishing themselves from mainstream brands. In the case of Fairtrade coffee, certified by the Fairtrade Foundation and bearing its mark, the appeal is linked to development goals operating through a minimum price paid to producers, coupled with a social premium. Fairtrade Labelling Organizations International (the FLO) describe this as a 'communal fund for workers and farmers to use to improve their social, economic and environmental conditions' (FLO n.d.c). The higher price paid by consumers to cover the extra cost is justified through moral claims about benefits to producers and environments. By offering shoppers a relationship with those people and places, mediated by the cup of coffee that the buyer drinks, development outcomes are attached to an ethic of consumption.

The growth in popularity of such 'relationship' coffees has attracted attention in the retail sector as well as from scholars, whose work on Fairtrade, and on ethical consumption more generally, has focused increasingly on its commercial success. While earlier works were divided between largely unsubstantiated optimism and critical pessimism, the spotlight has now settled upon tensions between the establishment of producer–consumer links as a positive force on the one hand, and on the other the fact that those links are established in, and so are undone by, neoliberal market relations.[1] As writers have increasingly observed, everyone, whether mainstream suppliers, non-governmental organisations (NGOs) or celebrities, is after a piece of the fair-trade pie (Daviron and Ponte 2005; Fridell 2007; Goodman 2010; Jaffee 2007; Raynolds 2002; Renard 1999, 2003). The goal these writers have set themselves has been to try to understand, and perhaps resolve, the contradiction that seems likely to exist when one tries to pursue moral and social goals through the market. This chapter follows in that vein, but differs from them in an important way. Most of the work that I have mentioned is written from a Northern perspective. There is little attempt to identify the complexity of relations from a Southern perspective, which is to say at the production end; the range of actors, and the social, economic and moral worlds they move in, are given scant recognition. This is important for a movement that wants to forge connections between consumers and producers.

This chapter raises two issues discussed in the Introduction to this volume. The first is 'ethicality', whereby Fairtrade transposes an idealised economy of direct relations onto the market. Ethicality is a response to the Washington consensus and the rise of the deregulated market since the 1980s, and it operates through particular social and moral idioms. While the old idea of a moral economy has long been juxtaposed to market rationality, this becomes especially problematic when specific ethical ideas coming from the North are inserted into world markets, so that Northern morality 'goes global' in the way that Lill Vramo describes in this volume.

Both those who see ethical consumption as a sort of moral neocolonialism and those who want to consume ethically in order to extend the reach of their values in the world are making two assumptions. The first is that the economy exists in the form it is presented to consumers. The second is that producers want the same thing as consumers. There are reasons to believe that neither assumption holds. It has long been understood from studies of coffee production that small-farmer economies are cross-cut by class, ethnicity and gender, and so resist easy assumptions about their morality (Ortiz 1999; Roseberry 1983; Seligson 1980; Stolcke 1995). What is more, while farmers and cooperative personnel may well seek good, guaranteed prices for their coffee, there is also evidence that they appreciate the freedom to speculate in the market (Luetchford 2006). That is, after all, what commodity production entails. So, whereas consumers see fair trade as morally and socially driven, cooperative personnel and growers regard it as a more or less rewarding tactic within the market world of economic relations and transactions.

To broach the question of ethicality, this chapter opens with an analysis of the claims and rhetoric of the Fairtrade scheme taken from coffee packages on the supermarket shelf. Coffee has a distinct social life in the world of consumption, which lends it power as a medium for conveying a broad range of messages, a power that it shares with cocoa, described by Amanda Berlan in this volume. It offers, as Wolfgang Schivelbusch (1992: 19) tells us, a 'motley catalogue of often mutually contradictory virtues'. While these often focus on the qualities of the product and on the relationships established and reproduced through its consumption, there is also an underlying association with the peasant form of production. For drinkers of fair-trade coffee, ethicality rests upon a rejection of alienated objects traded through an economy that neoliberalism has made ever more abstract and impersonal. That rejection is made manifest in social economies, imagined through unalienated relationships and realised by 'cutting out the middleman', by seeming to shorten or eliminate the distance between producers and consumers. Small family farmers and their cooperatives are easily advertised as fitting this bill, so they tend to define ethical coffee production. The trump card for fair trade is the idea that, with the purchase of the coffee, the goodwill of shoppers is communicated unproblematically to identifiable development subjects with whom the purchaser has established a moral relationship. In this, of course, it is not just the growers who are produced. Consumers are as well: they can imagine scenarios and outcomes from their actions, in the way that Vramo (this volume) describes, and are encouraged to consume accordingly.

The second issue that frames this chapter, also raised in the Introduction to the volume, is the relation between economy and society. While cooperative managers, farmers and workers all have social and moral commitments, tensions and contradictions arise among these when they are lived through commodity exchange, which includes fair trade. We can identify these tensions in the production and processing of coffee, and so see how different groups relate to each other and negotiate the gap between social commitments and economic considerations. Accordingly, the second section of the chapter problematises long-distance ethical action through the market by examining the tensions that arise as the social and moral aims and commitments of different people interact with the production of coffee in its commodity form. These tensions point to the contrast between simplified representations of social relationships aimed at the consumer, and the political economy of coffee in Costa Rica.[2] I will be concerned with three groups of people involved in production: cooperative managers, farmers and landless labourers. In so far as they engage with fair trade, these people do so very much within the commodity realm, seeking better prices and more stable livelihoods, rather than long-distance social relationships.

By contrasting representations of fair trade in the North with Southern experiences, the chapter subjects ethical consumption to critical examination. While the effect of this examination may be to knock fair trade off its pedestal, my intention is not to destroy. Rather, I think that it is only by seeking to comprehend how fair trade is viewed and used by different participants, and by facing up to its limitations, that fair-traders, and ethical consumers generally, can pursue their ethical and political engagement with the relation between economy and society.

Fairtrade as an Ethical Brand

Shopping is a complex affair, a mixture of economic reasoning, social motive and moral value, not only for shoppers but also for analysts. From one perspective, people should relish the presentation of objects divorced from the conditions and practices that bring them to the shops, a fetishisation that makes it all the easier to work them into social projects and moral relations closer to home (Miller 1987, 1998). From another perspective, one that reflects renewed anthropological interest in Marxian and Maussian approaches to value (Graeber 2001), they should reject this fetishism and instead be concerned with commodity chains and their political-economic implications (Foster 2008; Harvey 1993). These two perspectives mirror the meanings enacted through mainstream and fair-trade or ethical coffees.

People have used coffee in both social and economic relationships since at least the seventeenth century. Economically, coffee is in that class of powerful stimulants that grease the wheels of industry, a role usurped from beer, providing a sober and hence more 'rational' alternative for workers (Mintz 1985; Schivelbusch 1992: 34). Additionally, it has long been used to facilitate business negotiations. It is no accident that the first coffee houses were established in the City of London at the dawn of the industrial era, when 'business' encompassed intellectual activity and pleasurable sociality, as well as commerce. Later, the beverage spread from the coffee house into the private parlour, where it became associated with a different kind of sociality: the family, the domestic space and women's coffee parties (Schivelbusch 1992). Advertising by mainstream brands often reflects this broad range of associations by depicting users at work and at play, revitalised by coffee, relaxed by it or engaged in humorous, often playfully ironic social situations (examples are on www.visit4info.com). Perhaps unsurprisingly, that advertising focuses almost wholly on consumers and consumption. One could drink most major brands without being aware that coffee is an agricultural cash crop. Even when advertisements depict production, as in the Kenco television advertisement portraying a gap-year student receiving lessons from a producer, they do so in a way that stresses the quality of the coffee's taste.

When the coffee being advertised is ethical, however, we get a contrasting message about economy and a different set of meanings for the coffee. Rather than hide production processes and leave the qualities of the beverage free for appropriation by consumers, Fairtrade brands, like brands that are certified by other, comparable organisations, offer a message about the conditions of its production and portray a way for shoppers to relate to those conditions. So, in contrast to the Kenco conventional gap-year student advertisement, their 'growing communities with Kenco' campaign shows how partnership with the certification agency Rainforest Alliance allows them to 'grow', hence develop, coffee-producing communities. The commercial features water pumps, school equipment and buildings, all sprouting from the ground before amazed onlookers.

To document the meanings projected by fair trade I draw on information from a number of coffee brands certified by Fairtrade and similar organisations, and especially the claims and values that are presented on their packaging. The brands are Nescafé Partners Blend, Kenco Sustainable Development, Clipper instant organic, Tesco Fair Trade instant freeze-dried, The Co-operative Fairtrade rich-roast instant, FFI Fair instant, Good African

Coffee, Tesco FairTrade medium strength, Percol Americano organic Arabica, and Cafédirect rich-roast. The first seven are instant coffees, reflecting the importance of this sector in the UK market; the last three are roasted and ground. Three of the coffees, two instant and one ground, are supermarket brands; two are produced by companies that have only Fairtrade products (Percol is a more conventional ethical business while Cafédirect has its roots in the world of NGOs); three are marketed by companies that sell both fair-trade and conventional coffee (Nescafé, Kenco, Clipper); two are directed at narrowed concerns (Good African and FFI instant). Except for Good African and Kenco Sustainable Development, all carry the Fairtrade mark of the FLO, which states that the product 'guarantees a better deal for Third World producers'.

As indicated above, conventional coffee companies commonly portray consumers in their advertisements enjoying the coffee in congenial social settings. Their packaging, on the other hand, rarely portrays people. Ordinarily, the package of conventional instant coffee suggests an immediate energy fix by depicting a steaming cup of coffee on the label, ready to be drunk, on the go, often combined with an image of coffee beans. As a rule, the package of conventional ground coffee is very plain, allowing the contents to be appropriated into a broad range of social settings and situations. The packaging for fair-trade coffee is different, routinely having images of people who grow coffee and of places where it is grown. Often this takes the form of a portrait of someone's face or upper body, sometimes set in a landscape, graphically connecting the product, the producer and the place of production (Wright 2004). In certain cases, particularly the fair-trade coffee produced by the big companies, the packaging does not portray anyone identified as the grower of the coffee in the package. For instance, Nescafé Partners Blend and Kenco Sustainable Development both picture men with ethnic features wearing sombreros, but there is no clue to who they are. Tesco Fairtrade instant has a photo of an unidentified man picking coffee, but says the image is 'for illustration purposes only'.

While the photographs present people to whom the purchaser can relate, the details of that relationship and the intended beneficiaries of the purchase are documented in the small print. The brands differ in the amount of information they provide, and hence in the degree to which they personalise the relationship between the people and the coffee. For example, the package for Tesco's medium-strength roast and ground tells us only that the producers are independently audited by the FLO and that they receive a premium payment that enables them to invest in their farms and their communities. Another large British retailer, the Co-operative, gives even less information on its Fairtrade rich-roast instant. There is the Fairtrade logo alongside a picture of an unnamed man winnowing coffee beans and another close-up of beans themselves, but all we learn of provenance is that the coffee is made in the 'UK using Brazilian and Colombian coffee'. In these cases the ethical and social claims are generic, and largely subsumed under the audit process that is part of the certification. Thus, in these examples the principle visible difference between the packaging of the conventional and the ethical brands is the certification mark and the human interest embodied in the photo. Specialist Fairtrade brands, on the other hand, give much more information, identifying producers, benefits and relationships. They do so by detailing the material advantages to producers, who those producers are and how they are involved in production, all linked to claims about the quality of the coffee in the package. Unsurprisingly, this has lead commentators to consider that Fairtrade defetishises commodities (Fridell 2007; Hudson and Hudson 2003; Jaffee 2007; Luetchford 2008; Lyon 2006).

The variations not withstanding, all the Fairtrade and other ethical coffee brands raise common themes, point to some link to producers and production, and thereby contrast themselves with conventional coffees. In their advertisements and packaging, then, these coffee brands distinguish themselves and justify their higher price in two ways. Firstly, they present negative ideas about the condition of growers producing conventional coffee. Secondly, they indicate that positive outcomes follow the purchase of fair-trade coffee. With few exceptions, the positive outcomes are stressed more than the undesirable nature of conventional production. Generally, the adverse effects of conventional production are invoked only to establish the distinctiveness of fair trade, and unlike the positive outcomes they are rarely elaborated. When the undesirable nature of conventional production is mentioned, as on the Tesco Fairtrade instant, there is a reference to such things as 'disadvantaged farmers and workers in developing countries', and it is often combined with an encouraging message that the purchaser can counteract this by buying the ethical coffee in the package. So, Clipper Organic tells us that 'these farmers are protected from exploitation' by the Fairtrade mark. The mistreatment of growers in the economics of conventional coffee, then, is invoked so that it can be countered by the social concern of the potential purchaser.

This sort of social input into the economy becomes explicit as we learn about the forms through which it is expressed. For Fairtrade coffee one such form is the aforementioned minimum price and social premium. The minimum price for washed Arabica beans was set at $1.21 per pound in 1989 and increased to $1.25 in 2008 (FLO 2007*a*), well behind the level of inflation over the years. On the other hand, the premium, only paid when the market price rises above the minimum, doubled from $0.05 to $0.10 per pound in 2007 (FLO 2007*b*), after remaining unchanged for many years. The minimum and premium have advantages for producer organisations (e.g., FLO n.d.*a*; Jaffee 2007; Luetchford 2008; Ronchi 2002) and are the basis for statements about the advantages of Fairtrade emphasised in the small print. Cafédirect tell us that 'growers are paid better prices' and that the company 'always pay a fair price', while Good African state that their prices 'ensure a profitable return for their harvest'. The packaging identifies other tangible benefits for growers, notably investment in infrastructure (such as roads, schools, medical facilities and community projects) and a better future (Percol Americano talks about 'a sustainable future for coffee communities'; Cafédirect ensure 'a better future' and 'improve the quality of life for everyone').

In this packaging, then, 'quality' refers to an unspecified, improved standard of living for producers. Sometimes it includes testimony of the efficacy of fair-trade coffee in implementing that goal. For example, Cafédirect rich roast presents Emiliana Aligaesha, from KDCU, Tanzania. She says that the 'growers are paid better prices', 'Cafédirect is not like the others' and she 'did not believe anything would change but now it is changing'. Such statements are designed to impart trust in the qualities of the brand; that it does what it says on the label. For consumers, of course, quality also refers to the material properties of the coffee in the package. Whereas most coffees tout those properties – rich, smooth, dark, full-bodied – fair-trade coffees attribute them to their relationship with producers. They do this when they link the properties of the coffee to the skill and personal care of the growers, which emerge out of their relationship with the coffee company. Cafédirect state this clearly: '[T]hrough our unique relationship with the growers, they have become experts in their trade, they give us the pick of the crop, so all the products are of the highest quality'. Good African support farmers 'to improve yields and produce beans of the very best quality'.

Having presented the benefits of fair trade, the packaging then links the coffee to particular kinds of people who endorse fair trade, commonly in photographs. Cafédirect's presentation of Emiliana Aligaesha in Tanzania is one example. FFI Fair instant has a photo of José Urley Flores from Aguados, Colombia, and while there is no comment from him, information is provided on his behalf. Good African has its beneficiaries, a group of about 25 young African children, shown standing with an adult who might be their teacher. Under the photo we are told that the company buys its coffee from growers on the slopes of the Rwenzori Mountains in western Uganda, allowing us to associate a place with the photograph.

Photographs are not the only way that people are invoked on the package. For example, reference is commonly made to small farmers, which reflects the Fairtrade organisation's goal of supporting associations of small coffee farmers, the only sort of coffee growers that the FLO certify. Cafédirect say that the company works with 'small-scale growers across the developing world', and FFI tell us that José Urley works on a small farm. It is easy for the purchaser to imagine such people working their land and taking their produce to market, and so it is easy to socialise the coffee by associating it with them (see Introduction this volume). These small farmers, and the coffee that they grow and that we consume, echo common ideas about the family, social relationships and well-being. These values are apparent in another notable category of beneficiaries, children. Good African mention children as a vulnerable group, FFI donate 20 per cent of its profits to Save the Children to 'improve children's education in coffee growing regions' and Percol give information on the charity

Coffee Kids, which is described as an 'international non-profit organisation established to help coffee farming families improve the quality of their lives'. Children, like small farmers, link the coffee and the potential consumer with the valued ideas of the family and personal relationships.

Just as the idea of small family farmers links the coffee to a valued social form, so does the idea of community. Tesco Fairtrade tells us that the premium payment enables growers 'to invest in their farms and their communities', Cafédirect put profits to help farmers 'build a better future for their communities' while Good African 'invest in community projects' and invite you to 'bring benefits to coffee farming communities throughout Africa'. But 'community', as Terry Eagleton (2000: 45) once observed, is one of those things everyone approves of, and he says that this is sufficient grounds to be 'darkly suspicious' of it. Many anthropologists have similar difficulties with the term, which evokes a bounded world of unchanging structures within which consensus and unchallenged hierarchies prevail. This does not tally with the messy experience of social life in the field, where conflict and power pervade social relationships.

The invocation of small farmers, families, children and community on the package encourages the purchaser to link the coffee with things that commonly embody affective, harmonious social relationships, as opposed to impersonal, self-interested economic ones. This invocation is misleading, but that does not distinguish the companies that sell these coffees from every other company that makes fantastical claims about its products. The issue that concerns me, then, is not whether these invocations are distortions. Rather, it is the nature of the distortion, and hence what is hidden behind the imagined social form.

Addressing this issue requires understanding the contradictions hidden behind the ethicality of the image of the small family farmer. Those contradictions spring from the tension between fair-trade's social values and the place of market relationships in the lives of the growers and others involved in the production of the coffee, and they resemble some of the tension surrounding local cheese production in Italy, described by Cristina Grasseni (this volume). One tension revolves around relationships and processes of inclusion and exclusion, and the relative power of different actors to affect them. A second revolves around the competition and calculation required by the market. We can document these tensions as they are encountered by different people at different links in the coffee chain.

Three sets of people who have distinct roles in fair-trade coffee are cooperative managers, landowners and labourers. In the next part of this chapter I consider these people, their relationships and their differences in the place where I did field work in Costa Rica on coffee, cooperatives and fair trade in 1998–99 and again in 2003. Although the information I gathered is specific to that place and time, it indicates the kinds of tensions that exist more generally when people have to negotiate the economics of coffee markets, the ethical content of Fairtrade and their own social and political commitments.

A World of Production: Fairtrade in Costa Rica

The first set of key people I will describe who are in the Fairtrade coffee market in Costa Rica are cooperative managers. The information comes from visits to the producer cooperatives involved in Fairtrade in Costa Rica; interviews with the managers; and examination of cooperative reports. In addition, it is based on visits and interviews carried out at the second-level cooperative, Coocafé, an umbrella organisation of nine Fairtrade producer cooperatives.

These managers are generally young or middle-aged professional men who live in rural areas close to the cooperatives that employ them. Their job is to mediate the relationship between the farmers who own the cooperative and so employ them, and the market. This involves managing the cooperative itself: buying the farmers' coffee and ensuring that the wet processing of the coffee is carried out efficiently in the cooperative mill. This work is important, for promoting and monitoring productive activities and improving processing facilities mean higher production, a better-quality product and better prices returned to the members. The managers' second area of responsibility is the external marketing of the coffee and the cooperatives. This requires business negotiations by phone, extensive national travel and some international travel. In this work the managers must deal with specific contradictions between social values and the dictates of economy. Key concerns are relationships with Northern alternative-trade organisations in the coffee market (ATOs), the level of participation of the different cooperatives in Coocafé and the interests of cooperative members.

While the coffee cooperatives that concern me, concentrated in Highland Guanacaste in northwest Costa Rica, have a moral and social mission, the means they use are rational and technical. A key event for them was the arrival, in 1985, of the Agro-Economic Consultancy (CAE) under the auspices of a German NGO. The Guanacaste cooperatives met the CAE's criteria for assistance: they were composed of small landowners who were marginal to the industry, had problems accumulating capital, had difficulty maintaining the volume and quality of their coffee and struggled with marketing (Orozco 1992). Between 1985 and 1987 the CAE sought to turn the cooperatives into organisations with a professional bureaucracy and trained staff that could compete in the industry. Regular meetings among management, agricultural technicians and administrative staff at the CAE offices eventually led to the formation of Coocafé, the second-level consortium of cooperatives. Coocafé is supposed to engage with the Fairtrade sector, building on an earlier association between one of its constituent cooperatives and Northern ATOs (Luetchford 2008; Orozco 1992).

Newer members are recruited if they have experience with Fairtrade markets or if they produce good coffee, and over the years Coocafé has expanded its membership, field of influence and commercial activities. Expansion benefits Coocafé because each cooperative that joins must invest a sum in Coocafé, based on its average production. With its expansion, Coocafé's political influence is increasing. It has representatives in a wide range of organisations, including Icafé, the national coffee institute. More recently, Coocafé was joined by Infocoop, the government institute for the promotion of cooperatives, as a 'strategic member'. Coocafé is expanding commercially as well. In the 1990s it took out an export licence and set up a marketing department. In 1997–98 its exports increased in volume terms by 101 per cent (to 35,091 sacks) and in money terms by 111 per cent (to 1,405 million colones, about $5.5 million) (from figures supplied by Coocafé).

Coocafé portrays itself as a success, and like the Caribbean banana farmers described by Mark Moberg (2008), the group has used Fairtrade to consolidate markets. Rational technical and administrative processes have been used to establish strong institutions based upon sound economic management implemented by professional business people (Ronchi 2002). However, this commercial relationship can sit uneasily with the values of Fairtrade, to which Coocafé is committed. These two realms are signalled by different terms, as the managers switch between speaking of the cooperatives as collaborative (*la cooperativa*) and as business (*la empresa*). We can consider how these tensions are manifest in relations with Northern ATOs, in dealings with other cooperatives and internally within cooperatives.

Late in the 1990s managers commonly complained that Northern ATOs were unwilling to listen to producers: they sent only junior staff to meetings with Southern cooperatives and did little more than dictate terms and conditions. So, while they valued their relations with some ATOs, they said that most wanted to deal only with poor and acquiescent coffee farmers. Managers contrasted this with their cooperative assemblies, in which, they said, open debate and an exchange of opinions is encouraged and policies are determined by members' votes. Perhaps mindful of this discontent, and in line with its policy of participation, the FLO admitted producer representatives on to its board for the first time in 2007. The FLO board currently has five members representing labelling initiatives, four representing producers, two representing traders and two representing outside bodies. That distribution reflects the concern to include the opinions of producer groups and so maintain the 'special relationship' advertised on the package (for details see FLO n.d.*b*).

However, negotiating deals in a complex coffee market is different from allowing producers the chance to air their opinions, and a key area of tension is participation in the Fairtrade market. While some producer groups routinely sell most of their coffee through the Fairtrade network, others struggle. In both 1999 and 2003, Costa Rican managers complained that Northern organisations had not managed to expand Fairtrade sales enough to absorb their cooperatives' production, much less the output of the 'unending queue' of producer groups joining the system. As a result, Coocafé's sales to Fairtrade fell from around 60 per cent of its total production in the 1990s to about 30 per cent in 2003.[3]

Combined with competition among producer groups, the limited size of the Fairtrade market can cause problems. For example, Coocafé was so successful that their Northern ATO partners argued that they no longer needed the preferential terms Fairtrade offered. Managers disagreed. They said that excluding them would be a punishment for accomplishments; that they succeeded because they were in a stable country and to bar them would be to punish them for Costa Rica's peaceful democracy. Further, they said that their exclusion would not be good business. It is true that they could not compete in terms of marginality and poverty with cooperatives in countries like Nicaragua, but they shipped what they were supposed to, when they were supposed to, producing the good quality coffee that Fairtrade needed to improve the image of their goods. They even offered to help train cooperative groups that sought to emulate them.

Here the tension between ethics and business in Fairtrade is clear. Even though the package on the supermarket shelf links the quality of the product with the special relationship between the Fairtraders and the growers, quality is about more than that. It is also about climate, soils, altitude, production techniques and processing facilities, as well as roasting and preparation practices. The growers who need Fairtrade's help are, however, relatively unable to produce the sort of high quality coffee that Fairtrade companies need if they are going to maintain and expand their share of the market. This means that when supplies are low and demand for coffee is high, the best cooperatives, the ones that have relatively little need for Fairtrade's help, can command high prices from ATOs by threatening to sell elsewhere. For instance, in 2003 prices were rising again, and the manager of Coope Llano Bonito, in the renowned Tarrazú production zone, told me Fairtraders would need to pay at least $1.60 a pound if they wanted their coffee. This bears out Smith's (2010) point that cooperatives in advantageous positions have tended to forsake Fairtrade outlets in favour of speciality markets as market prices improve. That tendency may account for the doubling of the premium paid to growers (from $0.05 to $0.10 per pound) when the market price of coffee rises above the Fairtrade minimum price of $1.25 per pound: without that higher premium, Fairtrade companies were finding it hard to get good coffee. Alternatively, when market prices fall below the Fairtrade minimum, the existence of that minimum assures that the cooperatives growing high-quality coffee will be interested in the Fairtrade market, and the quality of their coffee assures that ATOs will buy from them, rather than from cooperatives in less fortunate circumstances, which will be left out in the cold.

In this way, the Fairtrade ethical goal of helping the poorest farmers is compromised by commercial considerations, as Fairtrade buyers compete with conventional ones and with each other, both to purchase coffee from producers and to sell coffee to consumers. Costa Rican cooperatives are likely to do well because they are efficient producers of good coffee, not because they are especially deprived. However, as I have described, if they are to have a secure Fairtrade outlet for their crop they can not appear to be very successful. Coocafé managers can carry this off by stressing their members' marginality and relative poverty, based on the fairly small size of the constituent cooperatives and the relatively small amount of coffee their members grow (Coocafé n.d.; Icafé 1998).

The tension between advantage and deprivation does not appear only in efforts by Coocafé's managers to keep their Fairtrade contracts. It is apparent as well in processes of inclusion and exclusion, inevitably mediated by power relations. Those processes are manifest in the efforts by managers to secure good returns for their own cooperatives within the Coocafé group, especially when the price of coffee changes, and with it the attraction of Fairtrade. The Fairtrade guaranteed minimum price for coffee described above was set when prices were low; as I have argued, when prices rise growers are decreasingly attracted to the Fairtrade market.

Fluctuations in the attraction of Fairtrade complicate Coocafé's market engagement. As cooperatives and their members try to regulate their Fairtrade sales in response to market prices, tensions arise between the cooperatives that constitute Coocafé. For example, during the severe dip in market prices between 1999 and 2003 cooperatives sought to sell as much of their coffee as possible at the minimum price offered by Fairtrade, which was higher than the market price. As a result 'minor disagreements' emerged, such as occurred between Coopeldos and Coopesanta Elena. That dispute arose because Coopesanta Elena had secured what was considered a disproportionate share of the Fairtrade market, achieved superior prices, and so attracted producers away from nearby Coopeldos (Coopeldos 2002, 2003). Discussions at the Coocafé Administrative Council tried to resolve such difficulties, and by 2003 the Council had settled upon a system that apportioned sales to ATOs by the different cooperatives according to three measures: the scale of production of each cooperative (45 per cent), which clearly favours the larger cooperatives; loyalty in selling coffee through Coocafé (20 per cent); and a fixed quota for each cooperative to demonstrate 'solidarity' (35 per cent). Added to this is an agreed ceiling on the amount each cooperative could sell to Fairtrade customers, 55 per cent of any cooperative's total crop (Coocafé 1999).[4]

Those negotiations around sales show how Fairtrade, set up as an alternative to the commercial market, must compete both with and within that market (Fridell 2007; Lewis 1998; Luetchford 2006; Renard 1999, 2003; Smith 2007). Managers seek first to develop strategies that will produce the best prices for their members: that is their job. This commercial concern is tempered by obligations to the wider cooperative movement and by the need to work with partners in Coocafé. While economic goals are mediated by moral ideas, this does not extend to any broader commitment to Fairtrade, embedded as it is within the market and strategies around prices.

Cooperative managers do not negotiate only with buyers and exporters. They also deal with farmers, and here too there is a range of interests at work. Understanding these dealings and the views of the growers involved required long-term field work in a production zone, the area of El Dos, near the town of Tilarán. Interviews were carried out with about 150 coffee farmers in different settlements. Most were men in charge of commercial agriculture and the family farm, and all were members of Coopeldos. More extended interviews with landowners and local landless labourers were held in one settlement. These farmers produce coffee, milk and beef cattle, commonly in combination. The landless labourers mix more regular work, especially in the dairies, with casual employment in agriculture, particularly the coffee harvest.

Farmers vary in their relationship with the cooperative. Some are active *cooperativistas*, central figures in supporting and running Coopeldos. They tend to hold administrative positions on one of the different councils, attend meetings regularly and follow the guidelines set down by the cooperative agronomist. They rarely criticise the cooperative or its policies: they give vocal support to the organisation, see little or no contradiction between the social and the economic mission and are good for advertising the cooperative to outsiders. Beyond this core is a larger group of farmers who generally use the cooperative's facilities but are not averse to seeking more advantageous outlets for their coffee or dissenting from cooperative policy, both in private interviews and during meetings between members and cooperative staff. Dissatisfaction focused on the disadvantaged position of growers compared to processors, which includes the cooperative, in the division of profits, and on the proper social mission of Coopeldos.

Their dissatisfaction with the relative position of growers and processors is part of the long history of concern in Costa Rica with the ability of processors to swallow profits (Acuña Ortega 1985, 1987; González Ortega 1987). From the beginnings of the industry, early in the nineteenth century, control of coffee meant control of processing and export, not production. In the wake of the 1948 civil war a professional middle class came to power, under the leadership of José Figueres and the National Liberation Party (PLN). Thus began the stable democratic government and the social welfare for which Costa Rica is famous. More importantly, Figueres and his followers implemented policies to control the power of the dominant coffee interests and promote cooperatives (Cazanga 1987; Luetchford 2008; Paige 1997; Winson 1989). Regulating the industry was part of the package of social development, and has been described as a 'hymn of peace' (Paige 1997: 233) that quelled unrest from producers at the extortionate practices of processors.

However, continuing dissent, especially in the cooperative sector, raises questions about the equity of the current system and about the unanimity of cooperative members. For example, farmers complain that the cooperative and its employees 'eat the profits' and receive benefits, such as sick pay and holidays, that farmers never enjoy. Their resentment is compounded by ideas about what constitutes work. For farmers, to labour is to work with one's hands to produce value from nature. They contrast their proper work with administrators in the cooperative offices who 'only shuffle papers and do not really labour', and with intermediaries in the supply chain who 'make money without even handling the agricultural produce'. This principled resentment may underlie the suggestion that some farmers made that there was foul play: they wanted me to investigate where 'missing money' owed to them had gone. No doubt to quell such accusations, the cooperative aims to be transparent. At meetings they explained how they calculate the final payments to producers, the *liquidación final* paid almost a year after farmers deliver their crop for processing. Similarly, the cooperative manager explains at meetings how an export price of $125 for 100 lbs results in a payment to the producer of around $87 after 9 per cent is deducted for the processors' profits, a similar amount for processing costs, government taxes on coffee of just over 3 per cent, and income tax of 20 per cent (Coopeldos 1998).

While cooperative members tend to be divided between the enthusiastic core and the more critical periphery, the farmers and their relationships with the cooperative differ in a more fundamental way. In particular, they differ in terms of the amount of land they own and the amount of coffee they deliver for processing. Supporting the idea that Fairtrade growers are small farmers, over two-thirds of Coopeldos members grow less than 40 *fanegas* of coffee (1 *fanega* = 400 litres of coffee cherry), which is a good return from one hectare. By contrast, six members produce more than 240 *fanegas* (Coocafé 1999). More is involved, though, than the area of land under coffee and the amount produced.

For instance, farmers differ in their dependence on coffee. In the area around the village of El Dos, 32 farmers with larger holdings devote a relatively small part of their land to coffee, the rest being dedicated to beef and dairy cattle. These people are very different from the 57 coffee specialists in another area close to El Dos, who farm an average of just less than two hectares. Likewise, a farmer with less than a hectare differs from one with two or three hectares, the smallest holding that could support a family. Those with the smaller farms must supplement their coffee with wage labour or a small business. Small, specialist coffee farmers working roughly equal plots, as portrayed on the package, were hard to find.

When we analyse incomes from coffee, similar disparities emerge. The highest-earning member of the cooperative in 1998–99 received about $24,000 for coffee, whilst the lowest received $40. Overall, 9 per cent of the 521 registered members earned over 1 million colones (about $4,000), while 18 per cent earned under 100,000 colones (about $400). The rest earned either nothing (10 per cent) or an intermediate amount (Coopeldos 1999). Such differences call into question the Fairtrade representation of fairly uniform small family farmers. What is more, these figures are complicated by the fact that farmers may record all or part of their crop in the name of another family member for fiscal reasons, and that landowners often divide their income by registering half the coffee in the name of the sharecropper who works their land.

Sharecropping is another practice that creates differences and tensions that are ignored in Fairtrade imagery. Of the 151 households surveyed, 44 per cent have no land, and about half of these work other people's land for a share of the crop.

Such arrangements resolve labour problems for farmers, and they extend cooperative membership and access to the coffee market to the landless. One notch below landless sharecroppers are the landless workers, who themselves vary. For more permanent residents, labour agreements are of longer duration and the *peón* gets reliable employment, usually on cattle and dairy farms, which need fairly regular labour all year. Day labourers (*jornaleros*) are in a more precarious position. There is casual work in everything from cattle to construction, but the main employers of temporary and casual labour are in coffee.

While a farmer can cultivate up to two hectares of coffee alone much of the time, assistance is required for harvest. The first help mobilised is family labour, particularly the 'reserve army' of wives, daughters and young sons. The second is local, landless men and women. As the harvest intensifies, however, farmers rely on outsiders, mainly Nicaraguans (Luetchford 2008). Tensions arise between farmers and their paid workers, particularly the Nicaraguans. One area of tension is quality, where farmers and workers have different interests. Those picking coffee at harvest are paid for each 20-litre box they fill, and so want to pick as much and as quickly as possible. On the other hand, the farmer wants careful workers who gather what the cooperative requires, a high percentage of ripe fruit, and will do so without damaging the plants. A second area of tension is the reliability of workers. While local workers generally are dependable, as they are interested in maintaining their local social and economic ties, the same is not true of the Nicaraguans. They have no long-term ties to the place to maintain and no incentive to develop them. Accordingly, they frequently move on in search of more rewarding work without warning, and local people often revile them and consider them untrustworthy (Sandoval-Garcia 2004).

This section has offered an answer to a question raised earlier in this chapter, concerning the small family farmer invoked as part of the representation of Fairtrade coffee. That question was: how does this invocation mislead? My answer has centred on differences among those involved in producing the coffee in the package, differences made invisible by the picture of the smiling grower. To begin with, I pointed to one set of people who are central to that, coffee cooperative managers, and I described some of the tensions they confront in their work and in their relationship with cooperative members. I then described the different sorts of people involved in growing the coffee, looking particularly at farmers, with their different holdings, activities and strategies, and at labourers, with their different interests and local attachments. Many of the divergences of interest and many of the tensions described are generic to the coffee industry, some are specific to Fairtrade, but all are shaped by the economics of the coffee market and the other markets in which these different individuals are involved.

Conclusion

To conclude, I want to raise three points concerning Fairtrade as a form of ethical consumption. The first is about what is hidden and why it is necessarily obscured. The next is about ethicality, the idioms through which Fairtrade is realised, and what this says about moral ideas of the economy. The last is about agency, who is able to exercise it, and the repercussions for ethical consumption (De Neve, Luetchford and Pratt 2008; Doane 2010).

On the first point, Fairtrade presents itself through specific images of idealised economic forms, which are attractive but problematic. Societies of small farmers living in communities and working together in cooperative associations proffer a seamless web of coherent meanings that can be read by consumers and that mark Fairtrade as differing in kind, rather than only in degree, from conventional commerce. Whether or not that qualitative difference is necessary for the survival of Fairtrade coffee on supermarket shelves, it is likely to make that coffee more attractive to many of those standing in the aisles. To maintain that difference, however, Fairtrade imagery has to ignore questions of the differences, tensions and inequalities that exist among those who produce the coffee. Put more succinctly, Fairtrade needs to obscure differentiation in order to gain credibility.

In part, this addresses my second point, about ethicality and moral ideas of the economy. This concerns how the pictures on the packaging, while seeking to de-fetishise, in fact re-fetishise a complex political economy of labour and production relations. Small farmers producing primary goods, the image of ethical production for Fairtrade coffee, are strongly linked in the West with particular ways of life, relationships with nature and forms of economic organisation (Guthman 2004; Kearney 1996). Part of the imagery of family farmers is of egalitarian sets of people who own the land they work, making them autonomous, self-sufficient guardians of the environment. When they do join together, as in growers' cooperatives, they will do so in a voluntary and democratic way. They offer an image of agricultural production that is a standing rebuke to the exploited labourer working in poverty on a chemical-ridden plantation owned by a multinational company based in London or New York.

Western consumers are not alone in being attracted by the image of the small family farmer. That image is a key part of Costa Ricans' sense of their country's history. Coffee holds a central place in that history because it provided much of the revenue for consolidating the country in the nineteenth century (Hall 1991; Paige 1997; Williams 1994; Winson 1989) and because it has long been a source of rural livelihoods. In the national imagination, those were the livelihoods of smallholding farmers, who are taken to be the foundation of Costa Rican exceptionalism (Edelman 1999; Gudmundson 1986; Monge Alfaro 1980; Seligson 1980). In that imagination, the small, independent farmer is the historical foundation for a peaceful, harmonious and democratic society. Coffee farmers have long used this image for their own purposes. For example, they cast themselves as the guardians of the country's stability and prosperity when renegotiating the laws regulating terms with coffee processors (Acuña Ortega 1985, 1987; González Ortega 1987; Luetchford 2008: 41–46). Likewise, cooperative managers draw moral inspiration from their service to the small, marginal producer who is exploited but whose legitimate interests are also the interests of the nation (Luetchford 2008: 23–25).

Protecting the exploited small farmer takes me to my last point, which concerns agency and whence it is directed. Coffee consumers and producers may be worlds apart in the coffee chain, but in Fairtrade imagery they speak a related moral and social language, albeit recognising different means and aims. At the production end, the language is about how to sustain social relationships between people with different interests and about the problems of maintaining a moral economy in the face of market encroachment and the state's indifference (Luetchford 2008: 124–36). Among Northern consumers, on the other hand, the language is about participating in these relationships and maintaining that moral economy through market transactions. Fairtrade imagery encourages consumers to think that they can do this by 'choosing Fairtrade', and that their agency is crucial. Fairtrade certainly can help protect small farmers. However, and to echo a point made in the Introduction to this volume, collective institutions can do more. In Costa Rica, when prices rise above \$125 per hundred pounds of dried coffee, producers pay into FONECAFE, an insurance fund. When prices fall, they draw on this fund. So, when coffee prices were nearing historic lows in the 2000–01 season producers at Coopeldos received 23,600 colones per *fanega*. Fairtrade was part of this, a premium of 1,700 colones. On the other hand, 6,000 colones were from FONECAFE (Coopeldos 2002).

In this chapter I have presented Fairtrade as a limited market that has consistently failed to reconfigure relationships of power, or even to provide a satisfactory mechanism to guarantee livelihoods for coffee producers. This does not mean that Fairtrade has no useful effects. It has put a political agenda into the shopping basket, highlighted the tendency for conventional companies to profit from the separation of producer and consumer and raised questions about the bases upon which trade is established and the conditions it engenders. If, however, Fairtrade is to pursue its critical engagement with the economy, it should not be exempt from such scrutiny itself.

Notes

Field work was kindly supported by the Wenner Gren Foundation and The British Academy.

 1. Barratt-Brown's early work (e.g., 1990) reproduces popular ideas about links between producers and consumers, constructed as a mirror image of mainstream commercial relations. Other accounts (Lyon 2006; Jaffee 2007) remain generally optimistic. Experiences are seen to vary and obstacles identified, but the consensus is that cooperatives and coffee growers benefit from fair trade. The more pessimistic argue that fair trade is ineffectual in

combating local, regional, national and international power relations, and worry about contradictions between ethics and business in a neoliberal world (De Neve, Luetchford and Pratt 2008; Dolan 2008; Fridell 2007; Vramo, this volume).

2. As Berlan's (this volume) discussion of cocoa reminds us, of course, those simplified representations that depart from the actual processes and relations of production can be used to deter purchasers, as well as to attract them.

3. According to Carlos Vargas at Coocafé, the primary effect of Fairtrade is 'psychological' rather than financial. It encourages producers to continue working and boosts morale. This effect weakens, however, as a grower's sales to Fairtrade drop.

4. As well as documentary evidence from the internal Coocafé (1999) document, this issue was discussed at length at a meeting of the Coocafé board attended by the author that same year.

Bibliography

Acuña Ortega, Victor H. 1985. Clases sociales y conflicto social en la economía cafetelera Costarricense: productores contra beneficiadores 1921–1936. In *Historia, problemas y perspectivas agrarias en Costa Rica. Revista de Historia* (special issue): 181–206.

———— 1987. La ideología de los pequeños y medianos productores cafateleros Costarricenses, 1900–1961. *Revista de Historia* 16: 137–59.

Barratt-Brown, Michael 1990. *Fair trade: reform and realities in the international trading system*. London: Zed Books.

Cazanga, José 1987. *Las cooperativas de caficultores en Costa Rica*. San José, Costa Rica: Alma Mater.

Conroy, Michael E. 2001. Can advocacy-led certification systems transform global corporate practices? Evidence and some theory. (Working paper 21). Amherst: Natural Assets Project, University of Massachusetts. www.peri.umass.edu/fileadmin/pdf/working_papers/working_papers_1-50/WP21.pdf

Coocafé 1999. Definición de participación de las cooperativas en las ventas al mercado alternativo. Estándar de calidad HB Coocafé. Alajuela, Costa Rica: Coocafé.

———— n.d. Grupo Coocafé: clasificación de los productores, cosecha 1998–1999. Alajuela, Costa Rica: Coocafé.

Coopeldos 1998. Liquidación al productor para una fanega de café. *Charla sobre comercialización de café* (October). Internal document.

———— 1999. Compras. Departamento de Contabilidad, Sistema de Control de recibo de Café, Coopeldos (12 March). Internal document.

———— 2002. *Memoria annual 2001, Asamblea Ordinaria No. 43* (23 February). Internal document.

———— 2003. *Memoria annual 2002, Asamblea Ordinaria No. 44* (1 March). Internal document.

Daviron, Benoit and Stefano Ponte 2005. *The coffee paradox: global markets, commodity trade and the elusive promise of development.* London: Zed Books.

De Neve, Geert, Peter G. Luetchford and Jeff Pratt 2008. Introduction: revealing the hidden hands of global market exchange. In *Hidden hands in the market: ethnographies of fair trade, ethical consumption and corporate social responsibility* (eds) G. De Neve, P.G. Luetchford, J. Pratt and Donald C. Wood. *Research in Economic Anthropology* 28 (Special Issue): 1–30.

Doane, Molly 2010. Relationship coffees: structure and agency in the Fair Trade system. In *Fair Trade and social justice: global ethnographies* (eds) Sarah Lyon and Mark Moberg, pp. 229–57. New York: New York University Press.

Dolan, Catherine 2008. Arbitrating risk through moral values: the case of Kenya Fairtrade. In *Hidden hands in the market: ethnographies of fair trade, ethical consumption and corporate social responsibility* (eds) Geert De Neve, Peter G. Luetchford, Jeff Pratt and Donald C. Wood. *Research in Economic Anthropology* 28 (Special Issue): 271–96.

Eagleton, Terry 2000. *The idea of culture*. Malden, Mass: Blackwell.

Edelman, Marc 1999. *Peasants against globalization: rural social movements in Costa Rica*. Stanford: Stanford University Press.

FLO 2007*a*. FLO International adjusts Fairtrade minimum prices for Arabica coffee to cover costs of sustainable production. Bonn: Fairtrade Labelling Organizations International. www.fairtrade.net/index.php?id=721&type=123&cHash=6b86aa90 38&tx_ttnews[backPid]=614&tx_ttnews[pointer]=3&tx_ttnews[tt_news]=32

——— 2007*b*. FLO announces increase in Fairtrade premium and organic differential for coffee. Bonn: Fairtrade Labelling Organizations International. www.fairtrade. net/single_view1.html?&cHash=aabc0b31c5&tx_ttnews[backPid]=614&tx_ ttnews[pointer]=5&tx_ttnews[tt_news]=17

——— n.d.*a*. Arabica market price vs. Fairtrade minimum price (1989–2007). Bonn: Fairtrade Labelling Organizations International. www.fairtrade.net/fileadmin/user_ upload/content/Arabica_Price_Chart_89-07_01.pdf

——— n.d.*b*. How we are run. Bonn: Fairtrade Labelling Organizations International. www.fairtrade.net/how_we_are_run.html

——— n.d.*c*. What is Fairtrade? Bonn: Fairtrade Labelling Organizations International. www.fairtrade.net/what_is_fairtrade.html

Foster, Robert 2008. Commodities, brands, love and kula: comparative notes on value creation, in honour of Nancy Munn. *Anthropological Theory* 8: 9–25.

Fridell, Gavin 2007. *Fair trade coffee: the prospects and pitfalls of market driven social justice*. Toronto: University of Toronto Press.

González Ortega, Alfonso 1987. El discurso oficial de los pequeños y medianos cafetaleros (1920–1940, 1950–1961). *Revista de Historia* 16: 161–91.

Goodman, Michael K. 2010. The mirror of consumption: celebritisation, developmental consumption and the shifting cultural politics of fair trade. *Geoforum* 41: 104–16.

Graeber, David 2001. *Toward an anthropological theory of value: the false coin of our own dreams*. New York: Palgrave.

Gudmundson, Lowell 1986. *Costa Rica before coffee: society and economy on the eve of the export boom*. Baton Rouge: Louisiana State University Press.

Guthman, Julie 2004. *Agrarian dreams: the paradox of organic farming in California*. Berkeley: University of California Press.

Hall, Carolyn 1991. *El café y el desarrollo histórico-geográfico de Costa Rica* (Second edition). San José, Costa Rica: Editorial Costa Rica.

Harvey, David 1993. Class relations, social justice and the politics of difference. In *Place and the politics of identity* (eds) Michael Keith and Steve Pile, pp. 41–65. London: Routledge.

Hudson, Ian and Mark Hudson 2003. Removing the veil? Commodity fetishism, fair trade, and the environment. *Organization and Environment* 16: 413–30.

Icafé 1998. *Café declarado por los beneficiadores en la cosecha 1997–1998.* San José, Costa Rica: Icafé.

Jaffee, Daniel 2007. *Brewing justice: fair trade, sustainability and survival.* Berkeley: University of California Press.

Kearney, Michael 1996. *Reconceptualizing the peasantry: anthropology in global perspective.* Boulder, Col.: Westview Press.

Lewis, David 1998. Non-governmental organizations, business and the management of ambiguity: case studies of 'fair trade' from Nepal and Bangladesh. *Nonprofit Management and Leadership* 9: 135–51.

Luetchford, Peter G. 2006. Brokering fair trade: relations between coffee cooperatives and fair trade organisations – a view from Costa Rica. In *Development brokers and translators: the ethnography of aid and agencies* (eds) David Lewis and David Mosse, pp. 127–48. Bloomfield, Conn.: Kumarian Press.

————— 2008. *Fair trade and a global commodity: coffee in Costa Rica.* London: Pluto Press.

Lyon, Sarah 2006. Evaluating fair trade consumption: politics, defetishization and producer participation. *International Journal of Consumer Studies* 30: 452–64.

Miller, Daniel 1987. *Material culture and mass consumption.* Oxford: Blackwell.

————— 1998. *A theory of shopping.* Cambridge: Polity Press.

Mintz, Sidney 1985. *Sweetness and power.* New York: Viking.

Moberg, Mark 2008. *Slipping away; banana politics and Fair Trade in the Eastern Caribbean.* New York: Berghahn Books.

Monge Alfaro, Carlos 1980. *Historia de Costa Rica* (Sixteenth edition). San José, Costa Rica: Trejos Hermanos.

Murray, Douglas, Laura T. Raynolds and Peter Leigh Taylor 2003. *One cup at a time: poverty alleviation and fair trade in Latin America.* Fort Collins: Fair Trade Research Group, Colorado State University.

Mutersbaugh, Tad 2002. The number is the beast: a political economy of organic-coffee certification and producer unionism. *Environment and Planning A* 34: 1165–84.

Orozco, Jorge 1992. La consultoría agro-económica: un proyecto de la FES. In *Siete años ... por el desarollo campesino* (ed) Javier Martinez, pp. 19–38. Cañas, Guanacaste, Costa Rica: Consultoría Agro-Económica.

Ortiz, Sutti 1999. *Harvesting coffee, bargaining wages: rural labour markets in Colombia.* Ann Arbor: University of Michigan Press.

Paige, Jeffery 1997. *Coffee and power: revolution and the rise of democracy in Central America.* Cambridge, Mass: Harvard University Press.

Raynolds, Laura T. 2002. Producer–consumer links in fair trade coffee networks. *Sociologia Ruralis* 42: 404–24.

Renard, Marie-Christine 1999. The interstices of globalization: the example of fair trade coffee. *Sociologia Ruralis* 39: 484–500.

————— 2003. Fair trade: quality, market and conventions. *Journal of Rural Studies* 19: 87–96.

Ronchi, Loraine 2002. *The impact of fair trade on producers and their organisations: a case study with Coocafé in Costa Rica.* (Working paper 11). Falmer: Poverty Research Unit, University of Sussex.

Roseberry, William 1983. *Coffee and capitalism in the Venezuelan Andes.* Austin: University of Texas Press.

Sandoval-Garcia, Carlos 2004. *Threatening others: Nicaraguan migrants and the formation of national identity in Costa Rica*. Athens: Ohio University Press.

Schivelbusch, Wolfgang 1992. *Tastes of paradise: a social history of spices, stimulants, and intoxicants*. New York: Pantheon Books.

Seligson, Mitchell Allan 1980. *Peasants of Costa Rica and the development of agrarian capitalism*. Madison: University of Wisconsin Press.

Smith, Julia 2007. The search for sustainable markets: the promises and failures of fair trade. *Culture and Agriculture* 29: 89–99.

———— 2010. Fair trade and the specialty coffee market: growing alliances, shifting rivalries. In *Fair Trade and social justice: global ethnographies* (eds) Sarah Lyon and Mark Moberg, pp. 28–46. New York: New York University Press.

Stolcke, Verena 1995. The labors of coffee in Latin America: the hidden charm of family labor and self-provisioning. In *Coffee, society and power in Latin America* (eds) William Roseberry, Lowell Gudmundson and Mario Samper Kutschbach, pp. 65–93. Baltimore: John Hopkins University Press.

Tallontire, Anne 2000. Partnerships in fair trade: reflections from a case study of Cafédirect. *Development and Practice* 10: 166–77.

Thompson, Bob 1999. Lessons for fair trade. *Small Enterprise Development* 10 (4): 56–60.

Williams, Robert G. 1994. *States and social evolution: coffee and the rise of national governments in Central America*. Chapel Hill: University of North Carolina Press.

Winson, Anthony 1989. *Coffee and democracy in modern Costa Rica*. Basingstoke: Macmillan.

Wright, Caroline 2004. Consuming lives, consuming landscapes: interpreting advertisements for Cafédirect coffees. *Journal of International Development* 16: 665–80.

Chapter 3

'TRADE, NOT AID': IMAGINING ETHICAL ECONOMY

Lill Vramo

> These items are handmade. They have been created by a real person, not made by a machine. If I bought a gift here, I could imagine that I was giving a gift both to the recipient and to the people I was helping.
> (Customer in a Norwegian fair-trade shop)

As argued in the Introduction to this volume, ethical consumption is an effort to affect the economic realm by introducing into it values from the social, values that commonly are embodied in the objects that ethical consumers buy. Of course the effects that are sought and the values that are to be introduced will vary from place to place. In this chapter I describe how ethical consumers and those who sell to them in one particular place imagine the objects that confront them and the values that they embody.

I do so by tracing things of thread and woven material that are designed in Norway, produced in Bangladesh and returned to Norway for sale as special products in a fair-trade shop, which I call Fair Shop Ltd. The underlying aim of the business I describe is to support people in the South through trade, distinguishing their business from practices and notions of aid. As part of that, Fair Shop focuses on the material attributes of what they sell, rather than on the ethical nature of the trade. To a degree, then, Fair Shop resembles the local cheese consortia that Cristina Grasseni (this volume) describes. Even though they differ in many ways, both are concerned to use commerce to secure the well-being of relatively poor areas. Although fair trade is marginal in Norwegian markets and mentality, an ethical shift is evident in the increasing visibility of fair-trade goods and shops, as well as in campaigns to encourage ethical consumption. As this suggests, the management, staff and customers involved in this fair-trade initiative see the shift from aid to trade not as a rejection of ethical values, but rather as an expression of them.

Why is trade understood as a better way of being ethical than aid in Norway? The 'trade, not aid' ideology is my point of departure for exploring how people imagine proper or desirable market relations. Long-distance trade facilitates expressions of ethical concerns and images. However, it is also true that a yearning for connectedness with the world, for closeness to production and producers, is an important driving force behind ethical purchases and the overall trade. The wish to bridge the gap between Us and Them is kept alive by ideas of direct trade and of receiving goods through ethical channels. The duality of 'far away' and 'right here' is represented in the thing, the object that connects us to the distant while remaining free from context. In this seemingly disconnected and independent state, as I will demonstrate, the object becomes a vessel for projections and expressions of ethics as well as a means of converting commodities to gifts.

This chapter draws material from a study of a trading relationship between a Bangladeshi company and a Norwegian company conducted between 2003 and 2005. My overall aim was to gain information about the relationships and the dialectics between production and consumption, between producers and consumers and between North and South in a contemporary, long-distance trade relationship. 'Long-distance' refers to the spatial, cultural and socioeconomic distances that are part of the general separation of production and consumption in the world economy today. As Marianne Lien (2004*a*: 15, n2) points out, this distance gives rise to abstract relations between producers and consumers, also fuelled by the 'processes of abstraction that characterise the ways in which suppliers and consumers are made apparent to each other – for instance through an emphasis on brand name at the expense of structures of ownership or agency'.

In his study of North London, Daniel Miller explains that choices related to shopping involve a number of moral values and considerations that make shopping inherently contradictory and full of dilemmas (see the discussion in Dombos, this volume). Even though Miller finds that consumers are facing pressure to express altruism through shopping, he argues that altruistic shopping does not exist. Instead, people engage in 'ethical dialogues' inside their own heads or with others in order to explain and legitimate their purchases. Miller shows how consumers attempt to prevail over the guilt that is an underlying theme in these dialogues, through practices that he calls 'doing one's bit' or 'being good', his names for a variety of themes that arise in ethical dialogues in everyday consumption (Miller 2001: 130–1).

Here I will show how, as a result of both structural circumstances and marketing, fair-trade shops and ethical trade are arenas where the guilt and moral dilemmas related to shopping that Miller describes are absent or can be transcended. Due to the framing of fair-trade shops as *fair*, they make good arenas for transformations of guilt and give room for ethical dialogues related to creating and producing different kinds of meaning and hope. As I will show, the very distance between producer and shopper that causes the 'information deficit' and the impossibility of being fully informed that Lien (2004*a*: 5) describes, makes it relatively easy for Northern actors involved in ethical trade to imagine those producers and their trade in ways that contain hope and meaning. After all, calling what these shops do 'fair trade' implies that other trade is unfair, which reinforces the belief in these shops as unique moral spheres.

In this chapter I explore the relationship of distance, meaning and value in terms of what Fair Shop sells, especially textiles. I do so by describing how these textiles, the work process and ideas of trade and ethicality are culturally and locally embedded in the contexts of their production and consumption. Fair Shop is especially suited to this, for while the textiles are manufactured in the South, the cognitive, cultural production of these things as *special* things is carried out in the North. This division of labour maintains the traditional structure of the production chain, with the South producing the raw material while the 'value-adding' activities remain the privilege of the North (Wilkinson 2007: 237). As Said (2003) has pointed out, the Orient remains an integral aspect of Western material and intellectual civilisation and culture, both as the source of the silk and cotton we import and of the intellectual material to construct and constitute ourselves as different and perhaps more modern, civilised or developed (Vramo 2006: 18–19). I explore how images of the Other and the Other's context are used as material for producing ethical commodities or converting commodities into gifts or possessions. By examining the various ways things are fetishised as commodities through entangling and untangling processes on the way between producer and purchaser, I explore how Norwegian actors express, construe, imagine and practice social and ethical values through objects, consumption and trade. In other words, I explore the ways that ethical goods work as bridges to displaced hopes and ideals through what Grant McCracken (1990: Chap. 7) calls 'displaced meaning' strategies.

The actors involved in the fair-trade business, and their strategies and practices to distinguish aid from trade, reflect the normative and ideal division between gift and commodity found in Western thought (Mauss 1990 [1925]; see Carrier 1995). I explore this division between aid and trade, and the ethical reorientation that comes with the shift to trade, as a ritual to cleanse the relationship between First and Third World countries, with a yearning for balance as an underlying driving force.

The Ethical Reorientation

Internationally, trade increasingly is seen as a better tool for development than is aid.[1] While this turn towards trade as key to development in itself is part of a wider international trend and ideal (see Dolan 2009: 34–35; Wilkinson 2007: 235), it does not have the same context or meaning in all Northern countries. Here I will briefly present the background for this trend in Norway.

Terje Tvedt describes the field of Norwegian development cooperation as an example of a national 'do-gooder regime' which, in its own eyes, has created a moral society within an evil and cynical world. This do-gooder regime has a special standing and legitimacy in Norway. The deep-rooted, historical self-image of being a good nation has rarely been contested in the country (Tvedt 2007: 621). Marianne Gullestad (2007) shows how, through evangelism, the long-term relationship between Norway and the Other has played a decisive role in the constitution of the Norwegian welfare state as well as in shaping Norway's relationship to the South.

Criticisms of the baleful unintended consequences of development activities are common (notably Escobar 1995; Ferguson 1994). Gullestad points to some of these consequences in the effects of what she calls the evangelist 'goodness regime'. One is a continuing confirmation of the social and cultural gap between giver and recipient in North–South relations, a common feature of development gifts (Stirrat and Henkel 1997: 69). Another is that the generous givers, almost without exception, are implicated in the recipients' potential humiliation. As Knut Nustad (2003: 21) points out, a distinct disconnection between the giver and the receiver is typical for development gifts, because the systemic connection between First World wealth and Third World poverty is ignored, and the poverty of the recipient country is explained instead in terms of particular local difficulties. So, the aid gift, besides sustaining the unequal relationship between donor and recipient, may provide the solution to the particular local problem but it ignores other and more systematic ones (see also Ferguson 1994; Stirrat and Henkel 1997).

Yet another unintended effect involves a change in the perception of giver and recipient. Over time, through a process involving key people on the receiving end, the problematic relationship between a generous giver and a grateful recipient has become redefined as a relationship between what Gullestad (2007: 233–36) calls a 'foolish giver' and a 'crafty taker'. This redefinition has been accompanied by a growing concern with corruption among Southern aid recipients, marked by anti-corruption protocols in development projects funded by the Norwegian Agency for Development Co-operation. I suggest that the idea of the crafty taker also tends to put the foolish giver in a humiliating position, and that the turn to ethical trade in Norway is partly a response. Appropriately, there is widespread optimism that an increase in trade is part of the solution for Third World countries, in contrast to an idea of 'merely giving', which is to say, aid.

Assuming that the asymmetrical historical relationship between North and South has produced what might be called 'relational discomfort', I suggest that the move away from aid is part of a ritual to cleanse the foolish giver found in these relationships.[2] The slogan 'trade, not aid' expresses both faith in trade as the key to development and a demarcation in relation to aid and charity. Trade and aid, thus, can be seen as two different modes that, in different ways, represent Norway's relationship to the wider world. These two modes reflect well-known conceptions in anthropology, namely gift exchange and commodity exchange, and imply the ideal-typical relationships these two modes create and represent. This has been described by Chris Gregory (1983: 104):

commodity exchange is an exchange of alienable objects between people who are in a state of reciprocal independence that establishes a quantitative relationship between the objects transacted, whereas gift exchange is an exchange of inalienable objects between people who are in a state of reciprocal dependence that establishes a qualitative relationship between the subjects transacting.

Making a distinction between trade and aid is important in the design, presentation and operation of the fair-trade shop that forms the basis for this study. By applying ideas from economic anthropology to my ethnographic material, I will draw attention to these practices as part of a ritual cleansing of the North–South relationship. Afterwards, I examine fair trade as an arena where cultural hopes, values and ideals are expressed and preserved through customers' understandings of the Other and the Other's context.

Fair Shop Ltd

The Norwegian company Fair Shop Ltd endorses 'trade, not aid'. By giving products access to the Norwegian market and conducting what the chairman of the board calls 'normal trade', the underlying intention is that the respective countries and individuals involved in the trade will benefit. The senior management in the company believe that if they are to succeed, the business needs to induce Norwegian customers to make purchases because of their appreciation of the products as material objects, not because they wish to help. A designer employed by Fair Shop Ltd explains:

> If we are going to compete with multinational companies – such as, for instance, Nike – in order to reduce the exploitation in this world, my opinion is that in order to work on those problems, we have to play by the same rules. This means that if we should be dependent on customers who appreciate pillows with mirrors or African bowls in crazy colours, I think we are doing ourselves a disservice. Instead we should, for instance, give Bangladesh the opportunity to see what we actually buy because we find it attractive or appealing, not because we think it is the right thing to do if we want to help. You should enter Fair Shop and not notice ... that it is a fair-trade organisation. You just walk in because they have very nice pillows and really, really nice chairs.

As this shows, Fair Shop Ltd has a clear strategy for both the customers and the products that enter the shop. The objective is that customers should be interested in the products and not in the people who produced them. This means that the company draws a strict line between what they term the 'concept', which is the good intention of helping producers, and the 'business', where, like the head of Cafédirect mentioned in the Introduction to this volume, they want to play by the same rules as other market actors. The products are to be sold in a *real* market sphere, in what the chairman referred to as 'normal trade': an idealised market exchange where the transaction takes place between independent actors. For such a transaction to occur, the potential purchaser can not be motivated by pity for the producers or by a desire to help them. Such motives indicate a social or moral link between purchaser and producer that contradicts the idea of autonomous transactors, and so have to be cleansed from the shop arena. Instead, the products have to be appealing or attractive enough in themselves to draw the customers over the threshold and into Fair Shop. As I will show, however, this separation of the concept from the business is an ideal, rather than a reality that has been achieved: the ethical message does reach attentive customers in Fair Shop.

An Ethical Arena

Fair Shop is in a good location in a city on the west coast of Norway, its large windows facing a busy street with people passing by and looking in. The shop can be characterised as a gift and interiors shop with a coffee bar attached. Small, white lettering on the shop window proclaims the name of the shop (an English-sounding woman's name) followed by 'fair trade by', and then the name of a Christian organisation. Because the name and the slogan are small and not in Norwegian, the message of a moral shopping arena is presented in a rather quiet way. White glossy boxes hang from the ceiling in the shop windows, each prominently displaying a silk cushion: light blue, darker blue, yellow, light green, purple. The cushions' gleaming silk threads represent the Fair Shop 'concept colours'; that concept, and the business based on it, reflects the work of marketing professionals and designers in the North. Besides the brightly-coloured cushions, Fair Shop sells items ranging from place-mats and runners to wooden articles, knitwear, cards and books. A large colour photo of the hands of an artisan is hanging on one of the empty white walls. The runners, tablecloths and place-mats are produced by the 'Sewing Section', a production unit in Bangladesh where I also did field work.

The products and concept of Fair Shop Ltd are designed with a target group in mind. As Michele Micheletti (2003: 108) points out, the growing visibility of ethical trade has been based on the identification of a broad category of 'political consumers'. This broad category is approached by the company, however, as normal consumers who will engage in normal trade. The company wants customers to choose the products due to what they call a real interest in those products. The chairman of the board expresses this objective:

> The purchase ought to be founded on desire rather than speculating on and hiding behind the wish to do something good. The products that are sold in this shop are to be bought because they are desirable. If not, we are beginning to exploit the idea of aid by saying that customers have to buy our products for other reasons. Then I believe you can attract a small following, but first of all that following is not large enough, and secondly I feel that we would be hiding behind the producers, and if I was a producer, I would never like that.

The company's insistence on a practice whereby customers are to be attracted to the objects themselves means putting the products in the foreground and forcing the producers out of focus.

Fair Shop recognises that customers might be moral creatures at the moment of purchasing. As a business, however, they do not want to appeal to this aspect of people or to the type of customer who they think is commonly motivated by such concerns. Instead, they want to appeal to the normal consumer. That sort of person is, of course, an abstraction. The sort of abstracting that is involved is described by Lien, who argues that 'the consumer' is constructed through processes of disentangling, where ties to other parts of life and the personality are broken: 'A consumer, in other words, rests upon processes of disentangling that cut the links to practically everything that makes any of us a person' (Lien 2004*b*: 61).

In accord with Lien's observation, Fair Shop envisions a certain way of shopping and deems alternative shopping behaviour as irrelevant. This idealised consumption practice corresponds to what James Carrier (1997) calls 'the market', referring to the notion of an idealised form of buying and selling. He is concerned with the market model as a cultural construction and a discourse with an elaborated theory of human nature and of the best means of promoting emancipation (Kahn 1997: 75). That market model rests on certain assumptions, and perhaps the most basic of these is that the world consists only of free individuals, the independent transactors of Gregory's description of commodity exchange.

Appropriately, the company has as its goal to frame Fair Shop as a normal shop that attracts customers acting as normal consumers according to the market model. In interacting with those customers, the shop assistants are to behave as normal shop assistants who are concerned with what is seen as normal shopping behaviour and preferences, namely what can be seen and touched: quality and design. This way of presenting the object is similar to conventional capitalist commerce, where the object is presented as a fetishised commodity, separated from the conditions and social relations that were involved in producing it and bringing it to the presence of the purchaser. In the presence of the consumer, such an object is seemingly as free as the individuals in the market model and should be assessed in terms of the relationship between 'look and feel' and price. The company's insistence that a better world should be achieved through capitalist commerce is a clear message: market relations are the way to goodness – the medium is the market.

Yet behind the counter at Fair Shop, another frame exists. Here the shop assistants, designers and senior management are free to think about and be concerned for the producers in the South. Reflecting this, a headache for the shop manager is the fact that Fair Shop customers do not purchase regularly or enough, resulting in a sporadic flow of orders to the Sewing Section. The words of the shop manager show how this commercial headache is also a moral concern: 'I feel sorry for them [the pieceworkers in Bangladesh].

Because it might be that we don't place an order for a month, and that makes me think: they ought to have some work to do. But I have enough goods and I can't order more. That is the situation.'

As the shop manager's statement indicates, the Bangladeshi pieceworkers are dependent on orders from the Norwegian fair-trade shop. This direct dependence, especially the pieceworkers' lack of rights and of the sort of wages that accompany regular work, is not communicated to customers in Fair Shop in Norway. Instead, the information reaching those customers is, as I shall show, diffuse and characterised by silencing and highlighting processes: some information eventually is conveyed about the producers' lives and their contexts, while other information is withheld along the way.

Such silencing and highlighting, which occur both consciously and unconsciously in the relationship between North and South, must be understood in a wider structural frame than this ethnographic example. By following certain images and discourses from the Sewing Section and the South that travel to the Norwegian context, I will focus attention on such processes of silencing and highlighting, and reveal that work processes and ideas of trade are locally and culturally embedded. This in turn demonstrates that meanings and values, including the values of fair trade, are irrelevant without contextualisation.

The Bangladeshi Context

As I have said, I did field work in Bangladesh in the Sewing Section, a production unit that makes runners, tablecloths and place-mats that Fair Shop Ltd sells in Norway. The Sewing Section directly employs six women as staff and production workers, and they have regular working hours, continuity of employment and a predictable workload. It also has another fifty women who are pieceworkers.

The Sewing Section is located on the first floor of a two-storey brick building in Netrapur, an urban area some ten hours by bus from Dhaka. The building is situated in a compound with a twenty-four hour security guard and a big, heavy gate that opens onto a heavily used main road. The women who work for the Sewing Section come from housing areas located two to four kilometres from the compound. They arrive on foot in small groups or individually. While buses and lorries rumble past them on the asphalt paving, they walk along the edge of the road until they reach the gate and the security guard lets them in. Whether there are orders to be filled determines when the women arrive and the frequency of their trips through the gate.

In Bangladesh there are two discourses related to women working outside the domestic sphere that are particularly important. These discourses, which I call the 'transformation discourse' and the 'decay discourse', both relate to a category of women who are referred to as 'poor', 'illiterate' and with 'no educational background'. The fifty pieceworkers at the Sewing Section belong to this category. I will begin by presenting the positive image found in the transformation discourse, and discuss its implications for the women at the Sewing Section.

Development programmes and the transformation discourse emphasise the positive aspects of women learning skills and of women moving out of their domestic sphere to work in the formal sector. Embroidery is not mechanised, requiring only a needle and an embroidery frame, and it can be transported easily between the Sewing Section and the household. The fluid character of this type of work partly explains why it is not seen as 'real' work. Pieceworkers do not enjoy the rights and wages that exist for regular, real work; piecework is characterised by sporadic orders, and thus irregular working hours and wages (Wilkinson-Weber 1999: 60–61). While the staff and the production workers have predictable wages, the amount of work, and hence the income, of the women who work on a piece rate depend on the flow of orders, the size of the orders and the number of women who want to embroider at the pertinent time. The pieceworkers in the Sewing Section are paid slightly above the average local rate for similar work. Even so, the money they receive is little enough that the women themselves define it as 'pocket money'. 'It is because we are poor that we come to the Sewing Section', the women whom I call Jarina and Ambia reply when I ask why they do this work.

The transformation discourse relies on the underlying assumption that paid employment has the same implications for women in the South that it has for women in industrialised societies. In the local context, however, embroidery work in exchange for money in piecework is associated with poverty. Furthermore, a woman working outside the home is not viewed as positively in Bangladesh as the imagery invoked by Fair Shop, described below, suggests. The ideal of separate spheres for men and women, in the institution of purdah, continues to be a powerful cultural ideal within Bangladesh (Dannecker 2002: 19). In accord with this, for those women whose families can afford it, seclusion is a sign of status and a state to be proud of (Gardner 2001: 210).

Consequently, when a woman in Bangladesh leaves her home to collect or deliver embroidery work, she demonstrates the household's poverty and low status. In this, the activities that are viewed positively in the Northern transformation discourse are viewed negatively in the Bangladeshi decay discourse. That discourse is a powerful social assessment of women who, like the pieceworkers in the Sewing Section, work outside the domestic sphere. In doing so, these women are acting in spaces not made for them, and in this they question the ideologies of female modesty and seclusion that are powerful in the country (Dannecker 2002: 42).

Transforming Women

Fair Shop, of course, frames the pieceworkers in the transformation discourse, which is closely linked to development discourse. In those discourses, Sarah White (1992: 2) points out, women are seen as the key to development of the society as a whole; at the same time they are the ones who have to be liberated. I want to illustrate this with the narratives of transformation that are part of Fair Shop's business, and also show how they form what Sarah Lyon (2006: 458) calls 'symbolic modes of connectivity'.

The senior management at Fair Shop Ltd travel to the Sewing Section in Bangladesh to place orders, guide the supervisors in new designs and keep in touch with their overall aim of fair trade. These trips are also important sources for inspiration and a time when the visiting Norwegians receive what I call 'narratives of transformation' from the producers. During the time I was doing my field work at the Sewing Section I observed three different visiting teams from the North, who all received the same simplified narratives about the producers. What characterises these visits is that they are short, the fact that pieceworkers are brought from their homes to the Sewing Section to act as regular workers, and that what is acted out between the producers and the visitors from the North follows a certain 'script', to use Goffman's term (1992).

Typically, one of the pieceworkers comes forward to tell her life story in Bangla. This is the essence of one such life story, as translated into English by the man I call Mr Singh, of the Sewing Section:

> Yasmin got married as a thirteen-year-old, what is known as early marriage. She is the oldest of seven brothers and sisters. Her husband was sent to jail. When he got out of prison, she divorced him. Her husband is a drug addict. Now Yasmin is twenty-five years old. Her life has been hard. Eight years ago she got in contact with the Sewing Section and learned her skills from Miriam, the supervisor. Yasmin now supports her family so that her two children can get an education.

In a Western frame of reference, Yasmin's story of moving from suffering and destitution to handicraft and self-support can be read as the single mother who breaks out of traditional bonds and becomes independent through paid work. When the senior management come back to Norway from their travels to production sites they re-tell stories like Yasmin's to the shop assistants.

Despite the company's policy that pity, producers and idealism are to be kept behind the counter, people at Fair Shop are aware that the products can be bridges to simplified narratives. This is made explicit when the chairman of the board talks to the shop assistants in a motivational sales meeting: 'Our guiding star, our motivation, is the dignity the work gives the producers. If we think of this for each product, it gives us a new way of seeing the products'. In the chairman's view, then, the shop assistants should see in Fair Shop's products the ideal state of producers in the South acquiring dignity through their work. This idea, that wage labour contributes to human dignity, stands in sharp contrast to the idea that receiving aid makes you inferior or dependent. In this way, the product functions as a bridge to Norwegian ideals of helping without having to engage in gift giving, and so without ending up in the humiliating position of the foolish giver. Thus it is that underlying the chairman's philosophy is the idea that work in exchange for money cleanses the business of any taint of aid.

The idea that paid work inevitably gives dignity to workers is common in Western thought. So is the idea that the money that comes from such work is a positive force in an evolutionary model that allows undeveloped places and people to reach new levels of development (Bloch and Parry 1996: 461–62). For Bangladeshi women, however, status and power are related to their relative control of resources in the household, most often their ownership of land, and not to wage labour, individual liberation or a career (Dannecker 2002: 53; Gardner 2001: 211).

Producing Value: The 'Good Narrative' from the Design Agency

In an interview, one of the Fair Shop designers, whom I call Toril, explained how the products that the shop sells are meant to communicate meaning and value in the Norwegian context. The following shows how the Other and the Other's context are a part of this process, through narratives about both the past and the future.

> Toril: A lot of time is put into the product, and the respect for the work, you know. It is handmade. It absolutely has to show that it is handicraft.
> Lill: Why?
> Toril: Because you know the story behind it, you can imagine that it is an actual woman, a family, or women who sit in the village and embroider a whole day and receive fair wages for their work. In addition to fair wages for the work they do, they get an education, they learn to read and write, they get to join educational programmes, their children can go to school, and they are able to build drinking wells in the village in order to get clean water. Those values behind [the concept] are really important, and these are values the customers ought to want to pay extra for.

In what this Norwegian designer says, the product is a direct link to the producers in the South. In her thoughts, one aspect of this is an idealised village where people are happy artisans using their hands in real work. Another aspect is movement into a better and more developed future where the water is clean, women are enlightened and liberated, children are receiving an education, wages are fair. Moreover, whatever Fair Shop policy may be, that designer sees the context of their production as something added on to the material nature of the things Fair Shop sells, something that makes them more valuable and more expensive. However, this additional value only exists in Norway: it does not reach the producers in Bangladesh.

This additional value is apparent also to the shop assistants in Norway. For them, work in a fair-trade shop raises a job that ordinarily is seen as having a low status to one that they experience as meaningful. As one assistant, whom I call Ida, said:

> Working in a shop is not a career path for me, but this is different because I work to benefit somebody. There are so many positive stories about it making a difference. I look upon this as aid. If we did not have this shop, lots of people would have been out of work.

Another, whom I call Marthe, said: 'I feel that I am important, that Fair Shop needs me. I like the fundamental attitudes and the principles of helping. That it is a concept of trade and not aid.'

What Ida and Marthe have to say are typical 'backstage' comments that illustrate how the idea of helping through providing work is alive behind the counter. This way of thinking seems to motivate the company's staff. On the other side of the counter, however, customers are supposed to be left alone, in that ideal market situation. The shop manager confided to me that some days she feels like forcing the customers to buy the products. However, out in the shop she conforms to the goal of the company, and so restrains herself, only speaking with the customers about what anyone can see: quality and design.

The idea that shop customers are supposed to choose objects on material grounds, rather than social ones, is something of a pretence. That is because customers get information about the products, but only *after* they make their normal market 'free choice', in accord with the view of senior management that what the shop sells has to be good enough to compete with regular shops in a normal market sphere. When a purchase has been brought to a successful close, an information card is slipped into the Fair Shop bag along with the item, and handed over the counter to the customer. The Southern producers are represented on these cards: '[I]n the new millennium, more than three hundred people – including prostitutes and others without hope in the queue for work – were energetically producing carpets, runners, handbags, cards' (Vramo 2006: 139). (The information may also given verbally, such as: 'These are handmade by poor women in Bangladesh'.)

The Fair Shop chairman said that if the information were given before the consumer had chosen, it might be offensive and frighten the customer away. However, because it is given after the moment of choice, the same information can function as a 'good narrative', making the product more valuable. The chairman said that information given in this way is positive: 'those customers have not bought the product because of that information, but still they have a good narrative to accompany the product, and that is the best thing that can happen'. In this way, it appears, customers are in a position to make connections to the producers through simplified narratives, or they can choose to treat the pillow as any other pure commodity. In other words, they can regulate the degree of stickiness in relation to the producer (Vramo 2006: 140).

Looking for Something Good: The Customers

Framing Fair Shop as good, with a strategic withholding of information, presents customers with a wide field for creating meaning. Despite the senior management's strategy of keeping the idealism behind the counter, most of my informants and customers associate Fair Shop with something morally good. Four comments illustrate this:

> 'Here I can shop with a clear conscience.'
> 'It's better to spend money here.'
> 'If you don't know what to give, you can always purchase something here. At least it is meaningful.'
> 'A good place to buy gifts for people who have everything.'

Customers have different ways of defining and understanding what shopping in Fair Shop entails or creates. Conversations with two customers in Fair Shop, whom I call Malin and Tone, illustrate how customers can deal with the possibility of taking part in something morally good.

Malin is nineteen and is living in a collective this term. She says she would tell recipients that she had bought their gifts in a fair-trade shop, because it gives more meaning to the gifts. She likes the things in the shop; even though they are similar to each other, she feels that they have individuality. 'This is because the products have been made by human beings', she explains. She went on, with the words quoted at the start of this chapter: 'These items are handmade. They have been created by a real person, not made by a machine. If I bought a gift here, I could imagine that I was giving a gift both to the recipient and to the people I was helping'. In Malin's remarks she moves beyond the objects themselves to express values regarding handicraft and ideals of helping people in the South. In using Fair Shop items as gifts, then, she imagines herself linked with two sets of people, those who make what she buys and those who receive what she gives. Through ideas of direct trade and bridge building, then, Malin imagines the producers behind the products, and by conjuring up real people whom she knows, she imagines that she can give the purchase as a gift. By defining the transaction as a gift, Malin shows how trade can be comprehended as aid.

Tone is a regular customer dropping into Fair Shop after a workout to buy an organic apple and to browse in the interior department, which she enjoys. Tone is twenty-eight, cheerful and extrovert. Today she is going to exchange a silk cushion. 'It was the wrong colour', she explains. As we walk around in the shop, she enthusiastically tells me that she loves the atmosphere here, the concept and the products. She thinks it is important for all people to have something to do. 'Then they feel useful instead of useless', she says. She tells me that she thinks the shop's concept contributes to a feeling of self-worth among people in the South through being useful. We stop by the notebooks from a market in Bangladesh. She opens one of them and explains that she bought such notebooks, which she likes a lot, on an earlier occasion. She thinks that one of the books is more Bangladeshi than the other because it has a pattern and is not so sweet looking. She likes how the pages stick slightly, and she thinks it makes the book soft. She strokes the pages. 'The sheets of paper are softer than in other books, it makes them good to write on with a ball pen', she says. A thought hits her; she looks at me and says: 'It is somewhat selfish. I buy the book and get a nice thing, and then I help the people down there at the same time. It is a bit selfish'.

Wandering around in Fair Shop as a shop assistant with Malin, Tone or other customers is rather different from serving customers in ordinary shops. The conversations readily turn to the imagined effects of purchasing products in Fair Shop, linked to personal ideals of helping people without means. Purchasing is associated with being able to help others and with the hope of creating a better and fairer world. In this way the shift from aid to trade is not a rejection of ethical values, but rather an expression of them. Yet this mixing of aid and trade, or aid in a market context, feels slightly problematic, as Tone says. In a more general understanding of aid, there is a belief that development assistance is a pure gift, one that is given freely and selflessly, without thought of return. However, Fair Shop customers get something in return, an appealing object. This makes those shoppers uneasy, even if also doubly pleased.

Fair Shop has the ability to transform consumption into something morally good, with the products as important vehicles for personal and cultural hopes, values and ideals. What I call a 'normative add-on' to the product and the shopping helps the customers in Fair Shop to transcend the dilemmas and contradictions inherent in shopping, such as concerns about being too materialistic, or about products and shopping being alienating and without meaning. Those add-ons also transcend the dilemma of having to choose between close relations and distant Others (Miller 2001: 133–34; see the discussion in Dombos, this volume), as Malin demonstrates by establishing close relations through a 'double gift', although in one of those relations the Southern producers of Fair Shop's 'Norwegian Design' remain indebted recipients.

Conclusion

I have argued that fair trade functions as a good arena for producing meaning and expressing ethics in the North, while the effects in the South are diffuse and largely imagined, rather as they are among the coffee growers that Peter Luetchford (this volume) describes. Values and hopes of creating a better and more equal world are alive in Fair Shop, when customers browse or purchase objects produced in the South.

Because of the ways that Westerners commonly think of market transactions, the relationship between Norwegian customer and Southern maker is seen as free and equal. While this may be a fairly common Western assumption, it takes on distinctive significance among the people who buy at, work for and run Fair Shop. I pointed to this significance when I said that seeing ethical consumption in that way is part of the cleansing ritual by which Norwegians, and Norway itself, attempt to trade themselves out of being the foolish giver. Historically, the national image of 'being good' has stemmed from and been sustained by aid, charity and peace-brokering activities. As these sources of our goodness become increasingly problematic, moral action shifts from aid to trade. I have shown how such a shift opens up an arena where it is possible to 'help the others and get a nice thing at the same time' without being perceived as that foolish giver.

That cleansing ritual has strict rules regarding customers' and shop assistants' behaviour, the dissemination of information, the design process and the role of the products in the process. The product is the material object which, in an untangled state at the moment of transaction, can liberate Fair Shop from running an aid programme, give people in the South dignity and independence through wage work, and provide customers in the North the opportunity to shop first and foremost out of desire. This means fetishising those objects, untangling them conceptually from their actual existence before their life in the shop. That untangling, in turn, reinforces a lack of simultaneity in the relationship between North and South, turning Fair Shop into an apolitical and opaque arena, one of high hopes for the idealised producers, yet disconnected from those women walking to the compound gate in Netrapur, their work and their lives.

This fetishising is not, as I have noted, complete. Although it does so only in small letters on its front window, Fair Shop does present itself as fair trade, something people who have bought there know already. However, this fair trade does not focus on specific producers who benefit, in the way that bags of ethical coffee commonly carry pictures of and stories about the growers. There is, then, little of the personalisation that is common in fair trade. Much of the reason for this seems to lie in the Norwegian concern not to be taken as foolish givers, in which case portrayals of the producers might be seen to echo the cunning presentation of wily takers. Rather, customers appear, in effect, to be asked to trust Fair Shop to assure that this does not happen, and they seem happy to do so. This trust in the institution may not, moreover, be peculiar to Fair Shop or to Norway, with its ambivalent perception of producers in the Third World. In his description of ethical coffee, Luetchford (this volume) observes that the bags of the Co-operative's own brand contain almost nothing beyond the Fairtrade mark. It may be that the Co-operative stores, perhaps because they are a cooperative, are trusted by their customers in a way that other large retailers are not, and that Fair Shop is.

In this chapter, I have shown how Fair Shop products are useful as bridges to spheres where both individual and cultural ideals and values can be sought, just as, in a different way, the ethical things they buy can be bridges for the Palermo residents that Giovanni Orlando (this volume) describes. As bridges to spheres where the world is fairer, simpler and less alienating, they become vehicles that can take us to who it is we wish to be. The shop serves as an arena for assisting distant Others, which makes fair-trade objects especially good not only to purchase but also, in Lévì-Strauss's terms, to think. I have demonstrated how fair-trade shops and fair-trade businesses constitute accessible arenas that both transcend individual dilemmas related to shopping and empower employees working in ethical trade.

Several conditions are present in creating an arena for building bridges and imagining worlds. The company's strategy of withholding information before a purchase, combined with the distance between Bangladeshi producers and Norwegian consumers, make fair-trade shopping a suitable arena for displacement strategies. The gaps and distances in the chain between the Sewing Section and Fair Shop managers and customers are the ground where visions and narratives of what that trade is and does can flourish and evolve. At the same time, the ideas of direct trade draw the Southern producers closer in to an imagined community where 'they are just like us', striving to get recognition and liberation through wage work. This does not involve only the creation of imagined Third World producers. In addition, as I said at the outset, it removes from view the structures of relationships between the North and the South, so that the cause of things like poverty in Bangladesh is located in the peculiarities of Southern countries (Nustad 2003: 26–28). Or, in the words of one Fair Shop employee, 'when the South gains more expertise in our standards, design, fashion and trade, they can become as developed and rich as us'.

Fair Shop is an arena where cultural hopes and ideals are preserved through customers' creative processes, where the Other plays a key role as material for creating bridges to imagined and desired worlds. Through these processes of memory and creation, simplified and decontextualised images of the Others are maintained and reproduced. As I have argued, 'being good' through fair trade is more of a tribute to the market model and the sovereign consumer than a serious attempt to bridge the gaps in the world economy. The constructed consumer, spared the unsavoury and complex aspects of world trade, is left to choose in what appears as an apolitical arena where the connection between the reality of piecework and the nice place-mat remain unclear.

Notes

1. Gavin Fridell (2007) has a thorough examination of the historical (and theoretical) origins of the fair trade movement. A distinct reorientation has been evident, from an earlier emphasis on the role of the state and on developing a distinctly alternative market, to its current conformity to neoliberal globalisation and embrace of the ideology of free trade.
2. Stirrat and Henkel (1997: 73) refer to another strategy to avoid the charge that development donors and their agents are patrons, formulated in the slogan 'helping the poor to help themselves'.

Bibliography

Bloch, Maurice and Jonathan Parry 1996. Introduction: money and the morality of exchange. In *Sosialantropologiske grunntekster* (ed) T.H. Eriksen, pp. 455–87. Oslo: Ad Notam Gyldendal.

Carrier, James G. 1995. *Gifts and commodities: exchange and Western capitalism since 1700*. London: Routledge.

―――― 1997. Introduction. In *Meanings of the market* (ed) J.G. Carrier, pp. 1–67. Oxford: Berg.

Dannecker, Petra 2002. *Between conformity and resistance: woman garment workers in Bangladesh*. Dhaka: The University Press Limited.

Dolan, Catherine S. 2009. Virtual moralities: the mainstreaming of Fairtrade in Kenyan tea fields. *Geoforum* 41: 33–43.

Escobar, Arturo 1995. *Encountering development: the making and unmaking of the Third World*. Princeton: Princeton University Press.

Ferguson, James 1994. *The anti-politics machine: development, depolitization, and bureaucratic power in Lesotho*. Minneapolis: University of Minnesota Press.

Fridell, Gavin 2007. *Fair trade coffee: the prospects and pitfalls of market-driven social justice*. Toronto: University of Toronto Press.

Gardner, Katy 2001. *Global migrants, local lives: travel and transformation in rural Bangladesh*. Oxford: Clarendon Press.

Goffman, Erving 1992. *Vårt rollespill til daglig*. Oslo: Pax Forlag AS.

Gregory, Chris 1983. Kula gift exchange and capitalist commodity exchange: a comparison. In *The kula: new perspectives on Massim exchange* (eds) Jerry Leach and Edmund Leach, pp. 103–17. Cambridge: Cambridge University Press.

Gullestad, Marianne 2007. *Misjonsbilder: bidrag til norsk selvforståelse*. Oslo: Universitetsforlaget.

Kahn, Joel S. 1997. Demons, commodities and the history of anthropology. In *Meanings of the market* (ed) James G. Carrier, pp. 69–98. Oxford: Berg.

Lien, Marianne 2004a. The politics of food: an introduction. In *The politics of food* (eds) M. Lien and Brigitte Nerlich, pp. 1–17. Oxford: Berg.

―――― 2004b. The virtual consumer: constructions of uncertainty in marketing discourse. In *Market matters: exploring cultural processes in the global marketplace* (eds) Christina Garsten and Monica Lindh de Montoya, pp. 46–66. Basingstoke: Palgrave Macmillan.

Lyon, Sarah 2006. Evaluating fair trade consumption: politics, defetishization and producer participation. *International Journal of Consumer Studies* 30: 452–64.

McCracken, Grant 1990. *Culture and consumption*. Bloomington: Indiana University Press.

Mauss, Marcel 1990 [1925]. *The gift*. London: Routledge.

Micheletti, Michele 2003. *Political virtue and shopping*. Basingstoke: Palgrave Macmillan.

Miller, Daniel 2001 *The dialectics of shopping*. Chicago: University of Chicago Press.

Nustad, Knut 2003. *Gavens makt: Norsk Utviklingshjelp som Formynderskap*. Oslo: Pax Forlag.

Said, Edward W. 2003. *Orientalism*. London: Penguin.

Stirrat, R.L. and Heiko Henkel 1997. The development gift: the problem of reciprocity in the NGO world. *Annals of the American Academy of Political and Social Science* 554: 66–80.

Tvedt, Terje 2007. International development aid and its impact on a donor country: a case study of Norway. *The European Journal of Development Research* 19: 614–35.

Vramo, Lill 2006. *Trade not aid: en antropologisk analyse av rettferdig handel mellom Norge og Bangladesh*. Oslo: University of Oslo.

White, Sarah C. 1992. *Arguing with the crocodile: gender and class in Bangladesh*. London: Zed Books.

Wilkinson, James 2007. Fair trade: dynamic and dilemmas of a market oriented global social movement. *Journal of Consumer Policy* 30: 219–39.

Wilkinson-Weber, Clare M. 1999. *Embroidering lives: women's work and skill in the Lucknow embroidery industry*. Albany: State University of New York Press.

Chapter 4

'TODAY, ONE CAN FARM ORGANIC WITHOUT LIVING ORGANIC': BELGIAN FARMERS AND RECENT CHANGES IN ORGANIC FARMING

Audrey Vankeerberghen

In its early days, organic agriculture emerged as a critique of mainstream agriculture, food and consumption. More recently, the success enjoyed by organic farming has led to its recognition and regulation through public policy and to its insertion into commercial food markets. Organic farming today tends, therefore, to be shaped by market forces and the public institutions that it initially criticised.

The change in organic farming that I present in this chapter echoes the 'conventionalisation thesis'. That is based on studies of organic agriculture in California carried by out Julie Guthman and her collaborators (Buck, Getz and Guthman 1997; Guthman 2004a, 2004b), and others have discussed its relevance in other contexts (e.g., Best 2008; Coombes and Campbell 1998; Hall and Mogyorody 2001; Lockie and Halpin 2005). The thesis is that organic farming has gradually ceased to be a radical critique of conventional agriculture, instead becoming only slightly different from it. That is, the production and distribution of organic foods have become dominated by firms whose practices are far closer to those of the mainstream than they are to the organic movement's ideal of sustainable agriculture. While Belgian agriculture differs in important ways from what Guthman describes, especially concerning the importance of large businesses, something is going on there that resembles conventionalisation.

This trajectory of organic agriculture illustrates some of the consequences of the growing popularity of ethical consumption and the expansion of ethical consumption commerce mentioned in the Introduction to this volume. It also creates an ongoing challenge for participants in the organic farming movement to affirm the distinctive features of their activities in the context of mainstream food production. This chapter seeks, therefore, to explore the perception that Belgian organic farmers, and particularly the farmers from the Walloon region, have of this trajectory and some of their reactions to it.

'Organic farming' is an ambiguous concept, and this ambiguity is important for understanding the challenges faced by those in the movement. On the one hand, it is described as an alternative production method without any synthetic chemicals (de Silguy 1991: 33), and the stress is often put on its holistic approach to the relationships and balance among soil, plants and animals (Aubert 1970). Such a description views organic farming in terms of material inputs and agronomic processes, and those are what underlie the codification of 'organic' in European Union (EU) regulations, national specifications and government subsidy schemes. On the other hand, organic farming is often described as an ideological, social movement (Kaltoft 2001) that envisions a fundamental change in farming: 'the development of organic farming signifies an important new type of interrelationship between agriculture and society' (Michelsen 2001a: 4). In this view, organic agriculture is a movement uniting producers and consumers with common concerns and values, a movement that offers a collective commentary on the relationship between the economic realm of agriculture and the social realm. As such, it echoes the tension between the realms of economy and society described in this volume's Introduction.

'Today, one can farm organic without living organic', the words of one organic farmer, reveals the tension between the economic and social dimensions of organic farming (all translations are by the author). They do so because they speak to the development of organic farming both as a set of technical practices and as a way of life based on a distinctive set of values. In order to better understand the sentiments expressed by that farmer, the first part of this chapter describes the emergence of the organic farming movement in Belgium, and in particular in the Walloon region, the values and principles underlying it and the changes this movement has undergone in the past few decades. As will become clear, those changes have made it possible for the techniques to become separated from the values and the way of life, at least in the eyes of those farmers who express a feeling of loss of control over the production norms and principles of organic farming. This sense of loss has led those in the organic movement to redefine the movement's values and principles in order to maintain its influence, the topic of the second part of this chapter.

Organic Farming Disjointed

The development of the organic movement in the Walloon region is embedded in the European one. I start with the ideas on which that movement was built.

Three main currents of thought are usually considered to be the basis of organic agriculture in Europe. The first is the anthroposophy of Rudolph Steiner, a philosophy of life that gave birth in the 1920s to 'biodynamic agriculture', which sees the farm as a closed and self-nourishing system. The particularities of biodynamic agriculture include the use of an astronomical sowing and planting calendar and of herbal and mineral preparations as compost additives and field sprays (Steiner 2006 [1924]). The second current emerged in the 1940s in the United Kingdom, from the work of Sir Albert Howard. He stressed the role of the organic material in soil (humus) and the use of composting (Howard 1940; see Conford 2001). The third current is 'biologic' agriculture, arising in Switzerland in the 1930s and advocated by Hans Muller and Hans Peter Rusch. It stresses the importance of the fertility of the soil for the fecundity of life in general (Rusch 1972), of the autonomy of agricultural producers and of short distribution networks (de Silguy 1991: 11). While these three currents have been important historical influences on diverse organic associations and unions, in the Walloon region only biodynamic agriculture survives as a distinct, named school of thought with a distinct body of practitioners.

It was in the 1960s that organic agriculture in the region began to be organised into groups, unions and associations that united organic farmers, consumers, agronomists, physicians and intellectuals. This movement was shaped by three currents. One is biodynamic agriculture, mentioned above, which has its own distinct networks of producers, consumers and associations linked with broader anthroposophist networks. A second current came with two French agronomists, Raoul Lemaire and Jean Boucher. They founded their own organic fertiliser company in the 1960s and made extensive use of lithothamnion (a type of seaweed) as fertiliser, and their followers have attracted some criticism from those within the organic movement because of the commercial aspect of Lemaire and Boucher's work. A third current, also originating in France, was that of *Nature et Progrès*, an association of producers and consumers established in 1964. This association dissented from the predominant view of agriculture, trade and consumption. Instead, it emphasised short distribution networks, with no, or few, traders standing between the producer of organic foodstuffs and the consumer.

Different practices that are identified as 'organic' have emerged from these three different currents. They include a series of agronomic principles and agricultural techniques intended to stimulate the health of the soil, animals and human beings, including crop rotation, homeopathic veterinary medicine, mixed-farming techniques and no use of chemicals. These practices also include the consumption of local products, short distribution networks and small-scale farming, which are seen as economically, environmentally and socially better than conventional industrial farming and the existing system of food distribution. Taken together, these diverse practices seek to address concerns with human health, quality of the soil, animal welfare, the economic and social success of small-scale farming and the personal relationship between producers and consumers.

The founding values and practices of organic farming persist in many ways, but also they have evolved in tandem with changes in the larger society. For example, the events of May '68 were associated with a 'back to the land' movement that brought new people to the countryside, a more global concept of ecology and a growing interest in organic agriculture and organic food. Another important event is the foundation of the International Federation of Organic Agriculture Movements (IFOAM) in 1972, which played an important role in the definition of organic principles and values. The organic values identified in its charter became a major international reference in the organic movement: 'Organic agriculture is based on: the principle of health, the principle of ecology, the principle of fairness, the principle of care' (IFOAM n.d.*c*).

Early Adopters of Organic Farming

The stories of early adopters of organic farming reflect the three historical currents and their underlying principles described above. To illustrate this, I describe several farmers who converted to organic practices in the 1960s and 1970s. Those descriptions, and the other ethnography presented in this chapter, are based on my doctoral field research on Walloon farmers, carried out from March 2007, to April 2009.

One is Peter, who has been an activist in the first Walloon organic farmers' union as well as in *Nature et Progrès*. His story begins with his concern about a chemical herbicide. 'Three grains of this were enough to kill a pheasant. I thought: "Damn, such a violent poison!" What if something remained in the earth afterwards?' Then, by coincidence ('but there is no coincidence', he told me), he read a book by a French agronomist explaining organic farming and its principles.

> It was so obvious for me, 'coming from the land'. His argument was so logical, from the earth to human consumption. It was about considering the balance of the soil and the plants, about prevention and anticipation, about another way of working, much more coherent than the 'reacting way' of modern agriculture.

At that time, one of his children had a recurrent health problem. He and his wife tried to cure it with herbs, and were successful. This brought them a bit closer to what he called the 'organic way of thinking' or 'of living', one characterised by 'natural methods' of agricultural production and disease prevention, homeopathy, healthy food and a better relationship with consumers. In order to forge that better relationship, his wife started a small shop on the farm to sell their own produce.

Another is Henry, who was the president of the regional organic farmers' union for a couple years. His parents were farmers, but he first worked as an employee in a farmers' union. When he lost his job, he and his wife decided to start a farm. They had heard about organic farming through *Nature et Progrès* and were attracted by it: 'a small farm, no chemicals, direct sale to the consumers'. They began to process their own milk into dairy products to sell at the farm. They practised biodynamic agriculture for a while, but dropped it because it demanded a lot of work and time. Today, they describe themselves as being 'peasants' and work for the preservation of small-scale farming.

Yet another is David. Like Peter, his first worry was about agricultural chemicals. In the 1960s he started to have a headache each time he used them on his fields. Out of curiosity, he went to a conference on organic agriculture given by Jean Boucher, one of the French agronomists mentioned above. He decided that this was the only agriculture that would protect soil fertility and human health, but he was concerned about its costs and yields. For this reason, he started with only a part of his farm in organic agriculture. He saw it was successful, and a few years later he converted his whole farm. His wife processed their milk into dairy products, sold mostly at the farm. A few years later, they learned about biodynamic agriculture and adopted it.

A fourth is Richard, who was involved with the regional organic farmers' union for a number of years. In the beginning, however, he was a small farmer at 'the top of the technology': he managed his farm to make it very productive, with advanced seed varieties and breeding stock and extensive chemical inputs. However, he began to question his way of farming when problems began to appear, such as a lack of roots in his grassland and recurrent mastitis in his cattle. This made him worry about the future of his farm and about his economic survival. 'The cows were giving [milk], the dairy was paying [for the milk] but almost everything was going to the veterinarian and the feed merchant. My wife told me: "We won't survive long like this".' He found a solution when he heard about organic farming from a farm counsellor who was working for the Lemaire–Boucher company. Although he converted to organic agriculture, he stresses that he practises it in a highly technical and agronomic way supervised by organic specialists. That is because he sees a healthy farm as one that is profitable. So, his goal is 'to produce quality but also quantity'. In this, he distinguishes himself from organic farmers 'who just let nature work'. In addition to advocating organic agriculture, he has emphasised the importance of family farming, and is proud that both his sons are working with him.

In describing their lives, these early organic farmers identify the adoption of organic agricultural practices as a means of expressing certain concerns and values. Accordingly, their stories reveal an era when social values and agricultural practices were closely linked: the farmers using organic techniques were motivated by the values underlying the organic movement, such as the health of the earth and of humans, the maintenance of soil quality, small-scale farming. This does not mean that there is no tension between their organic principles and the practical needs of farm management. For instance, one farmer told me: 'I bought non-organic straw for my cowshed this winter. It would be better to buy it organic, but it's more difficult to find and to organise the transportation, and it is much more expensive.'

Even though they may not have been able to follow organic practices completely, these farmers see in those practices an answer to concerns about their farm management and their lives. Equally, however, while early organic farmers saw organic agriculture as suited to values that they shared, such as human health and the preservation of the natural environment, they differed somewhat in the ways that they practised it, such as the importance that they gave to productivity or to technology. It is important to keep this diversity in mind to avoid a reification of old organic farming practices.

It is important also to realise that early organic farming had a clear social dimension. For one thing, most farmers were members of organic farming unions or associations, and so were involved in making the important decisions that affected the sector. They were members also because membership in organic organisations was a practical requisite to being certified organic: these organisations elaborated the specifications for organic agriculture. Early organic agriculture was distinctly social in another way as well, through the sale of farm produce. At that time, there were two ways for buyers to identify organic goods: personal relationships of trust between producers and consumers, or private organic standards, the specifications of which were elaborated by certain groups or associations of producers and consumers, such as *Nature et Progrès* in Belgium. These social links, among farmers and between farmers and consumers, as well as with associated scientists and intellectuals, meant that the early organic critique of mainstream agriculture was part of a larger social movement of individuals and their unions, associations and organisations.

According to the stories these farmers tell, today things are markedly different. We will see how the further development of organic farming has affected its nature and how the development of regulation and the organic food market have increasingly separated organic practices from their associated values.

The Evolution of the Organic Food Market and Regulation

The development of associations and unions made organic farming more visible and 'gave it a certain weight' in the eyes of government institutions. This was especially important for those in the movement who had been trying to obtain official recognition and the creation of a legal framework that would prevent 'cheating' in organic cultivation, trade and retail sale. The organic movement attracted government interest also because of growing concerns for the environment among EU politicians, and the associated desire to maintain the European countryside through appropriate sorts of agriculture.

The result of this coalition of interests was the first European Economic Community (EEC) regulation on organic farming in 1991, which said that 'in the context of the reorientation of the common agricultural policy, this type of production may contribute towards ... the protection of the environment and the conservation of the countryside' (EEC 1991: 3) (this was replaced by 834/2007 [EC 2007], which became effective in 2009). Under this regulation, the member states enacted new legislation or modified existing laws to implement aspects of the EU regulation, to cover some areas on which the EU regulation was silent (such as animal production until 1998 or catering) or to impose more restrictive rules (this was banned by the newer regulation). In Belgium, regulation of agriculture devolved to the regions in 2002.

The regulation specified the production methods and techniques that are allowed in organic farming and the conditions a product has to fulfil to be called 'organic'. It was based on different private specifications presented to EEC legislators, which linked organic production techniques with their associated values. However, the resulting regulation focused on the technical side of organic food production and processing and generally ignored the values associated with organic farming. The consequence, according to one commentator, was that 'the values underlying organic farming have not been codified in rules and regulations' (Darnhofer 2006: 156). Under that regulation, to be called 'organic' a foodstuff has to be produced in ways that satisfy the requirements of a 'control body', which is 'an independent private third party carrying out inspection and certification in the field of organic production in accordance with the provisions set out under this Regulation' (EC 2007: 5).

This gave 'organic' a legal status, but the role of control bodies in the process meant that organic producers' and consumers' associations are no longer involved in the certification process. This marked the culmination of the evolution of the definition of 'organic'. Originally a matter of diverse specification, often informal and based on trust, it became a matter of concern for the different organisations and associations within the organic movement, and then became a matter of legislation, enforced by commercial inspection companies authorised by individual European countries. However, this is not the end of the changes in definition and inspection because, as described below, several private specifications and standards persist.

Until the 1990s, the organic food market remained marginal. It was only a very small part of the global food market; organic produce was traded in restricted networks, mainly by direct sales from producers to consumers or through small organic shops. However, since the 1990s the organic food market has grown to meet increasing demand, reflecting a growing concern with the environment that was heightened by the food panics of the 1990s, typified by the BSE (Mad Cow Disease) and dioxin crises. This growth was facilitated as well by the introduction of a common EU specification for organic food. This growth in the market for organic food has brought with it a marked increase in the number of organic farmers in Europe. While some farmers are attracted by new market opportunities in the organic sector, others are concerned about ecological and health problems associated with conventional farming. For all these farmers, converting to organic production is made easier and more profitable by subsidies to organic farmers offered by the national governments of the EU member states, which began around the middle of the 1990s.

New Organic Farmers

As a result of this expansion, the emergence of ethical consumption commerce, a new type of organic farmer has emerged, one who sees organic farming and its products as a niche market (see, e.g., Best 2008; Van Dam 2005). Two brief cases will illustrate this new type.

The first is Albert, who breeds and rears beef cattle. He converted his business to organic techniques ten years ago because he had the opportunity to join the organic meat supply chain of a supermarket. The higher price he gets from this market, in addition to government subsidies, is economically attractive. He distinguishes himself from farmers who farm organic as a 'philosophy' or a 'way of life'. In his view, these farmers stress their own consumption and produce relatively little. He says that he manages his farm professionally and is concerned with the profitable sale of what he produces. His family does not eat organic food at home, except for the farm's own meat. In their opinion, the only advantage of organic meat over non-organic is better food safety.

The second is Christian. When he began farming he looked for a growing niche market and opted for sheep breeding. Ten years later, in 1997, he heard about organic farming and about a project that sold organic sheep meat to the supermarket sector. He found this attractive because he would not need to modify many of his techniques to fulfil the specification and because he could get a higher price by selling his meat as organic. When talking about his activities, he stresses the professional aspect of his farm and its profitability. He distinguishes himself both from the 'organic philosophers who do real in-depth work' and from the 'opportunists who farm organic only for the subsidy'.

Farmers like these do not take up organic agriculture primarily because of values such as human and environmental health or the relationship between producers and consumers. While they may appreciate these things, they adopt organic farming mainly because of its commercial advantages. The emergence of these new organic farmers with their clear commercial orientation has been made possible by changes in market demand and EU regulation. With the expansion of the market for organic food, especially with the appearance of organic products in supermarkets, the trade in organic goods increasingly takes place in conventional market transactions; personal relationships lose their importance. In addition, a farmer can meet the EU specifications without being motivated by the principles and values that historically were associated with organic agriculture. Finally, with the appearance of an official 'organic' label, personal relationships between producers and consumers, whether directly or through their participation in a union or association, are no longer necessary.

This has created a situation in which a farmer can produce an organic commodity in order to satisfy someone else's ethical aspirations. A farmer may convert to organic production because he thinks that it will help him stay in farming or bring him a bigger profit, or because he wants to diversify his production. But whatever the farmer's reasons, so long as production conforms to the EU regulations, the products are labelled 'organic'. So labelled, however, they may well embody for consumers the organic values that these farmers might ignore, such as the preservation of the environment and respect for human health.

Re-assembling Organic Farming

It is always like this, when the regulation comes from on high.

This statement by an organic farmer reveals a sense of alienation from an organic regulation imposed by the state, as well as a negative view of its consequences. The story of one farmer and his wife who took up organic agriculture in the 1970s illustrates that alienation and those consequences. This couple have a small farm, and they are more concerned with the values of the form of agriculture that they practice than they are with their profits or the volume of their production. As well, they have always sold their dairy products through short distribution networks: local markets and a small shop on the farm.

Today, they point out the risk of 'being satisfied' with a minimal application of the official specification:

> In short distribution networks, there is a control exercised by the consumer over the producer. This control encourages the farmer to do his best. People were buying our cheese because it was made 'with love' … we were working the best we could! Today, we tend to rely on the specification. If we fulfil its requirements, we think 'it's okay', while we could do even better. Before, the farmer's soul offered the guarantee that his products were truly organic.

In his view, then, the formal specifications have the contradictory consequence of leading some producers not to do the best they could. This farmer also mentioned a financial constraint leading him to lower the quality of his work. This couple's dairy products today have to compete with what he called 'industrial organic production' sold in supermarkets. To survive, they need to cut their production costs, which means sacrificing some of their organic principles. In particular, they have had to sacrifice their self-sufficiency by reducing the range of what they produce and, as a result, have to buy more of their agricultural inputs.

In my research I observed that farmers often are ambivalent about EU regulation. They say that it gives them official recognition, which has improved their previous low standing in the eyes of conventional farmers. As well, it prevents cheating and brings important financial support. At the same time, many organic farmers complain about the purely technical orientation of the regulation and the absence of values and ethics in it. For instance, an organic farmer involved in a union said: 'The essence of organic farming, the philosophical principles and the values that have driven the organic movement since its beginning, are not reflected in this regulation. This is a big mistake.' This farmer pointed to the way that the regulation allows for the import of organic apples from New Zealand as an example, because the pollution caused by the air transport does not fit with the ecological values he sees in organic farming.

Farmers' complaints about the way that EU regulation does not respect the original values of organic farming resemble what Michael Herzfeld (2005) says of Cretan shepherds' attitudes towards the state and of their rhetoric of nostalgia. Those shepherds regretted the disappearance of the system of reciprocity that regulated the theft of livestock before, whilst simultaneously asking for state intervention to curtail it. In our case, organic farmers express nostalgia for a bygone era when the personal relationship of trust between the producer and the consumer was enough to guarantee the organic quality of the product. They deplore the 'damaged reciprocity' (Herzfeld 2005) that made official regulation unavoidable for the continuation of organic agriculture, a regulation that, as I said, many in the movement supported.

Feeling of Loss in the Organic Movement

The development of regulation in organic agriculture has led many farmers to fear that they are losing control of the direction of the movement and of organic practices. Walloon organic farmers are not alone in this, for a similar situation is reported among organic farmers in California (Guthman 2004a: 172) and in Denmark (Michelsen 2001b: 80). I want now to consider the ways that those in the organic movement react to this, creating new dynamics and collective actions. Their initiatives are interesting because they reveal the different perceptions of what organic farming should be.

Blaming the Regulation

A draft of new EU regulation of organic agriculture was released in 2007. Given what I have said so far, it should be no surprise that many in the organic sector said that it did not respect the basis of organic farming and that it would lower organic standards and reduce the quality of the organic products. A Walloon consumers' and producers' association, *Nature et Progrès Belgique* (2007), produced a petition, *Sauvons la bio*, that denounced this draft. It included the following:

> This new specification on organic farming is on many aspects unacceptable and represents a true regression compared to the present specification fixed in the regulation 2092/91:
>
> 1. the use of synthetic chemicals is not clearly forbidden any more;
> 2. the contamination of organic products by GMO [genetically-modified organisms] is accepted to a maximum rate of 0.9%, the same as for products from conventional agriculture; ...
>
> The two first points neglect the specificity of organic agriculture.

The petition, which says that the basic principles of organic agriculture are endangered in this new regulation, obtained considerable public support: 65,000 signatures, mostly from producers, consumers, environmentalists and activists. A demonstration was organised in support of it, and many demonstrators protested that consumer choice was threatened by the new regulation. One organic consumer said: 'Now, it is too much! We don't have the right any more to keep a small protected area of organic food!' In a telling instance of the way that many see the expansion of the economic realm threatening the values of the social realm, many demonstrators protested against the way that lobbying by supermarkets and agribusiness influenced the specifications: 'Money always fucks up everything!' said a man who had been an organic farmer for fourteen years.

The petition was presented to the members of the European Parliament. In the end, Parliament supported the petitioners, but the Agriculture and Fisheries Council voted in favour of the new draft (the Belgian, Italian, Greek and Hungarian Ministers voted against). In reaction, the association that launched the petition proposed creating a new private standard called 'Organic Plus'. According to the leaders of the association, this would respect organic values and principles, would 'be faithful to the first organic farmers', mostly with a guarantee of no GMO contamination. It was seen as a way to keep a clear differentiation between organic and non-organic products. This attempt echoes the reaction of some Bitto cheese producers described by Cristina Grasseni (this volume). These producers thought that the criteria for producing Bitto cheese had relaxed over time and no longer led to real Bitto cheese. Some of them established a new consortium, setting stricter production rules to maintain what they saw as the proper product.

However, while the attempt to influence the regulation of organic farming through petition, demonstration and the creation of an Organic Plus standard was popular, it was not supported by the entire organic farming movement in the Walloon region. The existence of this lack of support reveals the diversity of perception and opinion regarding regulation and its effect on the future of organic agriculture. So, many were opposed to the new regulation but did not agree with the idea of Organic Plus. They said it would discredit organic farming and confuse the consumer, 'who is already lost with the amount of labelling'. Yet others agreed with the new regulation. They argued that, as GMO crops are expanding in Europe, GMO contamination has become unavoidable. If the new regulation forbids GMO contamination, farmers whose crops are contaminated will be refused certification, so a change in regulation is necessary for the survival of organic farmers. Another argument against Organic Plus was that if Belgium did not authorise GMO contamination, food processors in the country could lose their Organic Plus certification if they bought raw materials from countries in the EU that allow GMO contamination. The result, in the words of one organic food processor, is that the 'Organic Plus standard could weaken the organic food chain'.

The Participatory Guarantee System

I said that dissatisfaction with EU regulation generated ideas for alternative forms of certification, such as Organic Plus. Another of these forms is the

Participatory Guarantee System (PGS), advocated in Belgium by *Nature et Progrès*. It attempts to provide alternatives to the current system of control and certification in organic farming, especially to counter some of the negative effects of the certification bodies, the 'independent private third parties', imposed by EU regulation. Supporters of this initiative put forward two main arguments. The first was that the cost of certification under the EU regulation is prohibitive for small farmers and processors. The second is that the official regulatory systems are not able to guarantee the quality, integrity and coherence of small, diversified organic systems (Roure 2007: 26).

The PGS as an alternative certification system emerged in the 2000s. However, the concept is based on certification systems in use in some European countries before the establishment of the EU regulation and its independent control bodies and also used in other countries all over the world. It relies on internal 'investigation' (preferred to the more repressive-sounding 'control') among the members of an association. Producers, consumers and other professionals involved in the association visit the producers and check to see if they have met the specifications. It works, then, as a form of collective evaluation. An advantage of this system is that those having trouble meeting the requirements for certification could benefit from the advice of the professionals who are assessing them. The practitioners of this method stress the importance of this sort of exchange of experience and knowledge, which is missing in the official system. The result is not simply certification, it is also the continuous improvement of practice.

Supporters of the system stress that it is based on values such as consumer trust, transparency and civic control: 'PGS programs offer a complementary [to the third-party system], low-cost, locally-based system of quality assurance, with a heavy emphasis on social control and knowledge building' (IFOAM n.d.*b*). In addition the system, unlike the EU third-party certification, links organic values and organic practices: 'In the majority of cases Participatory Guarantee Systems do not only guarantee the credibility of organic produce, but are closely linked to local and alternative marketing approaches' (IFOAM n.d.*a*).

This system deviates from the EU regulation, which states that both the inspection and certification must be performed by an independent control body. However, some in the movement doubt that these commercial bodies can be independent. One activist organic farmer put it this way: 'Can a body being paid by its clients pretend to be independent?', and as noted in the Introduction to this volume, this is a reasonable question to ask. The IFOAM is currently seeking recognition of Participatory Guarantee Systems in the EU regulation. This recognition is important for Walloon farmers interested in the system, for that recognition is necessary if they are to get government grants and financial backing.

It is worth noting that the Participatory Guarantee System does not break with the idea of labelling and certification and, therefore, does not depart from the basic structure of the existing system. A more radical response to the negative effects of official control and certification is non-certification, and indeed some organic farmers do not want to be controlled and certified under any formal system. They prefer to sell their products without any certification, directly to consumers in a relationship of trust. Such farmers stand outside of the official system of organic farming: they are not allowed to use the official organic label; they are not formally recognised as organic farmers; they can not benefit from government subsidies.

The Working Group on Legislation

Another way farmers can try to influence regulation and policies is to participate in unions and associations officially recognised in the organic farming sector. Such bodies are in direct dialogue with government institutions and have, to a certain degree, the opportunity to give direction to the organic farming sector. One example is a working group on legislation that was established by one of the Belgian associations of the organic movement. This working group aims to be a forum for discussion on issues related to legislation concerning organic agriculture, such as a modification in the regulation. The group has representatives from various associations and unions that are officially recognised by the organic farming sector, and it aims to take a unified sectoral position on the issues being considered.

The group first came into existence in 2005 to provide a forum for those concerned with organic farming to debate issues that concerned them. Officials in the Walloon Department of Agriculture also hoped that it would become a body that they could consult as representative of the whole of the organic farming sector. As indicated by the range of responses to the revision of EU regulation, however, representing the entire sector is difficult, if not impossible. The diversity of the sector is illustrated by the debate about organic chickens that took place in 2007 and 2008, a debate that also illustrates in condensed form the consequences of the historical evolution of organic farming that I described previously.

EU regulation and the development of the market for organic food have allowed the emergence of a set of newer organic breeders whose concerns and rearing practices are very different from those of the older organic breeders. These newer breeders began to appear around the year 2000. They are generally bigger than the older ones, having around 10,000 chickens, and they work with companies that coordinate the entire production chain. Those companies will organise the building of chicken houses, the supply of chicks and of feed and the slaughter and marketing of chickens for all the breeders in the group. The chickens are sold to supermarkets in Belgium and adjacent countries, and so are subject to competition from chickens produced in places that may have different certification standards.

Michael is the administrator in charge of one of these 'chicken commodity chains'. He was first an advisor in a poultry company, but eventually decided that he wanted to run an organisation that would produce and sell premium chickens. 'I thought it was interesting to have, on one the hand, a standard chicken with an affordable price and a perfect bacteriological and chemical quality and, on the other hand, a product of high quality like the "Red Label" in France.' He approached the poultry company where he worked, but they were not interested. As a result of the dioxin crisis in 1999, some poultry farmers decided to do something other than produce battery chickens. A few years later, as supermarkets were beginning to look for premium chickens in response to growing consumer demand, Michael's company decided to get into the production of premium chicken, and Michael was able to implement his idea. The company opted for the organic standard and set up their production chain in accord with EU regulation.

Opponents of the new breeders generally have been producing organic poultry for a long time. As well, they tend to be what is called 'small breeders', having a stock of only a few thousand chickens at most, and they tend to sell their poultry through short distribution channels, using shops on their own farms, nearby markets or small organic shops. With their short chains, they do not export their produce and so are not materially affected by differences in the organic standards of different countries that affect the new, larger breeders and the companies that oversee the production chains. The difference between the new, more purely commercial breeders and their older opponents illustrates the bifurcation of the organic sector that has been described elsewhere (see, e.g., Goodman and Goodman 2001; Lockie and Halpin 2005; Michelsen 2001*a*).

A breeder named John is an example of these older breeders. Initially he practised conventional battery farming. However, he switched to organic production for two reasons. The first was recurrent disease among his birds that was killing them but that he could not identify, prevent or cure. This turned him against battery farming. The second reason came from his wife's experiences selling their poultry in markets. She concluded that it was unprofitable to try to sell the same sort of chicken that was being sold in the supermarkets. It would be better, she thought, to offer a distinctive, local, premium product such as free-range chicken. John began to sell such chickens, and started organic rearing a few years later. At that time, in the 1970s, there was no official standard, and farmers who wanted to produce organically conformed to the specifications of a producers' and consumers' association. He says that he has very good relationships with his clients, based on trust and mutual understanding. In fact, for some of his clients the personal aspect of the relationship is as important as the organic one: they like to buy 'John's chicken'. He could continue being a poultry farmer without the organic certification, but he is certified because it enables him to sell to organic shops, to be on the official lists of organic farmers, to participate in organic trade fairs and similar events and to get government grants.

The new breeders try to influence regulation in order to resolve the particular problems that they confront, efforts that are seen by some as an attack on the values and ethical principles associated with organic chicken-rearing and with organic farming in general. Those who object to the influence of the new breeders reject what they perceive as a loss of their own control over the regulation, in favour of industrial agriculture. Both the new breeders and their opponents seek to influence regulation through their participation in the working group that I have described.

An example of the differences between the newer and older breeders is the dispute over the age at which organic chickens can be slaughtered. The details of the regulation of the minimum age for slaughter of chickens certified as organic are complex. The result of the complexity, however, is that in many EU countries the minimum age is 70 days, while in Belgium it is 81 days. The cost of rearing their chickens eleven extra days reduces the profit of the Belgian breeders who compete with breeders from elsewhere in the EU. Worried about this reduced profit, two administrators of Belgian chicken commodity chains asked the regional Department of Agriculture if it were possible to harmonise EU poultry slaughter regulations. This request created debate in the working group on legislation mentioned above.

That debate initially focused on the taste of organic chicken. On one side were those, primarily small breeders, who argued that 81 days was necessary to produce high-quality meat because this is the time needed for a chicken to mature and become tasty. On the other side were those, representing the chain producers, who said that the taste would be just as good with a chicken slaughtered at 70 days. They argued that selective breeding had produced strains that mature earlier. Perhaps reflecting their main concern, to produce premium chicken that was clearly different from the conventional battery chickens, normally slaughtered at about 40 days, one large breeder said: 'A slaughter at 70 days maintains a clear difference from standard chicken meat and that is the most important thing.'

While the discussion focused initially on taste, it quickly became a broader debate on organic agriculture. The representative of the smaller breeders claimed that there would be a decline in quality: 'We are producers, we are not going to lower our quality requirements!' Then, a producers' and consumers' association representative joined in, supporting the smaller breeders and arguing not only against the proposed slaughter at 70 days but also, more widely, against the larger-scale chain operations. This representative said that such an operation:

> doesn't respect the values that underlie organic farming like the respect for and the balance of the natural cycle. To import chicken feed for the export of chicken meat does not make sense. We do not agree with the combination of organic farming with non-organic farming on the same farm [which is common with the larger-scale chain farms]. We are against a low-price commercialisation for the supermarkets. The request is unacceptable because it comes from conventional breeders who don't know anything about organic farming!

A representative of the large-scale chain operations rebutted that defence of complex organic values by invoking market logic: 'We must be realistic and pragmatic: the chicken breast convinces the consumers! [i.e., taste matters, not the age at slaughter] We must defend ourselves from the Netherlands, from Italy, let us go ahead!'

It is interesting to note that both groups used similar arguments, but often for different purposes. For example, each group attached importance to animal welfare and to respect for the environment, but for different reasons. For the defenders of the 81 days, these things are important because they are part of the essence of organic farming and all that this implies. On the other hand, for the larger-scale producers they are important for commercial reasons, because they sell chickens: 'the consumers like to think that the chicken they eat had run in a grassland' is the way it was put by a chain administrator.

Conclusion

Organic farming was born as an alternative to mainstream agriculture and consumption, and farmers have understood it in different ways. Organic agriculture was seen as an alternative farming method, as an alternative to the entire commercial food chain, as an alternative way of consuming and as an alternative way of living. As an alternative, organic farming has always existed in relationship to conventional agriculture, in two ways. Firstly, it has existed in the constraining context of agriculture policy and farmers' organisations that are oriented toward conventional agriculture (Lynggaard 2001: 85). Secondly, its identity as a form of agriculture has depended on its being seen as different from conventional agriculture. The challenge for organic farming is, thus, to keep the distinctiveness that constitutes its identity: 'organic farming must – in order to be successful – promote itself as an alternative' (2001: 86).

This challenge has been made more important by the changes that organic farming has undergone in the last few decades. The success of the organic farming movement has led to the insertion of organic agriculture into public policies that today define its standards and its practices. This has intensified the integration of organic agriculture, at least its technical side, into the economic and institutional system of mainstream agriculture and the food trade.

Such a development is not unique to organic farming. Some argue that fair trade, which emerged as a radical social movement in opposition to the deregulation induced by neoliberal policies, has become a mainstream, niche market dependent on corporate producers (e.g., Doane 2010). As a result, the fair trade movement now rests on a paradox: in seeking social and environmental goals, it pursues a market-based solution to the very problems arising from free markets (Lyon and Moberg 2010). This corporate mainstreaming of course poses challenges for the realisation of fair trade's development aspirations (Dolan 2010).

This process of being adopted by large companies attracted by the growth of consumer demand has made it imperative that the people involved in the organic farming movement promote and reassert its values and principles if they are to remain different from conventional agriculture. One member of an organic farming association summarised this success and the challenges it brought: 'When what I was denouncing as an avant-gardist became obvious and was appropriated by the economic system, I partly won. Now, I must work for more purity and for a greater respect of the norms by the people who took up my ideas.'

The partial victory of organic agriculture that I have described has, as I have said, produced a feeling of loss among many in the movement, as they see what they were doing being turned into government regulation and appropriated by conventional commercial firms. As I have also said, it has generated new ideas and new movements. People involved in these initiatives seek to reintroduce the values and ethical principles that they believe define organic farming. In practice and over time it appears, then, that identifying organic agriculture has been an evolving process. Those in the organic movement have had to redefine 'organic' as the term has changed its meaning because of changes in legislation and in the activities of companies in the food sector. This evolution may be inevitable when producers concerned with a set of social values confront other producers whose commercial orientation leads them to adopt the marks of those values in order to increase their profit. It may be inevitable, that is, when the social and economic realms intersect in the marketplace.

The cases I have presented illustrate the current dynamics of this redefinition of 'organic'. They also, however, demonstrate the problems such efforts face, caused by the divergence of opinion about what organic farming ought to be and about the characteristics that distinguish it from conventional agriculture. These divergences, debates and disputes point to a larger question: Who can legitimately define organic farming and give direction to this ethical movement?

The Introduction to this volume urges us to see ethical consumption as an instance of something that has been going on for centuries: that is, efforts to protect people's social values from what they see as the threats posed by an encroaching economic realm. As I have shown in this chapter, the organic agriculture movement is one such effort, for it seeks to protect long-term values concerned with human and environmental well-being from the threats posed by an increasingly rationalised, intensive and expanding industrial agriculture, with its consistent and narrow pursuit of sales and profit.

That Introduction also directs our attention to the risks posed by ethical consumption commerce. Once more, as I have shown in this chapter, organic agriculture illustrates that risk. The very success of the movement has, in many ways, led to a profound change in what the shopper sees in the food store. The organic apple or chicken that had been the product of a farmer's practices and values is now organic only in the technical sense: the farmer who produces it need conform only to technical requirements contained in EU regulations. It is this change that led that member of an organic farming association to say that he had won, but only partly.

Acknowledgements

I would like to thank the FNRS (National Fund for Scientific Research) for supporting my Ph.D. research, and Pierre Petit and Priscilla Claeys for their suggestions and advice on this chapter. I would also like to acknowledge the tremendous support of Robyn d'Avignon, who spent hours revising my English.

Bibliography

Aubert, Claude 1970. *L'agriculture biologique*. Paris: Le Courrier du Livre.
Best, Henning 2008. Organic agriculture and the conventionalization hypothesis: a case study from West Germany. *Agriculture and Human Values* 25: 95–106.
Buck, Daniel, Christina Getz and Julie Guthman 1997. From farm to table: the organic vegetable commodity chain of northern California. *Sociologia Ruralis* 37: 3–20.
Conford, Philip 2001. *The origins of the organic movement*. Edinburgh: Floris Books.
Coombes, Brad and Hugh Campbell 1998. Dependent reproduction of alternative modes of agriculture: organic farming in New Zealand. *Sociologia Ruralis* 38: 127–45.
Darnhofer, Ika 2006. Organic farming between professionalisation and conventionalisation: the need for a more discerning view of farmer practices. In *Proceedings of the European joint organic congress on organic farming and European rural development*, Odense, Denmark, 30–31 May, pp. 156–57. www.wiso.boku.ac. at/fileadmin/_/H73/H733/pub/Biolandbau/2006_Darnhofer_Odense.pdf
Doane, Molly 2010. Relationship coffees: structure and agency in the Fair Trade system. In *Fair Trade and social justice: global ethnographies* (eds) Sarah Lyon and Mark Moberg, pp. 229–57. New York: New York University Press.
Dolan, Catherine S. 2010. Virtual moralities: the mainstreaming of Fairtrade in Kenyan tea fields. *Geoforum* 41: 33–43.
European Community (EC) 2007. Council Regulation (EC) No 834/2007 of 28 June 2007 on organic production and labelling of organic products and repealing Regulation (EEC) No 2092/91. http://eur-lex.europa.eu/LexUriServ/LexUriServ. do?uri=OJ:L:2007:189:0001:0023:EN:PDF
European Economic Community (EEC) 1991. Council regulation (EEC) No 2092/91 of 24 June 1991, on organic production of agricultural products and indications referring thereto on agricultural products and foodstuffs. http://eur-lex.europa. eu/LexUriServ/LexUriServ.do?uri=CONSLEG:1991R2092:20060506:EN:PDF
Goodman, David and Michael Goodman 2001. Place, space and networks: geographies of sustainable consumption. In *Exploring sustainable consumption* (eds) Maurie J. Cohen and Joseph Murphy, pp. 97–119. Oxford: Elsevier Sciences.
Guthman, Julie 2004a. *Agrarian dreams: the paradox of organic farming in California*. Berkeley: University of California Press.
——— 2004b. The trouble with 'organic lite' in California: a rejoinder to the 'conventionalization' debate. *Sociologia Ruralis* 44: 301–16.

Belgian Farmers and Recent Changes in Organic Farming **117**

Hall, Alan and Veronika Mogyorody 2001. Organic farmers in Ontario: an examination of the conventionalization argument. *Sociologia Ruralis* 41: 399–422.
Herzfeld, Michael 2005. *Cultural intimacy: social poetics in the nation-state* (Second edition). New York: Routledge.
Howard, Sir Albert 1940. *An agricultural testament*. London: Oxford University Press.
International Federation of Organic Agriculture Movements (IFOAM) n.d.*a*. Organic standards and certification. Bonn: IFOAM. www.ifoam.org/about_ifoam/standards/index.html
——— n.d.*b*. PGS FAQs – General questions about PGS. Bonn: IFOAM. www.ifoam.org/about_ifoam/standards/pgs/PGS_FAQs_1.html#FAQ1_1
——— n.d.*c*. The principles of organic agriculture. Bonn: IFOAM. www.ifoam.org/about_ifoam/principles/index.html
Kaltoft, Pernille 2001. Organic farming in late modernity: at the frontier of modernity or opposing modernity? *Sociologia Ruralis* 41: 146–58.
Lockie, Stewart and Darren Halpin 2005. The conventionalisation thesis reconsidered: structural and ideological transformation of Australian organic agriculture. *Sociologia Ruralis* 45: 284–307.
Lynggaard, Kennett S. C. 2001. The farmer within an institutional environment: comparing Danish and Belgian organic farming. *Sociologia Ruralis* 41: 85–111.
Lyon, Sarah and Mark Moberg (eds) 2010. *Fair Trade and social justice: global ethnographies*. New York: New York University Press.
Michelsen, Johannes 2001*a*. Recent development and political acceptance of organic farming in Europe. *Sociologia Ruralis* 41: 3–20.
——— 2001*b*. Organic farming in a regulatory perspective: the Danish case. *Sociologia Ruralis* 41: 62–84.
Nature et Progrès Belgique 2007. *Sauvons la bio*. Jambe: Nature et Progrès Belgique.
Roure, Karine 2007. *Les systèmes de garantie participative*. Uzès, France: Nature et Progrès.
Rusch, Hans P. 1972. *La fécondité du sol*. Paris: Le Courrier du Livre.
de Silguy, Catherine 1991. *L'agriculture biologique*. Paris: Presses Universitaires de France.
Steiner, Rudolph 2006 [1924]. *Agriculture: fondements spirituels de la méthode bio-dynamique*. Genève: Editions Anthroposophiques Romandes.
Van Dam, Denise 2005. *Les agriculteurs bio, vocation ou intérêt?* Namur: Presses Universitaires de Namur.

Section II

ETHICAL CONSUMPTION CONTEXTS

The second set of chapters in this volume pursues a point made in the Introduction. That is the observation that even though ethical consumption is concerned with the relationship between economy and society, it is a practical activity that is shaped by the context in which consumers exist. These chapters consider a variety of such contexts and their effects on people's ethical consumption, and so help answer the question posed at the end of the introduction to the previous set of chapters: why and how do people become ethical consumers, and with what results?

The first chapter in this section investigates a variety of motives for ethical consumption, motives that reflect people's personal and social situation. Tamás Dombos's 'Narratives of Concern: Beyond the "Official" Discourse of Ethical Consumption in Hungary' begins with an important point. Organisations encouraging ethical consumption present images of it and of the people who practice it that can be as problematic as the images of producers considered in the preceding section. Those images are contained in what Dombos calls the 'official discourse' of Hungarian organisations advocating 'conscious shopping', as ethical consumption is called in that country, a discourse not materially different from what is found in most of the rest of Europe and North America. These images turn out to look a lot like the market transactors of much economic thought. In that discourse, ethical consumers are fairly autonomous individuals who may be concerned for their locality and the people in their lives, but are not defined by them in any significant way. They are enlightened in the sense that they are sceptical about the claims made by corporations for what they sell and about the will and ability of governments to bring about change. Accordingly, in the official discourse individuals rationally select purchases in light of their concern for the environment and trade justice. From what Dombos presents in his chapter, however, few ethical consumers in Hungary fit that image.

In contrast to the uniform image in the official discourse, Dombos describes five people who represent in relatively pure form the motives and contexts common in the people that he studied. In doing so, he shows that people's decision to be ethical consumers and the values that concern them range from a desire for taste and distinction to a virulent Hungarian nationalism. Thus, while they are concerned to protect the social realm from the incursions of the economic, they value different aspects of the social.

There is another point that Dombos makes that deserves mention. As he explains, Daniel Miller (2001) has argued for a distinction between the morality and the ethics of shopping. The former is concerned with the well-being of the shopper's immediate social circle, especially the family; the latter is concerned with the well-being of distant people, of the sort that buying Fairtrade-certified products is supposed to help, or the well-being of the environment in some abstract sense. Miller argues that the dictates of morality, prime among which is thrift, trumps the dictates of ethics, which require greater spending. What Dombos says indicates that we ought to be careful not to read more into this distinction than Miller may have intended. The immediate social circle, the Us of Miller's morality, is a fluid group. As some of Dombos's cases demonstrate, it can include those well beyond the household, those who might seem distant strangers at first glance.

This blurring of Us and Them appears in the next chapter in this section, Giovanni Orlando's 'Critical Consumption in Palermo: Imagined Society, Class and Fractured Locality'. It describes people who are 'critical' consumers, the Italian equivalent of 'ethical' consumers, and shows how their ethical consumption is shaped by their context, especially the political economy of Palermo, and of Italy more generally, since the 1960s and 1970s.

In the eyes of many, that city has been dominated by an alliance between the Christian Democrats and the Mafia. The result was the creation of a city with a corrupt, clientelistic system that saw the enrichment of those on the top, the impoverishment of those on the bottom and indifference to the condition of the city itself. Seeing the city and its government, and indeed the Italian government, in this way, the people Orlando describes saw no point in conventional electoral politics. Instead, like some of the Hungarians that Dombos described, in their despair they embraced critical consumption as the only way to effect change.

In embodying the relationship between history and people's ethical consumption, Orlando's Palermo shoppers find echoes in those who frequent the Fair Shop that Lill Vramo described in her chapter. As she notes, Fair Shop's advocacy of 'Trade, not aid' reflects the changing historical situation of Norway, especially the public concern that the country's previous generosity had turned into foolish giving to crafty recipients. With aid thus tainted, trade has to be made more fair. The ethical consumption that both Orlando and Vramo describe, then, is affected in important ways by the history of a place and of the people who live there.

I said that Orlando's chapter echoes Dombos's in warning us against too facile an interpretation of Miller's distinction between a morality and an ethics of shopping. That is because the people Orlando describes saw much of the Palermo middle class as Us, concerned for the city and repulsed by its corruption. The fact that the vast majority of those people were unknown is immaterial, just as it is immaterial that the fierce Hungarian nationalist that

Dombos describes had no knowledge of the vast majority of the Hungarians who were her Us. For both, ethical consumption was a way to support an Us, even if only an imagined one, that is much more extensive than the circle of family and close friends.

The chapters in this section that I have described thus far indicate the ways that people's historical situations influence their decision to consume ethically. The remaining chapters in this section are concerned with a different aspect of the context of ethical consumption. That is the social corollaries and consequences that such consumption has for ethical consumers. These can affect how people practice ethical consumption and, indeed, whether they continue or abandon it. The first of these chapters describes Swedish ethical consumers. It is Cindy Isenhour's 'On the Challenges of Signalling Ethics without the Stuff: Tales of Conspicuous Green Anti-consumption'.

Isenhour is concerned with ethical consumers who think it important to consume less and, like Dombos, she presents a set of cases that illustrate different forms of that consumption. For many of the people she describes, the shift to reduced consumption is also a shift to a more prestigious form of consumption. For some, that means selecting only the items that have the least adverse effect on the environment. For others, that means searching for secondhand items that are fashionable. For yet others, that means buying the highest quality model of the item that they want. With these tactics, these people can consume ethically while demonstrating that their reduced consumption is a matter of choice rather than necessity. Put differently, and in the words of Isenhour's title, it is a way of 'signalling ethics without the stuff'.

As she describes, this is especially important for middle-class Swedes because their cultural norms encourage high levels of consumption, particularly of household goods. While Sweden may be unusual in the strength of those norms, the problem that these ethical consumers face is likely to appear generally. Wherever people signal their social standing through the objects that they possess, those who want to reduce their consumption risk signalling a reduced social standing. The tactics Isenhour describes serve to assert social standing through the quality and rarity (and cost) of possessions rather than the quantity. Isenhour's chapter shows, though, that this does not always work. As one of the people she describes complained, people 'think that you are poor or that you're not well educated, that you don't have nice taste or that you are not successful'. And as she notes, those with a deep and long-term commitment to an ethic of consuming less are likely to withdraw from many of their old social networks. They find new friends who share their ethic or find themselves with fewer friends.

Isenhour's chapter points to the way that people's adoption of ethical consumption can carry social costs. Some of the Hungarian ethical consumers that Dombos discusses experienced these costs as well, either in conflicts with other members of their circle or in a reluctance to talk about their ethics for fear of alienating friends and acquaintances. And if the social cost is high enough, of course, people will abandon their ethical consumption. This is what happened to some of the people described by Peter Collins in the next chapter in this section, 'Ethical Consumption as Religious Testimony: The Quaker Case'.

As indicated in the Introduction, Collins's chapter is important because it shows how something that looks very much like modern ethical consumption, the modest consumption of Quakers, can rest on principles and values, and can seek ends, that are very different. These Quakers are not saving the world, they are focused on the bit of God that is in everyone; they are not responding to threats to the environment or distant others, they are heeding biblical injunction. As well, they are not the autonomous individuals of the official discourse that Dombos describes: their consumption is not a spontaneous reflection of their own volition. Rather, it is defined and enforced by the Quaker movement as a whole: failure to conform means expulsion. Here, then, modest consumption is not an individual choice, but instead rests on an elaborate social mechanism of the sort alien to many of the images and much of the rationale of ethical consumption.

I said that Collins's chapter provides another instance of what Isenhour describes, the social costs that ethical consumption can entail. For some of the Swedes that she describes, those costs included a degree of social isolation. For some of the Quakers that Collins describes, there was much more involved than loneliness. Those are what he calls the 'dynastic' Quakers, prosperous merchants and manufacturers around the middle of the nineteenth century. As Collins describes, these people operated at a disadvantage. The rules of Quaker consumption prevented their participation in many of the social activities undertaken by their non-Quaker fellows: the hunts, the balls, the dinners and so on.

In one sense the result may have been the sense of isolation that Isenhour describes, but there was more to it. That is because the social events were the frame in which valuable information circulated and useful acquaintances could be made. They were, in other words, important for the continuing prosperity of these dynastic Quakers, their businesses and families. As Collins notes, many of those Quakers found the price too high to pay. They abandoned their faith and so freed themselves to live more easily the lives that their social equals expected of them.

Isenhour and Collins describe one aspect of the context of the practice of ethical consumption, its social corollaries and particularly its social costs. The final chapter in this section also describes those corollaries and costs. However, it does not address the effects of the signals that ethical consumption can send. Instead, it describes the social effort and tension that can follow from the decision to consume ethically and from the decision to produce things for ethical consumers. That chapter is 'Reinventing Food: The Ethics of Developing Local Food', by Cristina Grasseni.

Like Orlando, Grasseni is concerned with critical consumers in Italy, but her focus is on the north of the country rather than on Sicily, in the south. As I indicated, her chapter attends to both the makers and the purchasers involved in ethical consumption. The makers are those involved in the production of cheese that is considered 'authentic', and hence suited for ethical consumption. Echoing and extending the points made in the Introduction about ethicality, she shows how the production of authentic, traditional Alpine cheese is no simple reproduction of ancestral practices. Such a cheese has to be recognised, its authenticity and its tradition made legible, which means in practice that it has to be certified in one way or another so that it can be slotted into what Grasseni, invoking Michael Herzfeld (2004), says is a global hierarchy of value.

As she describes, this is a process in which social, economic and political interests come to bear. They do so in ways that are likely to be invisible to ethical consumers, and they can illuminate the complexities and compromises that lurk behind the 'ethical' in ethical consumption. Which is more important, the well-being of the goatherds who historically have made the cheese or the well-being of the dairies in the broader, declining region in which they live? One definition of 'authentic' points in the first direction, another points in the second. Who is entitled to use the traditional name, those who happen to be the main cheese-makers when certification is being sought or others whose historic claim is equally valid even if they make little of that cheese now? Again, different answers benefit different groups of people, both of whom merit support.

Grasseni's description of consumers raises similar issues. In part that is because the groups of people she describes take their consumption very seriously indeed. They are not content with a certification that what they buy is Fairtrade, organic or the like. Rather, they seek to locate and inspect the sources of what they buy. The result is that these groups have to do a lot of work finding sources that they like, arranging orders, collecting foodstuffs, storing and distributing them. This reflects what they want their consumption to be. However, it means that there is the risk of tension in these groups, the risk that they will divide into those who do the work and those who reap the benefit.

For Grasseni's Alpine cheese-makers, ethical consumers, dairy owners and provincial officials, producing and acquiring something that is identifiable as ethical requires a lot of time and attention, as well as the balancing of conflicting legitimate interests. The people and the effort that she describes are different from Isenhour's Swedes and Collins's Quakers. However, all three chapters agree on one point. The official discourse of ethical consumption, which shares with the economic realm a focus on autonomous individuals, is deceptive. The decision to become an ethical consumer and the effects of that consumption, like the creation, recognition and acquisition of ethical items, all locate ethical consumption in a web of social relationships, whether intended or not, desired or not. Moreover, if Orlando's *palermitanos* and some of Dombos's Hungarians are any indication, that consumption is intended to extend and strengthen those webs. The household Us that is taken to be the focus of Miller's moral consumption, like the market actor of the economic thought that ethical consumption often invokes, seems far less significant than it appears at first glance.

Bibliography

Herzfeld, Michael 2004. *The body impolitic: artisans and artifice in the global hierarchy of value*. Chicago: Chicago University Press.
Miller, Daniel 2001. *The dialectics of shopping*. Chicago: University of Chicago Press.

Chapter 5

NARRATIVES OF CONCERN:
BEYOND THE 'OFFICIAL' DISCOURSE OF
ETHICAL CONSUMPTION IN HUNGARY

Tamás Dombos

The last few years have brought a significant increase in ethical consumption in Hungary. When a group of activists decided to start a promotional campaign for fair-trade goods in April 2005, they had to drive to Vienna, pack the boot of the car with fair-trade coffee and tea and drive it back home. Today there are several wholesalers dealing with fair-trade products, which are widely available (Fairvilág Szövetség n.d.). Organic goods have been available in specialised farmers' markets and shops since the middle of the 1990s, and by 2009 organic consumption had become fairly common, as shown by the increased role of supermarkets in the distribution of organic food (Szente 2004) and by the introduction of own-brand organic products in large supermarket chains. The growing prominence of consumption as an arena for advancing social and political causes is also shown by the number of consumer boycotts called for during the past decade (Gulyás 2007: 114) and the spread of alternative food networks (Kiss, Simonyi and Balázs 2009).

   That increased availability of ethical products and growth of consumer activism has run parallel to a shift in consumer politics and a growing public engagement with ethical consumption. While environmentalist organisations with an anti-consumerist orientation have operated since the middle of the 1990s (Harper 1999, 2006), the founding of organisations such as the Association of Conscious Consumers and the Fair World Fair Trade Alliance marks the emergence of a different politics of consumption, not opposition to consumer society as such, but instead consumers' engagement with environmental and other ethical issues. Hungarian versions of international events such as Buy Nothing Day! and Fair Trade Day, and the publication of a series of educational materials and practical guides to consuming more ethically, provide the discursive background to the spread of ethical products and related consumption practices.

If one looks at what I call the 'official' ethical-consumption discourse, which is produced by activists and organisations firmly embedded in the global network of the ethical-consumption movement, one finds a more or less coherent narrative about ethical consumers. They are presented as people who recognise the social and environmental impact of their consumption, leave behind their previous consumerist orientation and start living and consuming more consciously. Ethical consumption appears as a rational activity that is made viable by the growing availability of information about products and their production contexts, an activity reaching beyond the individual as it promises to become a force transforming business practices through the signalling system described in the Introduction to this volume. The slogans 'voting with your money' and 'consumption as public participation' suggest an ongoing struggle to break down the boundary between citizens and consumers.

However, if we move beyond that official discourse, propagated by a relatively small circle of activists and organisations, we find a much more diverse world of orientations among those who identify themselves as ethical consumers. In this chapter I build on an ethnographic study of self-proclaimed ethical consumers, to show the heterogeneity of ethical and political concerns that motivate everyday ethical consumers in Hungary, the diverse ways in which ethical consumption is incorporated into these people's lives.

In showing that heterogeneity, I echo another of the points made in this volume's Introduction. That point is the problematic nature of ethicality, the ways that subtle processes not readily visible to consumers shape the ways that an ethical state of affairs is represented and comes to be understood, for instance non-exploitative coffee production (see also Luetchford, this volume; Vramo, this volume). The corollary of that discussion of ethicality is that other, and perhaps equally valid, ways of representing and understanding the ethical disappear from view. In this chapter I describe an analogous state of affairs. In particular, I am concerned with the ways that the most visible and influential discourses of ethical consumption, which Hungary shares with the rest of Europe and North America, portray ethical consumers in terms of some attributes rather than others and identify some things rather than others as ethical concerns. In this chapter I seek to uncover some of these other attributes and other things.

Theoretically, I start with the point that consumption is a social practice fraught with contradictions. In *The dialectics of shopping*, Daniel Miller (2001) analyses a series of contradictions, one of which is especially pertinent here, what Miller calls the contradiction between the ethics and morality of consumption. When asked, people commonly claim an altruistic concern for distant others by taking environmental and other ethical issues into account in their purchasing decisions. However, only a small minority actually buy ethical products. This common pattern is widely described in the literature as a 'words/deeds inconsistency' (Newholm 2005: 107). Miller (2001: 134) explains this contradiction with reference to what he calls the morality of consumption, the 'dutiful attempt to save money on behalf of the household at large'. This moral duty is incompatible with the ethical concern for distant others, because ethical objects that would satisfy that concern commonly cost significantly more than ordinary objects. Miller says that people will be likely to buy those ethical objects only when the values that they embody are moral as well, when they secure the well-being of the shopper's family. This is most apparent in the case of objects that are seen as environmentally sound. Purchasing them, says Miller (2001: 126), is motivated by a 'strong sense of self-interest based on the idea that non-Green foods will be harmful to the purchaser … [and a] concern for the effects of the products on … [one's] family rather than any wider concern for the health of the world at large'.

Roberta Sassatelli elaborates on the point implicit in what Miller says, that the motivations that drive shoppers are complex and that their practices do not always reflect the labels (like 'ethical consumption') commonly applied to them. She (2007: 188) notes that 'many of the practices which come under the umbrella of political consumerism might indeed be conducted by consumers who have in mind meanings and objectives other than the strictly political'. Shoppers at second-hand shops can be motivated by the environmentalist desire to avoid new objects, as well as by the desire to save money. Preference for food produced locally can reflect a commitment to reduce carbon emissions, express solidarity with local producers and increase local tax revenues, as well as a belief that eating what grows in your own area is healthy. As Terry Newholm (2005: 114) puts it, the problem lies in the fact that 'attitudes cannot be "read off" behavior or vice versa, not least because of social mediation and the varied meanings associated with particular practices.' These authors, then, warn us of a situation parallel to the point made in the Introduction about ethicality. Just as presentations of coffee growers focus on some constructions of an ethical state of affairs rather than others, so popular presentations of ethical consumption focus on some sorts of people and some sets of values rather than others.

The research underlying this chapter is part of my doctoral project, 'Ethical consumption in Hungary: discourse and practice'. This uses participant observation, interviews and discourse analysis to investigate how entrepreneurs, activists and consumers co-construct the market as a politicised space. These actors are linked by a myriad of communicative channels (discussion boards, newsletters, media campaigns, advertisements) through which meanings attached to ethical consumption are circulated. In this chapter I am concerned especially with the Association of Conscious Consumers, which I describe below, and a group of ethical consumers connected to it through their subscription to its bi-weekly electronic newsletter.

The first part of what follows focuses on the framing of ethical consumption by the Association in its various publications, including its website, quarterly magazine and electronic newsletter. The second part compares this framing with five narratives of everyday ethical consumers, each committed to the Association but showing radically different ethical consumption. The final part considers how the findings should inform our understanding of ethical consumption, an understanding that needs to treat ethical consumption not so much as a unified social movement in opposition to ordinary consumption, but as an assemblage of everyday moralities of consumption and selective re-appropriation of ethical-consumption frames.

The Association and its Notion of 'Conscious Shopping'

Tudatos Vásárlók Egyesülete, based in Budapest, was founded in 2002. Strictly, its name translates into English as 'Association of Conscious Shoppers', but 'Association of Conscious Consumers' better reflects its orientation and is the common English form of its name. It has been important in the recent development of ethical consumption discourses in Hungary and is still the only organisation in the country that is devoted solely to ethical consumption. It presents itself as concerned both with consumer protection and with the natural environment, thus combining elements of the first and third wave of consumerist movements (Lang and Hines 1993). This combination of aims is manifest in the name of the organisation: 'consciousness' signals both the value-for-money orientation characteristic of first-wave movements and the ethical consciousness prominent in third-wave consumerist movements.

According to its charter, it aims at 'winning people over to the idea that purchasing decisions have to be made carefully, looking beyond the usual price–quality considerations: taking into account, for example, the environmental and social performance of the manufacturer of a given product, the ecological features thereof or its impact on the consumer's health' (TVE n.d.*a*; all translations are by the author). The charter also describes the Association's commitment to the 'development of new types of consumer values, that is, a new lifestyle and identity'. The 'conscious shopper' in the Association's name was chosen with that new identity in mind, for it is a label that would attract people while avoiding the ambivalent connotations 'ethical consumer' has in Hungary. As one of the founders said, even though they were strongly focused on ethical consumption, they thought 'ethical' could be perceived as too pretentious, 'consumer' too alienating.

The Association quickly became important. It has a permanent staff, and by 2007 a budget nearly double that of the average Hungarian non-profit organisation (Központi Statisztikai Hivatal 2009), 85 per cent of which comes from the government and the European Union. It is a founder and member of the Ecological Consumer Protection Working Group, the Fair World Fair Trade Alliance and the Alliance for European Consumer Protection, all in Hungary, and is part of the international network of consumers' organisations, which includes Consumers International, the Consumer Citizenship Network and Transatlantic Consumer Dialogue. The Association's activities focus primarily on education: it runs media campaigns (e.g., Buy Nothing Day!) and school programmes, publishes the quarterly magazine and bi-weekly electronic newsletter already mentioned, maintains a list of organic shops and corporate social responsibility programmes, and does some research and consultancy work for various state agencies.

The views of the Association are nicely summarised in a widely-circulated document, *The twelve principles of the conscious shopper* (TVE n.d.*a*). At its heart is the claim that consumption is a form of voting: 'Shopping is based on your decision. You can decide whom and what you support and whom/what you do not. You do not have to support environmental pollution, chemicals, child labour and the mass production of foolish, harmful and useless products' (TVE n.d.*b*). The document goes on to give practical advice about what, where and how to consume, considering issues ranging from packaging and waste disposal to advertisements, environmental pollution, animal rights, health and the advantages of fresh and natural local products.

In *The twelve principles* and other publications, the Association presents a message about consumers, consumption and the world in which they exist, and it resembles much of what is contained in presentations of ethical consumption in other parts of Europe and North America. A number of themes stand out in that message, and I present them in summary form here, in two sets. One set deals with the state of the world and the task that conscious consumers face. Firstly, the world is a tightly interconnected entity where everything has a reason and an impact, and no decision is without consequence. Secondly, corporations are powerful entities that constantly seek to circumvent regulations. Thirdly, the state is powerful and could, through regulation, have a positive influence, but currently is slow to enforce the regulations it has enacted and to respond to new challenges. Fourthly, conscious consumers can take over the task of the state and enforce existing regulation, as well as put pressure on corporations in areas where regulation currently does not exist. The other set of themes relate to conscious consumers themselves. Firstly, conscious consumers are rational actors free to make decisions. They are constrained by lack of information and corporate pressure, but both of these can be overcome by higher levels of awareness. Secondly, conscious consumers do not have a gender, class or ethnicity, but are deeply rooted in their local (not national) community. Thirdly, ethical consumption is closely allied with progressive politics built on values of accountability, solidarity and political participation.

Beyond the Official Discourse

To explore how people's ideas matched those of the Association, I posted an advertisement in the Association's electronic newsletter, 'looking for people who think it is important to pay attention to ethical and political considerations in their consumer decisions'. This technique was chosen to reach people who are regularly exposed to the Association's ideas and who identify with the ethical-consumption movement, but who are not as tightly linked to the organisation as staff members and volunteers are.

A wide range of people responded to my advertisement, although the overwhelming majority had high levels of education (all but a few had completed college or university courses of study) and a significant majority were women. About two-thirds of them were living in or around Budapest, with the remainder living in other urban areas. In spite of their relatively high level of education, their income varied from those living on social benefits to people in top managerial positions who are paid five to eight times the average Hungarian wage. The youngest informant was 26, the oldest 54, with the majority in their 30s. Their living arrangements did not diverge significantly from the Hungarian average, though single-person households were slightly over-represented even when age was taken into account.

I conducted interviews of 2–4 hours with people responding to the advertisement. These covered their life history, the organisation of their daily life, the patterns and organisation of their daily consumption, their consumer aspirations and their attitudes towards wealth, money, brands and advertisements. I asked no direct questions about ethical considerations during most of the interview, because I wanted to know if people would bring these up spontaneously. Aspects of ethical consumption not brought up by the respondents were covered by more direct questions at the end of the interview. After the interviews I asked respondents if I could accompany them in their shopping routine, a technique Miller (1998, 2001) used. This allows one to see people's consumption practices, and so use what they do to complement what people say in their interviews. During the shopping trips we discussed why people choose one product over the other, their past experiences with and aspirations about the items that are available, and their opinions about the environment of shopping: their fellow consumers and the advertisements placed in retail outlets.

Not surprisingly, all of the informants were keen readers of the Association's newsletter and identified themselves as conscious consumers. In addition, they reported, or at least aspired to, consumer behaviour that is usually associated with ethical consumption: participating in boycotts of various products or retail establishments; paying attention to the environmental consequences of their consumption, such as choosing simpler packaging and avoiding chemicals; sorting their waste; consuming organic food regularly. Yet the meanings they attached to ethical consumption and their stories of how it fits in their respective lives showed significant diversity.

To show this diversity, I will describe five respondents who represent different types of ethical consumption. These five are distinctive in the clarity and consistency of their approaches to ethical consumption; the majority of informants were less cogent in their accounts and less clear-cut in their actions. Unlike these five, then, most people recounted a more fragmented and ambiguous story, combining bits and pieces from two or more of the orientations I describe.

Ethical Consumption as Moral Duty – The Story of Veronika

Veronika (all names are pseudonyms) is a forty-year-old mother of a one-year-old child. She is currently living on state child allowance with her parents, who are pensioners, outside the capital. Veronika has a working-class background: her mother was a shop assistant, her father a locksmith. She left school at fifteen and started working in a series of low-paying jobs. She completed her secondary education in an evening school, and then applied for admission to the state higher-education system. She was not successful, and ended up attending a private teacher-training college of alternative pedagogy, which she financed by working night-shifts. Her interest in languages and travelling (and her limited resources) led her to take a language course funded by the Indian government, and subsequently she taught in India for several years. It was there that she met her husband. She returned to Hungary to renew her visa, and discovered that she was pregnant. She has not met her husband for over 18 months and had to move back to her parents, even though her relationship with them is severely strained.

For Veronika, ethical consumption started with the banal refusal to litter as a child, which turned into more conscious environmentalism when she faced what she saw as the filthy conditions in India. It was the search for alternatives to disposable nappies that drove her to an on-line group of environmentally conscious mothers. This group is her primary source of information about such issues, and also her primary social network. In the past few years Veronika gradually switched to organic consumption, not only because she thinks it is healthy, but also because she sees non-organic production as harming the environment and as linked to worker exploitation and child labour. As part of this, she stopped using what she called 'chemicals' (including detergent and toothpaste) and, until very recently, ate only organic foods. For both economic and ideological reasons she relies heavily on second-hand charity shops, items handed on from relatives and friends, and home-made clothing and tools.

Veronika feels guilty about being unable to afford to live up to the strict standards she sets for herself, even though she thinks she does more than most people in her financial situation. She blames most people's failure to consume ethically on what she sees as the moral crises of Hungarian society, marked by a lack of concern for the environment, ethnic intolerance and cheating at work and on things like taxes and payment for public services. Veronika finds it difficult to understand why others do not share her commitment:

> This is such a universal human value, this is needed for normal life. One can say about ideologies that I think this way and you do the other way, and this should be respected. But there is nothing to respect here, this is the only thing acceptable … to respect the environment and the other person …. I believe that everything in the end is up to individual responsibility.

Veronika exemplifies an ethical consumption in which consumption decisions are strongly shaped by a universalistic moral outlook that overrides, or at least competes with, other considerations. In Veronika's case this moral framework is a type of humanism combined with environmentalist considerations: she often refers to Rudolf Steiner's anthroposophy and the balance between human freedom and social responsibility. References to Steiner and the affiliation with Waldorf Schools, based on Steiner's thought, appear in the accounts of several respondents. The link between ethical consumption, especially organic consumption, and the Waldorf School movement is remarkably strong in Hungary. The twenty-five Waldorf Schools were the first regular institutional consumers of organic produce in the country, and they were important in promoting green consumption among the parents of children enrolled there.

Steinerian humanism is, however, not the only universalistic morality that provides a motive and framework for ethical consumption: religious orientations, especially varieties of progressive Protestantism, can do so as well, as shown by several other respondents. Both moral systems stress individual responsibility. For those, like Veronika, who embrace such moral systems, ethical consumption is not seen simply as a way to influence economic practices or to bring about social or political change. Rather, it marks a personal commitment to live an ethical life.

Ethical Consumption as Political Resistance – The Story of Julia

Julia is in her late twenties, a handicraft teacher and irregular university student who lives in a better-off district of the capital with her mother, a pensioner. Julia's narrative projects a strong sense of downward mobility: she completed a degree in agricultural engineering only to find that her previous qualification as a handicraft teacher offered better job prospects. She feels she is working more every year but earning less, as prices continually rise. She links her misfortune to the failure and wrong-headedness of government policies, a theme that appears regularly in our interview. Julia currently has one thing on her mind: how to get enough money to complete the renovation of a house she bought in rural Hungary, which would allow her to escape the capital.

Julia recounts a long history of environmental sensitivity that was not initially connected to her consumption. She became a committed ethical consumer only recently, at the same time that she became more active politically as a result of discussions with a number of friends affiliated with an extreme right-wing party. For her, buying Hungarian is not the only concern that shapes her purchasing decisions, but it is the strongest: she sees this as a vital strategy to fight globalisation and the rule of multinationals. Although she deems exploitation inevitable, she feels it is worse if foreigners do it. In her narrative, foreign companies want to destroy the country, sell it off and make everyone slaves. The marketing and distribution of chemicals by companies that are indifferent to the harm that they cause is part of their strategy, and she stopped buying such chemicals about a year ago. Supermarkets and shopping malls are emblematic of this foreign colonisation, and she refuses to visit them. At the same time, Julia has a strong distrust of goods commonly associated with ethical consumption. She lives close to an organic farmers' market and laughs at the stupidity of people who are tricked into buying low-quality foods at high prices. For her, those selling organic products are as manipulative as politicians and people who run businesses, for they all are trying to squeeze as much money as possible out of people.

She contrasts these tricks with the tricks *she* uses in everyday life to get back at people setting immoral prices or taxes. Those are tricks to get everything from welfare provisions to swimming-pool tickets, and she spent a lot of time in the interview explaining how she was forced to use trickery to get into an exhibition promoting traditional Hungarian products and cuisine. For her, these tricks are not only a result of her financial situation, they are also part of a struggle against immoral business practices. Julia also invokes standard extreme-right political assumptions and values when she explains her consumption. She refuses to take out a loan to finish the renovation of her house because she is not willing to give any more money to the Jews. She no longer buys from Chinese merchants as she hates Chinese people. When she described her most recent purchase of clothes, a year earlier in a Transylvanian village, she added that she does not consider Transylvania to be abroad.[1] For Julia, collective mobilisation is the only way to solve the problems she sees around her, and she unfavourably contrasts Hungary to Greece and Italy:

> In those foreign countries people simply decide not to go to that particular shop, but here this wretched nation cannot do it …. National pride is much greater there, here it has been completely cut back. People should be given back their hope that if we come together we can change this situation …. If people would recognise the amount of manipulation, how stupid they have been, then everything would be easier. For me these two things [conscious consumption and nationalist sentiments] are inseparably linked.

Julia's case shows how ethical consumption can be associated with very different political orientations. While strong political views can contribute to ethical consumption, in most studies it has been found to be associated with a leftist political orientation (see, e.g., Andersen and Tobiasen 2004; but see Pratt 2007). In Hungary, on the other hand, it was the right-wing political parties and movements that urged people to pay attention to the social consequences of individual consumer choice. Nationalistic consumer mobilisation has strong historical roots in Hungary (see Kosáry 1942; Nyugat. hu 2007), and initiatives such as the 'Club for Hungarian Products' and 'Domestic Product – Domestic Jobs' appeared in post-socialist Hungary as early as the middle of the 1990s. The movement got a strong boost in 2002 with the establishment of 'civic circles' (see Halmai 2007) and a call by a former right-wing prime minister to buy only things with a product code that starts with 599, supposedly a marker of Hungarian origin.

Similar initiatives mushroomed: new labels promoting Hungarian products have been born (Magyar Termék, Hungaricum Club, Premium Hungaricum, Magyar Áruk), retail chains have appeared that specialise in Hungarian products or that emphasise their Hungarian nature (Magor, CBA – A magyar üzletlánc, Magyar Termékek Boltja); a whole subculture built around nationalist symbolism, consumer engagement and radical right-wing politics developed (Jeskó 2009). The movement is not limited to buying Hungarian products. It also incorporates other forms of ethical consumption such as buying organic food, seen as produced by traditional rather than modern industrial agriculture, and a preference for direct contact with farmers, to keep in touch with the unspoiled nationalistic sentiments of rural Hungary. At a recent event to promote social and environmental sensitivity in consumer decisions, one could find a tent promoting fair trade coffee next to a vendor selling traditional pottery with nationalistic political messages, a local farmer selling organic jam, a craftsmen selling hand-carved wooden maps of historic Hungary and a stall promoting solar energy.

What is distinctive about this sort of ethical consumption, however, is not its specific, nationalist content. Rather, it is the way that it links consumer choice to political action. This group of ethical consumers sees institutionalised politics as empty, enervated and governed by corporate interests. Ethical consumption appears as a means to reconstitute the true meaning of politics through active engagement with political issues in everyday life.

Ethical Consumption as Care for Family and Self – The Story of Agnes

Agnes is thirty-seven years old and a mother of two, currently expecting her third child. She works in a small, family-based consultancy enterprise together with her husband. Both of them were civil servants, but when they decided to move from the centre of Budapest to its suburbs they opted for a job with a flexible working schedule, to accommodate the arrival of their first child. Although Agnes never considered staying at home with her children full time, much of her day revolves around them: she never goes out for dinner, and mentions movie nights with her children as the main source of entertainment.

For Agnes, the prime concern in consumption decisions is ingredients, and her shopping takes hours as she meticulously checks most of the products she considers buying. She never buys processed food and tries to avoid 'E-numbers', the flavour-enhancers, stabilisers and the like that are identified on the label not by name, but by 'E' and a three-digit number. She even checks the things she regularly buys, because companies keep changing the ingredients and one can not be careful enough. Her concern with ingredients is driven by her concern for the effects of what the family eats on their health. Sugary drinks and salty snacks are strictly forbidden, and she is proud that her children follow her strict principles. She sums up her view as follows: 'You have to go beyond what looks good and what is cheap, and integrate other perspectives as well, most importantly how it affects your own and others' health.' She is very interested in organic food, but says she lacks the time and money needed to buy it. As this suggests, her purchasing choices are based primarily on price and quality; appearance is secondary. Indeed, attractive packaging makes her suspicious that the product is so poor that it needs the packaging to attract buyers. Her dislike of fancy packaging reflects her environmental concerns as well. Although she is a strong environmentalist, she quickly adds that it also pays off: a washing machine that consumes less water and energy is good for the environment and is economical. Similarly, she does not buy new things until the old ones wear out: if one buys new products only when the old ones no longer work, one does good for the planet and for oneself. Agnes refrains, however, from criticising other people for their consumer decisions. She thinks she has no real chance of convincing them, and her criticism would be taken as contemptuous and could harm her social relationships. Similarly, she is strongly interested in politics, but never participates in political discussions, because maintaining family and other social relationships is more important to her than expressing her opinions.

In seeing ethical consumption in terms of what is best for her family, Agnes reflects common public attitudes towards family values. Even though the demographic reality is more ambiguous, Hungarians still consider children and family life as the most important things in their lives (for an overview, see Neményi and Tóth 2003). Providing security and well-being for the family is a central tenet of Hungarian consumer culture (Fehérváry 2005).

Agnes illustrates how Miller's contradiction between the ethics and morality of consumption can be overcome by linking ethical and moral considerations in consumer decisions: what is good for the environment is also good for you and your family, and saves money. Indeed, as suggested by what I have described of Julia, the previous case, the boundary between the 'us' of Miller's morality and the 'distant others' of his ethics need not coincide with the boundary of the household. So, for instance, concern for health can reflect care for one's family, but equally it can reflect the desire to help maintain a healthy workforce, the desire to help ensure the survival of the nation and so forth.

The salience of mothers with small children among those who responded to my advertisement makes Agnes's sort of ethical consumption one of the most prominent. Concern for children's health helps account for that salience, but does not explain why these people engage in ethical consumption not directly linked to health. It seems likely, rather, that the heightened ethics of care associated with having children has a spill-over effect: having to care about another human being leads people one step further. The integration in the ethical-consumption movement of organic consumption with forms of environmentalism and concern for other issues means that parents are more likely to encounter materials that link other ethical considerations to consumer choice.

Ethical Consumption as Rational Calculus – The Story of Gabor

Gabor is a forty-year-old economist living with his wife and their three children. For fourteen years Gabor worked for the regional branch of a large, multinational company in a senior position, before leaving to start his own company. Change, however, was not limited to his work. Gabor became vegan, switched to natural personal-hygiene products and worked to transform his previous life, which he now considers shallow, monotonous and overly materialist.

In Gabor's ideal world he could trust manufacturers, farmers and shopkeepers to produce and trade things of good quality in ethical ways without harming the environment. In that world, he could go into a shop and choose what he liked. In his real world, however, shopping is a nightmare, where a host of concerns have to be considered and deliberated. He thinks most people simply avoid thinking things through carefully and are guided by irrational motivations and fears. He recounts several conflicts with his wife and his parents, which arose when he tried to convince them to change their habitual consumption practices. One example he recounts enthusiastically concerns household chemicals. He says that when people buy toilet fresheners, detergents or floor cleaners, they are driven by irrational fear, even hysteria, about bacteria. They never take into account how those things affect the environment. He says that he lives differently:

> I am first and foremost a man of facts, I cannot rest until I gather all the information available out there. Then comes the hard part: to consider all the different aspects and make the best decision, which is always a best-compromise at most …. I have principles that I would never contradict, the rest …. I'll try to weigh the options and find the best solution.

The image of ethical consumption promulgated by the Association includes the idea of the rational consumer who, like Gabor, overcomes corporate pressure by collecting and weighing information about products and their production contexts. However, very few of the people I studied identified strongly with that image. Interestingly, all of those who did were linked in one way or another to economics as a profession and used economic terminology to explain their daily consumer choices, invoking things like externality, trade-off, monopoly, consumer sovereignty and consumer satisfaction. This usage suggests that these people's ethical consumption is, at least in their own minds, closely tied to their profession and to the understanding of capitalist economies that it gives them.

This rationalistic vision of ethical consumption was often accompanied by some form of asceticism. For Gabor, for example, this meant the outright denial that he gets any pleasure out of buying things and his general frustration with never being able get the right product and always having to compromise. For others, asceticism appeared in a milder form, refusing to buy a lot of things, and instead focussing on a few, durable things of good quality, such as Cindy

Isenhour (this volume) describes among some of the Swedish ethical consumers that she studied. For these people, the best way to decide what to buy was to collect extensive information about the choices available, save the necessary money and make the purchase.

Ethical Consumption as Alternative Lifestyle – The Story of Kornélia

Kornélia is thirty-six years old, an activist in gender and Roma organisations who lives with her current partner, a university student, in a flat close to the centre of Budapest. She does not have a permanent job, but goes through cycles of work. When she runs out of money she takes on a job for a couple of months, then stops work and lives off the money she earned until it runs out, then takes on another job. Kornélia grew up in the 1980s in a family of 'alternative' intellectuals and belonged to an eccentric group that followed underground bands and bought their clothes in flea markets. In 1990 she decided to leave the capital: she got married and moved to rural Hungary to start organic farming. After a couple of years she and her husband, whom she subsequently divorced, returned to Budapest, where he became a truck-driver and she started working for a travel agency. They travelled throughout Europe, never staying in Budapest for more than a couple of weeks at a time. When the demands of her job changed, she decided to quit and started working with a non-governmental organisation, sometimes as a volunteer and sometimes for pay on specific projects.

Kornélia's engagement with ethical consumption goes back to 1990, when she and her husband embarked on organic agriculture primarily as a way to differentiate themselves from other local farmers. When they returned to Budapest from the countryside, they found it hard to maintain their organic consumption because organic food was almost impossible to get. They relied heavily on bringing organic food back from abroad themselves and on establishing relationships with producers in the countryside, of the sort described by Audrey Vankeerberghen (this volume) in her discussion of organic agriculture in Belgium. In fact, Kornélia still buys meat only through these relationships. Visiting farmers' markets, bartering with neighbours and picking their own mushrooms and fruits also play an important role in Kornélia and her partner's food provisioning. Although she eats organic foods, she is sceptical about the food sold at organic shops. Also, she finds the association of organic food with health and fitness regrettable: she is a proud smoker and enjoys alcohol. As this suggests, Kornélia is no ascetic and has no missionary zeal. Rather, good-tasting food, ethical considerations and distinction from others go together. This orientation is apparent in her explanation of what led her to establish relationships with farmers to get meat: 'I had no trust in that meat [available for sale in shops], and I had this romantic vision of supporting local guys, and it might be egoistic, but I simply love to eat well, I'd rather not eat than eat this shit …. I'm primarily a hedonist, asceticism is alien to me.'

Kornélia's story shows how people can become ethical consumers at least partly as a way to distinguish themselves from those who consume the normal things of everyday life. This echoes one of the points made in the Introduction to this volume. That is that varieties of ethical consumption can look very much like the sort of thing that Bourdieu (1984) described in *Distinction*, illustrated in this volume by some of the Swedes that Isenhour describes. This sort of distinction depends, of course, on the ethical items in question being fairly exclusive. Once those items become widely available they cease to signify social difference and thus have to be replaced with other items that are esoteric, either because they are hard to get or because their use requires specialist knowledge (of the sort that is important to some in the Slow Food movement: see Introduction). Kornélia's ambivalent attitude towards organic products is a clear example. When organic food was not available in supermarkets, it had great value for her. The effort invested in importing organic food from abroad, locating that one retailer who had organic tomatoes in Budapest in the 1990s and going as far as leaving the city to grow their own organic food brought pleasure and fulfilment that disappears when such food is routinely available in supermarkets. Rather than being political or rational, ethical consumption for Kornélia and her fellow non-conformist consumers is pleasurable, a phenomenon nicely summarised by Kate Soper's (2007) concept of 'alternative hedonism'.

Conclusion

These short descriptions show the diversity of values, aims and motivations that can underlie ethical consumption. While for Veronika ethical consumption is a moral duty beyond political considerations, for Julia it is primarily about expressing political views in everyday decisions. For Gabor it is about giving more prominence to rationality in decision making, for Agnes about expressing love and care for her family members. Gabor's ascetic tendencies are hard to reconcile with Kornélia's hedonism, while Agnes's self-sacrifice and insistence on decency stand in clear opposition to Kornélia's extravagant pleasure-seeking. Julia's constant efforts to win people over to the cause and Veronika's conviction that ethical consumption is a universal human value can be contrasted with Kornélia's conscious eccentricity.

Despite these differences, all five people view themselves as concerned consumers, people for whom every purchase carries weight. They also share a general distrust of producers and retailers, whom they criticise for their lack of concern for the natural and social environment. In this, these ethical consumers manifest the criticism of the orientation and practices of the economic realm described in the Introduction to this volume. In addition, however, the people I have described in this chapter criticise many of their fellow consumers, who they see as being too susceptible to advertising and prone to make hasty purchasing decisions. In this, these people distinguish themselves from 'consumer idiots' (*konzumidióták*; see Dombos 2004), mindless people who do not pay attention to what they buy. For many of those I have described here, distinction from these consumer idiots is an important part of their identity as ethical consumers.

These five cases, and the common tendencies that they illustrate, also allow us to reflect on what I described as the official discourse of the Association of Conscious Consumers. I want to do that by considering two of the ways that the official discourse differs from what my research reveals. The first concerns the Association's activist view of ethical consumption, the stress on rational purchasing decisions as a way to put pressure on firms to change their ways, which echoes the description of the economic signalling system in the Introduction to this volume. Only a few of the people I studied seemed concerned with this. Instead, most people seem driven by other motives, such as caring for loved ones, expressing one's political stance or rejecting elements of mainstream consumer culture. The second concerns the rather generic construction of ethical consumers in that official discourse. In that construction, ethical consumers are simply that, devoid of differentiations of age, sex, class, nation or politics. However, as what I have said in this chapter indicates, identities based on these attributes are important in motivating people to be ethical consumers. The nurturing mother concerned with her children, the Hungarian concerned with the integrity of the nation, the working-class critic of big business, even the wise economist, all are very different from the amorphous, asocial consumers of the Association's publications.

The Introduction to this volume makes the point that we need to be careful of the phrase 'ethical consumption', pointing out that not everything that looks, at first glance, like ethical consumption really deserves to be seen that way and that not everything that looks, at first glance, to be different from ethical consumption really deserves to be seen that way. Rather, it was suggested that we see ethical consumption as concerned with the relationship between economy and society, two realms of life commonly seen to reflect very different values and orientations. Certainly the people I have described here, self-proclaimed ethical consumers, fit that view of ethical consumption, for they all see the ordinary realm of economy as violating important values in the social realm, and they shape their purchasing decisions accordingly. However, they do so in no uniform way. Ethical consumption as a social movement may have called on these people to pay attention to more than price and utility, may have called on them to consider the moral nature of the context of the objects on offer. However, it seems, that call is received selectively, is reinterpreted and often diverted by people who have to reconcile it with economic constraints, familial expectations and an established sense of personal identity. Policing the borderlands between economy and society, then, turns out to take many different forms.

Notes

1. Transylvania was part of Hungary until the end of the First World War, when it was annexed by Romania as part of the Treaty of Trianon. Revision of Trianon borders is a key demand of extreme right-wing parties.

Bibliography

Andersen, Jorgen G. and Mette Tobiasen 2004. Who are these political consumers anyway? Survey evidence from Denmark. In *Politics, products, and markets: exploring political consumerism past and present* (eds) Michelle Micheletti, Andreas Follesdal and Dietlind Stolle, pp. 201–21. New Brunswick, NJ: Transaction Publishers.

Bourdieu, Pierre 1984. *Distinction: a social critique of the judgement of taste*. London: Routledge & Kegan Paul.

Dombos, Tamás 2004. From petit bourgeois mentality to consumerism: moralizing discourses on consumption in socialist and present-day Hungary. MA Thesis, Department of Sociology and Social Anthropology, Central European University.

Fairvilág Szövetség n.d. Méltányos kereskedelemből származó termékeket árusító boltok listája. Budapest: Fairvilág Szövetség. www.fairvilag.hu/termekek/boltok

Fehérváry, Krisztina E. 2005. In search of the normal: material culture and middle-class fashioning in a Hungarian steel town, 1950–1997. Ph.D. dissertation, Department of Anthropology, University of Chicago.

Gulyás, Emese 2007. Az etikus fogyasztás mint a közügyekben való részvétel. *Politikatudományi Szemle* 16(4): 112–26.

Halmai, Gábor 2007. The swamps of neoliberal hegemony: Polgári Körök in 'transitional' Hungary. Presented at the 'Changing Europe Summer School 2007', Warsaw, September 2–8.

Harper, Krista 1999. Consumers or citizens? Environmentalism and the public sphere in post-socialist Hungary. *Radical History Review* 74: 96–111.

——— 2006. *Wild capitalism: environmental activists and post-socialist ecology in Hungary*. Boulder, Col.: East European Monographs.

Jeskó, József 2009. Gyorsan terjed a Jobbikhoz kötődő ellenkultúra. *HVG* (27 November). hvg.hu/velemeny/20091127_jobbik_szubkulturak.aspx

Kiss, Csilla, Borbála Simonyi and Bálint Balázs 2008. Alternative agri-food networks in Hungary. In *Sustainable Consumption in Hungary* (conference proceedings) (eds) Edina Vadovics and Emese Gulyás, pp. 76–84. Budapest: Institute of Environmental Sciences, Corvinus University of Budapest.

Kosáry, Domonkos 1942. *Kossuth és a Védegylet: a magyar nacionalizmus történetéhe*. Budapest: Athenaeum Literary and Publishing Company.

Központi Statisztikai Hivatal 2009. A nonprofit szektor legfontosabb jellemzői 2007-ben. *Statisztikai Tükör* www.civil.info.hu/modules/News/20090316/A_nonprofit_szektor_legfontosabb_jellemzoi_2007_ben.html

Lang, Tim and Colin Hines 1993. *The new protectionism: protecting the future against free trade*. London: Earthscan.

Miller, Daniel 1998. *A theory of shopping*. Ithaca, NY: Cornell University Press.

——— 2001. *The dialectics of shopping*. Chicago: University of Chicago Press.

Neményi, Mária and Olga Tóth 2003. Differential modernization in Hungary: families and family values after transition. In *Changing family structure in Europe: new challenges for public policy* (eds) Marie-Thérèse Letablier and Sophie Pennec, pp. 77–85. Loughborough: European Research Centre, Loughborough University.

Newholm, Terry 2005. Case studying ethical consumers' projects and strategies. In *The ethical consumer* (eds) Rob Harrison, T. Newholm and Deidrea Shaw, pp. 107–24. London: Sage.

Nyugat.hu 2007. Magyar karácsonyt magyar ajándékokkal! Szombathely, Hungary: Nyugat Média és Világháló Egyesület. www.nyugat.hu/tartalom/cikk/31760_magyar_karacsonyt_magyar_ajandekokkal

Pratt, Jeff 2007. Food values: the local and the authentic. *Critique of Anthropology* 27: 285–300.

Sassatelli, Roberta 2007. *Consumer culture: history, theory and politics.* Los Angeles: Sage.

Soper, Kate 2007. Re-thinking the 'good life': the citizenship dimension of consumer disaffection with consumerism. *Journal of Consumer Culture* 7: 205–29.

Szente, V. 2004. Organikus élelmiszerek fogyasztási és vásárlási szokásainak vizsgálata Magyarországon. *Élelmiszer, táplálkozás és marketing* 1: 101–6. taplalkozasmarketing.hu/old/2004/food-nutrition-marketing-2004-12-Szente.pdf

TVE (Tudatos Vásárlók Egyesülete) n.d.a. A tudatos vásárló 12 pontja. Budapest: TVE. tudatosvasarlo.hu/12pont.html

——— n.d.b. *Alapszabály.* www.tve.hu/celjaink

Chapter 6

CRITICAL CONSUMPTION IN PALERMO: IMAGINED SOCIETY, CLASS AND FRACTURED LOCALITY

Giovanni Orlando

Historically in Palermo we've been a dominated people. Sometimes I see it also in our times. It seems to me we've really been changed in our DNA, we're very passive.

(Martina, 41, social worker)

I think that my shopping is worth a lot more as critical consumption than my voting. With my actions I do a lot more than simply with my vote. Because what am I doing with my voting? I'm delegating: 'you deal with it for me'. With my actions I'm doing something in that moment.

(Lorenzo, 36, salesman)

This chapter draws on anthropological perspectives to explore 'critical consumption' – as ethical consumption is known in Italy – in Palermo, a city in Sicily that is very different from the areas in Italy farther to the north that Cristina Grasseni describes elsewhere in this volume. It considers some of the shared characteristics of ethical consumption in the city, and especially the consumption of organic foods and what I call fair trade, which includes things certified by the Fairtrade Labelling Organization (referred to as Fairtrade in this volume) as well as things certified or traded by other fair-trade organisations, commonly called Alternative Trade Organisations. I elaborate on Palermo ethical consumption by examining why organic and fair-trade goods are identified by shoppers as valuable sites for critical consumption. I explore these issues by asking two, closely related questions: what do those who practice critical consumption in Palermo think it is for, and who do they think it is for?

Adopting a framework inspired by Mauss's (2002 [1925]) theory of exchange, fair-trade and organic shopping in Palermo can be interpreted as a current way for middle-class citizens to widen the circle of their desired society through the circulation of these ethical commodities. When they exchange these objects among family through household provisioning and among friends through formal gifts, these people's moral concerns, attached to those objects, circulate with them. In this sense, then, buying 'critically' makes their polity, largely conceived of as 'the city' (which they thought of in strongly negative terms), a better place. During conversations, in fact, they consistently set the values they perceived to be embodied in fair-trade and organic foods against the negative ones they considered to be dominant in Palermo's social, political and economic life. This answers my first question, what these people think ethical consumption is for.

This engagement with the local milieu can be viewed as a particular instance, with broadly political overtones, of a process by which consumers subsume objects commonly seen as bearing the marks of far-away ethics within a close-by morality (Miller 2001a; see the discussion in Dombos, this volume). Both fair-trade and organic agriculture are usually seen as dealing with fairly distant domains: the developing South with its marginalised producers in the former case, 'the environment' or the rural places where food is grown in the latter. In my case study, close-by morality was framed by a perception of the city as an imagined community. Together with some of the points Tamás Dombos (this volume) makes, this raises questions about the distinction Miller makes between the near, the realm of moral shopping, and the distant, the realm of ethical shopping.

This is a distinctive instance of political engagement in shopping. When explicitly asked, Palermo's ethical shoppers commonly referred to consumer power as a tool for advancing social change, as being one of the last avenues of action, of power, left today to people. This aspect can also be partly interpreted as reflecting the inherent power of exchange to produce and reproduce social relations. However, given the contemporaneous origins of fair-trade and organic farming and of neoliberalism, it also inevitably raises the question of the validity of the neoliberal ideology that sees market exchange, and thus consumer sovereignty, as capable of providing a solution to almost any problem. No study of ethical consumption can, therefore, ignore the ways that contemporary politicoeconomic patterns, themselves shaped by neoliberal policies, mediate individuals' (class-based) perceptions of the social effects of their purchasing power.

Following some of Bourdieu's (1984) suggestions, and as described in this volume's Introduction, the comparisons expressed by Palermo's middle-class ethical shoppers between their own consumption choices and those of other people pointed to complex processes of distinction (see also Isenhour, this volume). On the one hand, their shopping habits were set apart from those of people perceived as belonging to their own class or higher. In this case there was a shared opinion that ethical consumption is 'a matter of choice' that 'everyone' simply 'has to make', with income not being a factor taken into account (see the case of Veronika, in Dombos, this volume). Given the Maussian insight that these people's consumption is linked to their desire to extend their ideal of a better society, I suggest this form of distinction may partly be the result of what appears to be the declining social trajectory of the class fraction of the people in question.

On the other hand, when people described the shopping habits of those who were perceived as belonging to a lower class, two alternative discourses emerged. Some people saw economic status as a limiting factor, and so saw consuming critically as an impossible option for the poor, given the higher prices of organic and fair-trade foods. Others saw ethical consumption among poor people the same way that they saw it among those higher up the scale, as a matter of personal or 'cultural' choice, independent of economic circumstances. People who held this view tended to describe working-class consumption in negative terms. These findings clearly point to the role of class in determining the possibility of shoppers' engagement with ethical consumption's symbolic construction of economy and place. They also suggest a common erasure, for different reasons and in different ways, of the question of class inequality from the way these critical consumers perceive the applicability of the moral economies that they valued. This answers my second question, who do these people think ethical consumption is for?

With these two questions, this chapter can be considered as an extension to Palermo of the comparison sketched in this volume's Introduction between ethical consumption's goals, means and agents, in order to reveal what is contained in this idea of the relationship between economy and society. It does this, however, in terms of a set of people whose location is very different from what is taken to be the common location of ethical consumption, urban residents of core capitalist regions. Palermo is not such a place. Because the values of ethical consumption are likely to be shaped by the social situation of those who practise them, the city's ethical consumers see that consumption in unexpected ways: not only as a means to bring sociality or sustainability into economy, but also as a response to perceived dependency and political disempowerment.

The remainder of this chapter is structured as follows. In the next section I describe how the idea of ethical consumption is deployed in my analysis. I then continue with a brief overview of the phenomenon in Italy. This is followed by my ethnographic analysis. That analysis is based on data collected through participant observation, and 17 semi-structured qualitative interviews with 23 individuals (in some cases couples). Interviewees were contacted through network sampling, starting from a shop where I carried out participant observation, and moving away from it to include also various organised groups of critical consumers known as 'fair-purchase groups' (*gruppi di acquisto solidale*).[1] The people I describe, then, are not representative of Palermo ethical consumers; they are a set of these who illustrate one particular way in which the decision to shop ethically was shaped by local circumstance.

Reflecting on Ethical Consumption: History, Anthropology, Morality

A look at recent Anglophone studies reveals the many definitions of what might be considered similar phenomena: alternative consumption (Bryant and

Goodman 2004); sustainable consumption (Cohen and Murphy 2001); ethical or moral consumption (De Neve, Luetchford and Pratt 2008); political and ethical consumerism (Klintman and Boström 2006); political consumerism (Micheletti, Follesdal and Stolle 2004); 'green' or 'red' shopping (Miller 2001*a*). Clearly, ethical consumption is a slippery matter. Because small changes in naming something often stem from important differences in the way it is conceptualised, a working definition is useful here.

I define ethical consumption as the purchasing of goods, together with their consumption in complex webs of socioecological practices and imaginaries (Goodman and Goodman 2001), imbued with positive values aimed at reducing the economy's harm to humans or the environment. Klintman and Boström (2006: 401) provide a useful summary:

> Social, cultural, animal-related and environmental concerns that go beyond the immediate self-interests of the individual consumer or household. ... Consumer cultures, trends, the flows of raw materials and refined products keep travelling around the world in increasingly complex – and sometimes puzzling – ways. The debates, policies and practices surrounding these flows are the main bases for 'political and ethical consumerism'.

In the past decade or so, a body of scholarship has been developing, dealing with different phenomena that broadly fall within a definition of ethical consumption like the one just offered. Among such scholarship, the works that are of relevance to the argument developed in this chapter are those framing ethical consumption with respect to the gift (e.g., Luetchford 2008; Lyon 2006; Rajak 2009) and neoliberalism (e.g., Dolan 2007; Fridell 2007; Tallontire 2006).

I do not mean ethical consumption to be a neutral label, for it refers to phenomena embodying values that we consider, at least in principle, as positive ones. As Sayer (2000: 101) notes, 'critical social science require[s] critical, implicitly normative assessments of actors' accounts'. With the demise of radical political economy and the rise of poststructuralism, all normative assessment tends to be rejected a priori, 'thus undermining any basis for opposing the status quo' (2000: 100). Criticism, of economy in the case of ethical consumption or of ethical consumption itself in the case of an anthropological analysis, requires the idea of a more desirable, normatively better, alternative. Ethical consumption tries to engage with such an idea, and so should we. Of course, as anthropologists we have to acknowledge the pluralism of framings leaving open what actors include in 'positive' or 'negative' consumption, rather than use predefined categories of right and wrong (e.g., Greenberg 2004).[2] But as concerned individuals we should also not avoid broadly political engagement (Shukaitis and Graeber 2007). There is no reason to view research either as 'a site where academics can demonstrate their stance towards the world [or as] a place where the world stands as a potential empirical critique of our own assumptions about it' (Miller 2001*b*: 226); it can be both.

In the Introduction to this volume, ethical consumption is presented as a distinctive response to changes in economy and society that have been occurring for a long time. I will sketch these changes before turning to the ways that ethical consumption is a distinctive response to them.

Since labour, land and money have been commodified under market conditions (Polanyi 2001 [1944]), the economising mentality central to these shifts in social formation can appear as totalising. However, profit and commodification are not all-encompassing, and even in Western societies exchanges inspired by reciprocity are still central (Graeber 2001). Anthropology has shown how acts of consumption that appear selfish can be aimed at creating webs of affective relations, when commodities are put back in society by being given to, and used by, family or friends (Carrier 1995: 145–89; Miller 1998). This can be considered a result of human beings' broader moral economy. Re-inscribing the term in a century-old tradition from Durkheim (1984 [1893]) to Polanyi (1957), Sayer (2000: 79) defines moral economy as 'the ways in which economic activities – in the broad sense – are influenced by moral-political norms and sentiments', and notes how 'all economies – *including* so-called laissez-faire ones – are embedded in particular cultures'.

Ethical consumption differs from the ordinary kind in some important ways. Firstly, it is concerned with the broader negative effects of the economy on society and nature, which is not the same as the concern for one's household and friends that is part of ordinary consumption (see Miller 2001*a*: 111–44; the discussion in Dombos, this volume). Secondly, ethical and ordinary consumption each socialise commodities in different realms. For ordinary consumption, that socialisation occurs through the effort of choice and the use of the item purchased in social relationships. For ethical consumption, that socialisation occurs in the realm of production itself, through the effects of the signalling system (see Introduction, this volume). Thirdly, the socialisation in ordinary consumption is largely implicit, an unspoken consequence of provisioning the household. On the other hand, that socialisation is an explicit goal of ethical consumption, as illustrated in Peter Luetchford's (this volume) description of fair-trade coffee. Given that moral economy is concerned with 'norms and sentiments regarding the responsibilities and rights of individuals' that go from 'matters of justice and equality, to conceptions of the good ... [including] the treatment of the environment' (Sayer 2000: 79), then we can see ethical consumption as making one aspect of moral economy its particular, explicit concern (see Figure 6.1).

Critical Consumption in Palermo: Ethnographic Explorations

Italy is fertile ground for exploring ethical consumption, because it exhibits the entire range of those debates and practices surrounding 'social, cultural, animal-related and environmental concerns' mentioned above (e.g., Bovone

Figure 6.1. Ethical consumption as a subset of broader social and historical processes

and Mora 2007; some of these are illustrated in Grasseni, this volume). And because my concern is to keep the analysis close to its context of origin (Eriksen 2006), henceforth I will refer to 'critical consumption' (*consumo critico*), the term most commonly used in Palermo, and in Italy generally. I will start by situating Palermo in the broader Italian context of fair-trade and organic consumption. Very similar patterns emerge for both.

Recent national data (ISMEA 2005, 2007) show that the typical organic shopper lives in Italy's north-west (41 per cent; 9 per cent in the south), is a woman (83 per cent) aged between 35 and 44 (26 per cent), with secondary or university education in almost two-thirds of cases. With regard to income (Berardini et al. 2006), 35 per cent get between €1,680 and €2,480 per month (about $2,000–$3,000 and £1,100–£1,700 at the time), and 40 per cent get more. In Palermo, a set of four surveys of organic shoppers showed that they have a median age of 41–45 years; a median education of high school in two of the surveys and university in the other two; a household size of three; and median household income of €1,500 (about $1,800, £1,000) in two surveys and of €3,500 (about $4,200, £2,400) in the other two (Asciuto et al. 2003). With regards to fair trade, the typical shopper lives in the north of Italy (53 per cent), is a woman (55 per cent) between 35 and 44 years old, and has secondary (46 per cent) or university (43 per cent) education; she works as an employee, teacher or researcher (48.9 per cent), and has a monthly income of €1,501–€4,000 (about $1,800–$4,850, £1,200–£2,700) (61 per cent) (Manca and Vargiu 2007: 52). Unfortunately, there is no detailed information on fair-trade consumption in Sicily or Palermo.

Although the organic movement emerged before fair trade in Italy, as in the rest of the industrialised world, there is evidence that fair trade has been the driving force behind the diffusion in Italy of critical consumption's discourse, if not of its practice. In fact, from a commodity-network perspective the two initiatives function in very similar ways (Raynolds 2000), particularly with regard to consumption. However, the organic movement, apart from a relatively small fringe, lacks the emphasis on broader social transformation, a broader political connotation that is a distinguishing characteristic of Italian fair trade (Guadagnucci and Gavelli 2004; Grasseni, this volume; Vankeerberghen, this volume).

My ethnography of critical consumers in Sicily's regional capital is divided into three parts. In the first, I give examples of the negative perceptions of their polity that were widespread among my informants, focussing on opinions about the general quality of urban life, about the social system of patronage and about local right-wing politics and corruption, all closely linked to each other. In the second section I discuss the belief, widely held among the people I met, that their purchases gave them the power to change things, though they often regarded such power as an unfulfilled potential. In the final part I explore a particular instance of the previous discourse, the relevance of critical consumption for the city's different social strata. Because this study focuses on middle-class citizens' perceptions of Palermo, I provide a sketch of the city's stratification before introducing those I spoke with about these issues.

Palermo, which has been deeply affected by Italy's unequal development (Trigilia 1992), can be considered a hypertrophied tertiary city typical of the country's south (Crisantino 1990). Land reform, investments in industry and welfare services, and shifts in consumer preferences after the Second World War triggered migrations from Sicily's rural inland towards the city. However, Palermo never developed into a true industrial centre, instead becoming dependent for employment on the national government's funding of public-sector jobs. Although some of these socioeconomic and political features of the 1960s and 1970s have persisted to the present day, one local critic (Butera 2007: 191) has argued that 'our city has undergone a deep process of social transformation'. This is especially true of the city's economy and its once supposedly dominant public-sector workers (Chubb 1982), who are now part of a broader, more diversified middle class 'on which we basically have little information' (Butera 2007: 97).[3]

The 2001 general census (Comune di Palermo 2007) shows that 2 per cent of those in the labour market are employed in agriculture and fishing, 11 per cent in industry and 87 per cent in services. The census does not, however, tell much about Palermo's stratification, as it classifies the population into categories of 'entrepreneurs and professionals' (8 per cent; hereafter 'bourgeoisie'), 'public and private sector employees' (79 per cent) and 'self-employed individuals' (11 per cent). This classification does not distinguish between the middle class and the working class (referred to locally as *classi popolari*, 'popular classes'), which is markedly heterogeneous. It makes up the 'majority of the urban population' (Cole 1997: 28) and encompasses blue-collar workers, the poorest among the self-employed, the formally unemployed (29 per cent of the active population in 2001) and all those who are not officially seeking employment (Chubb 1982; Cole 1997: 27–32; see also Mingione 1988). What distinguishes these groups from the middle class is their very low and discontinuous income (Guarrasi 1978).

On the basis of their employment, two of the critical consumers I interviewed belonged to the bourgeoisie, the rest to the middle class; about two-thirds relied on some form of public-sector job (broadly defined, e.g., employee, teacher, doctor, researcher, public-service journalist). Those I spoke with were aged between 29 and 53 years, overwhelmingly women, often married and with children. Thus 'household provisioning', or shopping for the family (see DeVault 1991), was the wider context of their ethical shopping. Part of this provisioning was carried out at a small, cooperative–run shop that sold fair-trade and organic foods, both fresh (fruits and vegetables) and processed (e.g., pasta, breakfast items, snacks, etc.); another part involved two fair-purchase groups. One of these groups relied on the shop itself for organising a weekly vegetable box. Its members mostly belonged to an informal religious group involved in the local anti-war movement. The other group was entirely self-managed, dealing directly with wholesalers and producers, its original members coming from a far-left party.

Although their backgrounds differ, these critical consumers shared a genealogy – material for the older ones, symbolic for the younger – with Palermo's 'political' generation, which grew up with the anti-Mafia movement of the late 1980s. This was inspired by 'a loose set of universalizing values that include gender equality, human rights, and respect for the environment' (Schneider and Schneider 2003: 216), which at the time represented the blossoming of new, progressive values largely drawn from continental Europe's cultural milieu. Such values are largely compatible with what Palermo's critical consumers saw embodied in fair-trade and organic farming, as well as in the two fair-purchase groups: justice, responsibility towards people or nature, altruism, sustainability, 'caring' and so forth.

All in all, the individuals I met were ordinary, not noticeably interested in the markedly alternative ways of life found among some of those described by Dombos (this volume). They were new and old couples, often with children, working five days a week. They regularly shopped also at conventional retailers. In fact, almost all informants preferred shopping as close as possible either to their home or their workplace. For some, therefore, frequenting the ethical shop meant travelling farther away than they would have done normally. In the words of one of them:

> It's sad that this thing [critical consumption] should remain an ideological one, I mean it's something that appears to make you very modern, very informed, very intellectual, but that's nonsense! We've got the kids, we have to feed them, we have to eat ourselves, we're already stressed with the life we have. (Martina, 41, social worker)

The Circle of Society ... or the Archipelago?

Mauss's (2002 [1925]) point, that when objects are given they are never completely detached from the giver, means that when things circulate, social relationships are created and altered. From this perspective, the buying and giving of ethical goods is a way of fostering an ethical polity, because the values and sentiments of those who purchased them remain attached to these goods as they circulate. They are thus a means of widening the imagined circle of people's desired society. This was clearly the case for the critical consumers I met in Palermo, who shopped mainly with reference to gift transactions within their households, in the shape of the food bought for it during family shopping.[4]

Spreading their ethical values was important for these people, but also difficult. In our conversations, in fact, their actions often appeared as islands in a city marked by competition, corruption, inefficiency and resignation.[5] If we are to understand these people's beliefs about the importance of critical consumption, then, we need to understand how they saw Palermo.

Many of those I interviewed stressed how they felt alone in their shopping choices, surrounded by people who were indifferent to their values, not only friends and colleagues, but often also family members. Their sense of being alone is illustrated by statements like: 'If people know about it they say "good, you're doing a good thing", but then they don't modify their behaviour and keep buying as usual' or 'When I talk about my experience, they tell me "well done, it's a good thing", and then they change the subject of the conversation'. That sense was illustrated also by the ways people used 'difficult' when they talked about Palermo itself (*Palermo è difficile*), living in the city (*vivere qui è difficile*) or the general 'context' (*questo è un contesto difficile*). Often, these references conflated experiences of the social environment with that of the material one, many people seeing the deterioration of the latter as a function of the deterioration of the former.

> There's no idea of what environmental sustainability is. I've got the impression that by now the only thing that guides processes in our society in Palermo is the logic of profit, period. I mean there isn't even that capacity which I believe in other places, in other cities of the north [of Italy], there has been: the logic of profit can also include paths that don't destroy, don't cut the branch on which you're sitting. This idea just doesn't exist here: everyone is intent on cutting the branch on which they're sitting. (Gabriella, 50, doctor)

Given their age, education and political affiliation, the people in question were acutely conscious of the history that brought about the radical transformation of Palermo's social, economic and built environments, which a local human geographer once described as 'hyper-urbanization' (Guarrasi 1981). In the 1950s and 1960s, the agricultural belt surrounding Palermo was almost completely cemented over, without regard for planning regulations (La Duca 1994). Repeated disregard for building permits, zoning instruments, height limits and restrictions on the conversion of public land to private property, all gave rise to the present chaotic city. This is characterised by the fourth highest population density in Italy, inadequate services and infrastructures (especially those for mass transport) and a lack of green spaces.[6] At the same time, the old city and its inhabitants were left to decay. Palermo's people express their view of this change in their common name for it, *lo scempio* ('the disgrace'). The consumers I talked to thought the same.

The taking over of the construction boom by the dominant Christian Democratic party and by the Mafia, for electoral purposes and money laundering (with frequent overlaps), was basis for the city's poor development. It also reflected and strengthened Palermo's sociopolitical system of class relations: patronage or clientelism (*clientelismo*) (Chubb 1982). Clientelistic systems are based on forms of unequal exchange between two parties linked by dyadic ties, often characterised by the idioms of friendship and fictive kinship. Inequality, both economic and sociocultural, is key in explaining how patronage works (Gellner and Waterbury 1977). This is particularly true in Palermo, where people's social location made them more or less able to gain access to resources. This has perpetuated bad governance. As Jeffrey Cole (1997: 31) writes: 'Several consequences of the patronage system merit attention … generally poor and selectively provided services; a bloated, inefficient, and corrupt bureaucracy; a deteriorating historic center; unregulated urbanization; inadequate infrastructure'. Appropriately, the financial newspaper *Il Sole 24 Ore* (2008), in its annual assessment of the nation's best cities, ranked Palermo at 101 out of 102.

In their comparisons between the traits they saw in the local polity and the values they perceived in fair-trade and organic goods, the consumers I interviewed often referred to clientelism. In the words of one of them, well-placed to comment:

> My experience of working in the public administration is devastating. Because all the bad things you can think of from the outside, all the stereotypes, are nothing compared to what these places are in reality, where nothing exists which isn't – I don't mean meritocracy, that's science fiction – but not even the saving of human and economic resources. There are no rules, no laws that govern the functioning of these places, they are left to the initiative of the single councillor or director and are without any logic, sense of purpose, medium-term outlook, long term would again be science fiction. It's really depressing. (Fabrizio, 38, public employee)

For almost half a century, the Christian Democratic party was the core of this system, promoting it through its administration of national development funds. The party was extensively infiltrated by the Mafia, which linked clientelism and organised crime and led critical consumers, with their anti-Mafia heritage, to despise the centre-right political parties. This disgust continues, and today they oppose the coalition headed by *Forza Italia*, the party of the media owner and politician Silvio Berlusconi. It has dominated the region's politics since 1994

(Padrut 2007) and is perceived as the current party of patronage. One shopper told me: 'We suffer an administration that's what it is, which instead of making things better makes them difficult – we're already difficult in ourselves – I reach a point when I think: there's no hope!'. Another critical consumer explained:

> Superficially one would say [the city] has what it deserves, and what it wants after all, because what it wants is to satisfy certain personal interests it gives priority to, not giving any priority to the common interest. Why? Because the common interest isn't perceived as useful to one's personal benefit. Quite often this reason is linked to the knowledge that this type of political class and of administration can guarantee you in the future certain things, which in the end are mainly individual privileges. (Gianpietro, 34, university researcher)

Power and Place: The Economy as Tool

The linking of place to ethical economic values that I have described bears on what Daniel Miller (2001a: 111–44) has said about ethical consumption. Writing specifically about 'Green' shopping, he distinguishes between ethics, altruistic concern for distant others, and morality, concern for good and bad in one's own life (2001a: 133). He argues that ethical shopping faces an almost insurmountable contradiction. The consumer's moral concern for her household and friends, largely expressed by the ideal of thrift, can not be reconciled with the ethics of organic goods, which are relatively expensive. He notes (2001a: 137) that 'interest in Green or organic foods and other such concerns could be experienced not as a sign of the ethical depth of the shopper but as a sign that the shopper is more concerned to express their self-indulgent "issues"'.

As mentioned before, Palermo's critical consumers saw the values embodied in fair-trade and organic goods as about the opposite of what they saw as prevalent in their city. This seems to contradict Miller on the impossibility of bridging economic ethics and economic morality when practising shopping (see also Dombos, this volume; Vramo, this volume). The individuals I spoke with constantly appeared to subsume fair-trade's and organic's general (far-away) values with the close-by experiences of their lives: if not their immediate household then their immediate community, such as peers or workplace colleagues, who they thought part of a problematic polity.[7]

The critical shoppers viewed consumer power as a tool for social change, albeit in varying degrees. Some were very positive, others quite disillusioned. Overall, though, they saw the purchasing of fair-trade and organic goods as an action 'that can change things'. Key to the present argument were those instances in which such a general position was couched directly in terms of everyday political engagement. An example will illustrate this.

> I think today consumption is one of the things in which you can involve people who perhaps aren't available to go to meetings anymore, or to do the revolution, but who with their choices can make a difference. Individual choices are choices

that weigh on everyone's reality. Consumer choices are among these, and you can do politics also in this way. (Gabriella, 50, doctor)

Such 'politics' were largely of an oppositional nature, critiquing various aspects of capitalism.[8] At the same time, though, they were perceived by informants as detached from actual party politics, and consciously placed in realms of life considered extraneous to established political endeavours (this was the meaning of Gabriella's point about people not wanting to go to meetings).

Judith Chubb (1982: 98) has argued that conventional theories of patronage do not explain Palermo's social milieu, where the system 'works less through the distribution of benefits to all-comers than through the astute management of *scarcity*'. While scarcity is more of an issue for the city's popular classes, the middle class is also involved in patronage, though the manner of its involvement differs and its members manage to escape the more severe forms of clientelism. Cole (1997: 31) says that for the middle class, clientelism involves an exchange of favours (for jobs, promotions, bureaucratic mediation etc.), whilst for the poor it involves food, cash and job *promises*. This means the critical consumers whose values lead them to reject what they see as a 'culture' underpinning the city's patronage system, are still dependent on it to some degree. Their belief, sometimes hope, in the effect of consumer power can be interpreted as a reaction to the disillusionment and political disaffection engendered by their uncomfortable position. Perhaps more poignantly, they see themselves surrounded by people who do not view this as problematic. 'I see the *palermitano* [inhabitant of Palermo], he's the kind used to being the colonised, he's really colonised from all points of view, cultural, economic. He's got no freedom of thought. He's strong with the weak and weak with the strong' (Fabrizio, 38, public employee). And again:

> Yes, the *palermitano* is a colonised sort, but in a distinctive way. He has a strange receptivity, only for the worst that the coloniser can give him. If you see the behaviour on the street, in the traffic, at the Regional Government headquarters, et cetera, he has taken up precisely everything bad that can exist in a modern reality. (Viviana – Fabrizio's partner, 29, private-sector employee)

In some instances, though not that often, this feeling of disillusionment was contrasted with how people thought things are in the north of Italy:

> This summer I went on holiday with some people from Bergamo and Milan. And they were saying the worst stuff about the situation there, and I got really disappointed, I told them, 'How do you mean? You're taking even this hope away from me, I think of you as a civilised place.' … Anyway, I'm actually not convinced that it's like they say. In my view we truly hit rock bottom. (Brigida, 48, teacher)

I have said that both the fair-trade and the organic movements developed at the same time as the onset of neoliberalism in industrialised nations (Simmonds 1995), arguably as a response to that onset (De Neve, Luetchford and Pratt 2008). Making sense of what people say about the effects of consumer power, then, entails considering the degree to which the neoliberal ideology that sees the market as the solution to virtually everything has influenced the idea that shoppers have the capacity to ameliorate the social landscape (Johnston 2008). Considering that means understanding how contemporary politicoeconomic arrangements, still largely framed by neoliberalism, affect the new social movements, of which critical consumption is an example. What is the class position of those Palermitan citizens who feel disaffected by things Sicilian, and who turn to critical consumption as an avenue of action?

Perceiving the Local(s) through Critical Consumption

I have described the ways that critical consumers think about Palermo's polity at the level of imagined community. Those thoughts, however, are held by a specific section of the urban citizenry. Paradoxically, if Palermo has any underlying feature, it is that of being unequal and fractured. Thus, the final part of this exploration of critical consumption in the city dwells on how class sometimes acted as a factor shaping people's perceptions of different sections of urban polity, and hence the distinctions that they made between them.

During the course of the research, people often spoke in ways that resembled what Bourdieu (1984) describes of the relationship between class and processes of distinction. Individuals never talked explicitly about good or bad 'taste' (*buono/cattivo gusto*). Rather, they expressed 'judgement' (as in 'evaluation' or 'appraisal') through their discussions of why people from different classes did or did not engage in critical consumption. On the whole, they focused on those who did not engage in it. Such comparisons are an expression of taste in Bourdieu's sense insofar as they indicate that people saw a correspondence between classes of products and classes of consumers. This suggests that the model Bourdieu developed in *Distinction* might help us to understand aspects of critical consumption in Palermo.

Three outcomes are relevant here. The first one was unexpected. Although my initial focus was on those lower down the social hierarchy,[9] people spontaneously compared themselves with those whom they saw as being their class equals, and occasionally their superiors. A second result was how often people said things similar to 'I have a lot of difficulty finding points of reference in this city', such as friends, friendly colleagues, role models and the like. Finally, people appeared to possess their own approximate classifications of class structure in Palermo. These involved three layers: 'the rich people' (*le gente ricca*) on top, always seen as clearly different from the speaker; then the speaker's own class, sometimes referred to as 'those like me' (*quelli come me*) or 'the middle class' (*il ceto medio*); and at the bottom, almost invariably the periphrasis 'the inhabitants of popular neighbourhoods' (*gli abitanti dei quartieri popolari*).

I will consider first what people said about their class equals and superiors. Those I spoke to claimed that 'the problem' with the middle class, the absence of critical consumption, was 'a cultural one' (*un problema culturale*) or one 'of sensitivity' (*di sensibilità*) to the values in question. Typically, then, people ignored income as a factor, saying that ethical consumption is only 'a matter of choice' that 'everyone' just 'has to make'.

> I haven't got less money than a lot of other people, but I live in a house with a lot less furniture and which is a lot less beautiful, because clearly I spend money on organic, on books. … These are things that cost, so I can't afford other stuff. I have to make some choices. In the middle class there's a lot of difference between those who invest in a property [*nel mattone*] or in clothes, and those who invest in health. Apart from diet, health is something that I allow myself, but I don't spend money on jewellery. I haven't got jewellery. Many of my colleagues have a lot of jewellery. (Brigida, 48, teacher)

Most of these comments were made about class equals, rather than superiors. Following Bourdieu, it may be that people belonging to a fraction of Palermo's middle class that is declining relative to similar fractions react by distinguishing themselves through critical consumption.

Bourdieu (1984: 101) has argued that to understand taste as a product of class, one has to first identify 'the set of agents who are placed in homogeneous conditions of existence imposing … homogeneous systems of dispositions'. He uses occupation as an indicator of objective class, so that different occupations generate different 'class fractions' within a standard structure of dominant, middle and working classes. However, fractions are not defined only by occupation. They are also socially constructed 'by the structure of relations between all the pertinent properties which gives its specific value to each of them and to the effects they exert on practices' (1984: 106), which can include a variety of factors, such as sex, age, education, social origin, ethnic origin, political affiliation and religion (1984: 106–9). Their combination allows class fractions and the individuals within them to move in time up or down the social structure.[10] Using this framework, critical consumers belong to Palermo's middle class, often to one of its fractions that relies on state employment. Among the properties that make it a socially constructed class, the most important are arguably those of higher education, cosmopolitan left-wing beliefs, female gender and, perhaps, age.

In her insightful monograph, Chubb wrote (1982: 89):

> Public employees in Palermo have come to constitute the single most important component of the city's social and occupational structure … forming the core of the urban middle class. … The *impiegato* [public employee], in sum, has set the social tone of the city and in large part determined the directions of urban expansion, investment and consumption.

A quarter century has passed since then. Today, the anthropology of Palermo's middle class needs to be updated in the face of new economic and cultural trends. The middle class is no longer so uniform or so bound to employment in the public sector. Private-sector businesses in tourism, transportation, communications, informatics and research have been growing in the city since the mid 1990s (Comune di Palermo 2007: 125). Also, there have been political changes at both the local and national level, such as the diffusion of those progressive, 'European' values linked originally to the anti-Mafia movement (often led by public employees), and the birth of the new centre-right in the 1990s. These have affected the urban cultural milieu, have acted in different ways on various middle-class fractions and so have led to further fragmentation.

The public sector is not, then, a culturally monolithic bloc, if it ever was. Further, considering the low esteem in which public employees are held by Berlusconi's government, it is unlikely to 'set the social tone' any more, regardless of its size. In this context, it is reasonable that people who work for the state are left-wing, opposed to clientelism, feel generally politically disenchanted (perhaps also because of their gender) and perceive their position within the urban polity as declining. Critical consumption would allow them to distinguish themselves favourably from other middle-class fractions.

Ginsborg (2001: 66) has illustrated the emergence since the 1980s of two quite separate middle-class voices for the whole of Italy:

> [One was] heavily concentrated among small entrepreneurs and shopkeepers, was localistic, consumerist, strongly oriented both to self-interest and an overriding work ethic. The other, prevalent among those in education and the social services, in reflexive fringes of the professions and the salariat (all areas where a new female presence had made itself most felt), spoke a different language, not puritan but critical, not rejecting of modern individualist consumption but seeking to place it in a social context. ... The first [one], given the way in which state and economy had developed in Italy, was structurally much stronger than the second, and was destined to triumph, in political terms, at the beginning of the new century.

When critical consumers talked about the lack of fair-trade and organic shopping by members of the lower class (*abitanti dei quartieri popolari*), two views emerged that were generally mutually exclusive. The first, less prevalent, can be called the 'inapplicability argument'. In this view, economic status was seen as limiting their critical consumption because of the relatively high price of organic and fair-trade goods. Buying critically was thus regarded as impossible for the poor, with people typically replying 'that [i.e., working-class life] is another level' or 'that's another story', and also 'they've got other problems'. One person explained:

> There's minimum knowledge in a bourgeois middle class, a tiny amount amongst those who can afford everything, and almost none among the ultra-poor. I can understand the ultra-poor because they have to think about their more immediate lives, after all *they* are exploited *here*. There are problems of poverty which perhaps don't allow them to contemplate consuming something that costs more, maybe they would like to. Perhaps they haven't got enough to live on, so they say, 'First of all I

need to think about myself and then I can think about others'. A person who's got a full stomach can – actually should – take care of others. But how can somebody who has an empty stomach think of feeding someone else? (Lorenzo, 36, salesman)

However, people more often eschewed the inapplicability argument. For them, working-class people did not engage in critical consumption for the same reasons as their middle-class peers. This resulted in negative views of the consumption patterns of *popolari* strata, characterised commonly by statements like, 'They declare they are poor but they have huge cars/a brand new moped/ the latest mobile phone'. For these people, buying fair-trade or organic goods was still viewed as a matter of personal or cultural choice, not economic condition. Even though she recognised that critical consumption did cost more than some could afford, one woman still stressed cultural rather than economic reasons for the failure of the poor to be critical consumers:

> There's still a cultural problem, there's an ideological prevention. I'm definitely convinced that if the person from *Capo* [one of Palermo's historic working-class areas] can get his vegetables in the countryside, he does, because unconsciously he knows they're better than the ones he buys at the shop and come to him from outside. But then he thinks that going to an organic shop costs who knows how much, but he doesn't know because there's a sort of ideological prevention. He would never do it because it would seem to him he's acting like someone who spends money. If the greengrocer round the corner had organic food, and he knew what it was, and he found out it had the same price, I think he would buy it. There's a difficulty in spreading the culture. Because it's obvious that the person living in *Borgo* [another of Palermo's historic working-class areas] shops round the corner. He doesn't go to an organic shop because it would seem too strange to him. (Margherita, 40, journalist)

As mentioned already, the middle classes in Palermo generally escape a scarcity-based clientelism, if not one based on the exchange of favours, and this separates and insulates them from the lives of working-class people. And those lives are very different. Although they are describing the difficulty that the anti-Mafia activists from the middle class had when they tried to secure support from Palermo's working class, what Schneider and Schneider said is apt: 'Working classes are a challenge … not so much because they hold contradictory values as because these values speak to *the precariousness of their lives*' (Schneider and Schneider 2003: 231, emphasis added). Their insulation from working-class lives might help explain the way that many critical consumers perceive working-class consumption and values. This particular domain of consumer activism, then, reveals how 'the silencing of the language of class, not the disappearance of class issues, may be the most significant marker of the "new" social movements of the post-Cold War world' (Schneider and Schneider 2003: 192).

Conclusion

Until recently, fair-trade and organic goods, and the ethical consumption of which they are a part, were largely unknown to the wider public, having previously occupied what one author has aptly called the interstices of globalisation (Renard 1999). They were, as well, largely ignored by anthropologists. However, anthropologists have long dealt with issues that bear on the idea of ethical consumption, such as the interaction of economy with culture and politics, people's responses to power and domination, the place of exchange in the reproduction of society, the dynamics of class ideology. In this chapter I have shown how these classic anthropological interests can help to deepen our understanding of this volume's multifaceted topic.

Another characteristic of anthropology that helps illuminate ethical consumption is the discipline's concern with the time- and place-specific particularities of what is on the 'social ground'. That makes anthropologists especially sensitive to the diversity within ethical consumption. Though it may seem a transnational phenomenon, one should not gloss over its differences in different places, even while recognising the commonalities that exist. So, while ethical consumers try to use economic transactions to shape their world, we need to attend to the ways that their practical cultural and economic circumstances affect how they perceive that world and their consumption, as I have tried to do in this chapter.

I have approached Palermo as an example of ethical consumption within a region still often characterised by economic, cultural and political dependency. As I said previously, Palermo is hardly comparable to cities of equal size found in core capitalist areas. This is not simply because, from an ethnographic point of view, all sites are different. Rather, the question is what gives rise to such differences? Famously, early anthropologists who worked on Sicily adopted the world-systems paradigm and described it as a semi-periphery (Schneider and Schneider 1975). The specific politicoeconomic features of the island's productive base that influenced this interpretation have now largely disappeared, but the reality of the locale as one of modernisation without development has, in part, remained. The actions of those I talked to both reflected this state of affairs and reflected *on* it, for their critical consumption was a rejection of that state. But Palermo's history and political economy did not only motivate ethical consumers. In addition, through the city's class structure, it constrained the ways that this consumption would be practised.

From what I have said, it is clear how fair-trade and organic consumption in Palermo constituted practices of social production and reproduction. At one level, such practices were inspired by contemporary normative concerns for global economic activity, with their common motive of bringing sociality and sustainability into economy. But at another they were refracted through the politics of everyday life of some of its middle-class inhabitants, imbued with feelings of commitment, resistance and longing:

Palermo is a big city, varied … there are all sorts in Palermo. It is a strange city. You can find yourself having some great opportunities, which you wouldn't expect. But living here is very hard! I was one who left, and I came back. Because I didn't like living elsewhere, because I thought it was possible to stay, to give a hand. I belong to a generation that had many dreams, many projects, many idealisms. (Brigida, 48, teacher)

Notes

The data discussed in this chapter is part of my wider ethnography of organic farmers, fair-trade retailers and ethical shoppers, and of the networks they create, in Palermo and western Sicily. Funding for the larger project was provided by the ESRC (award PTA-030-2006-00260) and by the Royal Anthropological Institute (Emslie Horniman Anthropological Scholarship Fund 2006). For their comments on earlier drafts of this chapter, I would like to acknowledge: Catherine Alexander, Victoria Goddard, David Graeber, Keith Hart, Frances Pine, and the PhD seminar group at Goldsmiths College London. All shortcomings are, as usual, only the author's. Finally, I am grateful to Livia Alga for her constant support.

1. These schemes, now fairly common in Italy, are organised by local people to buy ethical commodities through direct channels (see Valera 2005; Grasseni, this volume).
2. Most people identify this discourse of ethical consumption as a positive one, even if they do not necessarily translate it into everyday behaviour.
3. A recent and engaging example of the long-standing North American scholarly tradition on the city (Schneider and Schneider 2003), although dealing directly with the cultural politics of the middle class, appears to have relied on studies of Palermo that still use data from Italy's 1981 general census.
4. Barnett et al. (2005) have recently explored similar dynamics. They propose the concept of 'moral selving' to point out how ethical consumers engage in this type of shopping to try to construct a moral identity consistent with their values and beliefs. Part of this process is achieved through 'educating' family and friends by involving them in the circulation of ethical commodities.
5. The data discussed here was elicited through a question asking 'How do you see your city with respect to the values [of fair-trade and organic agriculture] we have been discussing?'
6. In 2007, the annual report on Italy's urban ecosystems compiled by the environmentalist organisation *Legambiente* placed Palermo 85 out of 103 cities on various sustainability indicators (Legambiente 2007). Another report (Euromobility 2008) on sustainable urban mobility judges it 39 out of 50 large centres.
7. It is worth speculating why my conclusions differ from Miller's. Firstly, my research focused on people whom I knew to be regular buyers of fair-trade and organic goods. Miller, on the other hand, looked at ordinary shoppers. His point about the impossibility of bridging ethics and morals is, thus, based on data from individuals who were not regular ethical consumers. Secondly, my informants were middle class, and apparently better off on average than Miller's. This may have made thrift less important to them, and so made it easier for them to express care for the wider community. Class thus appears to have an important role in determining consumers' engagement with ethical consumption. Thirdly, these differences may reflect the differing ways in which the English and Italians engage practically with public spaces, and thus symbolically with the idea of 'community' (the former leading lives that are more private, more centred on the self and the household) (I thank James Carrier for raising this point).
8. Though I do not discuss it in this chapter, an important feature of the data is the fact that people construed ethical products through the coupling of opposing meanings. They opposed organic and conventional foods to each other as, respectively, healthy and

industrial, natural and risky. They also called upon dualisms of the rural and the urban, past and present. They also distinguished between a just trade, fair-trade, and an unjust one, constituted by globalisation and international exchanges between nations, but also more broadly by all trading that involved 'normal' economic actors.

9. A question already mentioned, 'How do you see your city with respect to the values we've been discussing?' was followed by one roughly phrased: 'Do you think the fact that Palermo has a lot of "popular neighbourhoods" (*quartieri popolari*) may have any influence on this [on the state of things the interviewee had just expressed answering the previous question]?' I emphasised middle-class citizens' opinions of their working-class fellows because I was interested in vertical class distinction. I soon discovered that my informants often were more interested in horizontal distinction.

10. Bourdieu (1984: 107–68) argues at length that the two most important properties of constructed class are cultural and economic capital, but I have found this too deterministic for my analysis (see Caillé 1988).

Bibliography

Asciuto, Antonio, Fabio Fiandaca, Giovanni Guccione and Giorgio Schifani 2003. The retail sector of organic food products: an analysis of overall consumer satisfaction and supply chain management in the main specialised retail outlets in Palermo. Proceedings of the 2nd Workshop on Organic Agriculture (GRAB-IT), Portici (Naples), Italy, 9–10 May.

Barnett, Clive, Paul Cloke, Nick Clarke and Alice Malpass 2005. Consuming ethics: articulating the subjects and spaces of ethical consumption. *Antipode* 37: 23–45.

Berardini, Lucia F., Fabio Ciannavei, Davide Marino and Francesco Spagnuolo 2006. *Lo scenario dell'agricoltura biologica in Italia*. Rome: Instituto Nazionale di Economia Agraria.

Bourdieu, Pierre 1984. *Distinction: a social critique of the judgement of taste*. London: Routledge & Kegan Paul.

Bovone, Laura and Emanuela Mora (eds) 2007. *La spesa responsabile: il consumo biologico e solidale*. Rome: Donzelli Editore.

Bryant, Raymond and Michael Goodman 2004. Consuming narratives: the political ecology of 'alternative' consumption. *Transactions of the Institute of British Geographers* 29: 344–66.

Butera, Salvatore 2007. *La citta sconosciuta*. Palermo: Kalòs.

Caillé, Alain 1988. Critique de Bourdieu. *Cahiers du Laboratoire de Sociologie Anthropologique de l'Université de Caen* 8–9(1): 103–213.

Carrier, James G. 1995. *Gifts and commodities: exchange and Western capitalism since 1700*. London: Routledge.

Chubb, Judith 1982. *Patronage, power, and poverty in southern Italy: a tale of two cities*. Cambridge: Cambridge University Press.

Cohen, Maurie J. and Joseph Murphy (eds) 2001. *Exploring sustainable consumption: environmental policy and the social sciences*. Oxford: Pergamon.

Cole, Jeffrey 1997. *The new racism in Europe: a Sicilian ethnography*. Cambridge: Cambridge University Press.

Comune di Palermo 2007. *Panormus: annuario di statistica del comune di Palermo*. Palermo: Comune di Palermo.

Crisantino, Amelia 1990. *La città spugna: Palermo nella ricerca sociologica.* Palermo: Centro siciliano di documentazione Giusepppe Impastato.

De Neve, Geert, Peter G. Luetchford and Jeff Pratt 2008. Introduction: revealing the hidden hands of global market exchange. In *Hidden hands in the market: ethnographies of fair trade, ethical consumption and corporate social responsibility* (eds) G. De Neve, P.G. Luetchford, J. Pratt and Donald C. Wood. *Research in Economic Anthropology* 28 (special issue): 1–30.

De Neve, Geert, Peter G. Luetchford, Jeff Pratt and Donald C. Wood (eds) 2008. *Hidden hands in the market: ethnographies of fair trade, ethical consumption and corporate social responsibility. Research in Economic Anthropology* 28 (special issue).

DeVault, Marjorie L. 1991. *Feeding the family: the social organization of caring as gendered work.* Chicago: University of Chicago Press.

Dolan, Catherine 2007. Market affections: moral encounters with Kenyan fair trade flowers. *Ethnos* 72: 239–61.

Durkheim, Èmile 1984 [1893]. *The division of labour in society.* (W.D. Halls, trans.) Basingstoke: Macmillan.

Eriksen, Thomas 2006. *Engaging anthropology: the case for a public presence.* Oxford: Berg.

Euromobility 2008. *La mobilità sostenibile in Italia.* Rome: Euromobility. www.euromobility.org/Conferenza_Stampa/50_città_08.pdf

Fridell, Gavin 2007. *Fair trade coffee: the prospects and pitfalls of market driven social change.* Toronto: University of Toronto Press.

Gellner, Ernest and John Waterbury 1977. *Patrons and clients in Mediterranean societies.* London: Duckworth.

Ginsborg, Paul 2001. *Italy and its discontents: 1980–2001.* London: Allen Lane.

Goodman, David and Michael Goodman 2001. Sustaining foods: organic consumption and the socio-ecological imaginary. In *Exploring sustainable consumption: environmental policy and the social sciences* (eds) Maurie J. Cohen and Joseph Murphy, pp. 97–120. Oxford: Pergamon.

Graeber, David 2001. *Toward an anthropological theory of value: the false coin of our own dreams.* New York: Palgrave.

Greenberg, Cheryl 2004. Political consumer action: some cautionary notes from African-American history. In *Politics, products, and markets* (eds) Michele Micheletti, Andreas Føllesdal. and Dietlind Stolle, pp. 63–82. New Brunswick, NJ: Transaction Publishers.

Guadagnucci, Lorenzo and Fabio Gavelli 2004. *La crisi di crescita: le prospettive del commercio equo e solidale.* Milan: Feltrinelli.

Guarrasi, Vincenzo 1978. *La condizione marginale.* Palermo: Sellerio.

———— 1981. *La produzione dello spazio urbano.* Palermo: Flaccovio.

Il Sole 24 Ore 2008. *Qualità della vita 2008.* Milan: Il Sole 24 Ore. www.ilsole24ore.com/speciali/qv_2008/qv_2008_province/qv_2008_province_settori_classifica_finale.shtml

ISMEA (Instituto di Servizi per il Mercato Agricolo Alimentare) 2005. *L'evoluzione del mercato delle produzioni biologiche.* Rome: ISMEA.

———— 2007. *Il mercato dei prodotti biologici: le tendenze generali e nelle principali filiere.* Rome: ISMEA.

Johnston, Josée 2008. The citizen-consumer hybrid: ideological tensions and the case of Whole Foods Market. *Theory and Society* 37: 229–70.

Klintman, Mikael and Magnus Böstrom (eds) 2006. Editorial. In *Political and ethical consumerism around the world* (eds) M. Klintman and M. Böstrom. *International Journal of Consumer Studies* 30 (special issue): 401–4.

La Duca, Rosario 1994. *Palermo ieri e oggi: la città*. Palermo: Sigma Edizioni.

Legambiente 2007. *Ecosistema urbano*. Rome: Legambiente. www.legambiente.eu/ documenti/2006/0926_ecosistemaUrbano2007/ecosistemaUrbano2007.pdf

Luetchford, Peter G. 2008. The hands that pick fair trade coffee: beyond the charms of the family farm. In *Hidden hands in the market: ethnographies of fair trade, ethical consumption and corporate social responsibility* (eds) G. De Neve, P.G. Luetchford, J. Pratt and Donald C. Wood. *Research in Economic Anthropology* 28 (special issue): 143–69.

Lyon, Sarah 2006. Evaluating fair trade consumption: politics, defetishization and producer participation. *International Journal of Consumer Studies* 30: 452–64.

Manca, Gavina and Andrea Vargiu 2007. Il consumo equo e solidale: impegno, distinzione, pratiche relazionali. In *La spesa responsabile: il consumo biologico e solidale* (eds) Laura Bovone and Emanuele Mora, pp. 31–55. Rome: Donzelli Editore.

Mauss, Marcel 2002 [1925]. *The gift*. London: Routledge.

Micheletti, Michele, Andreas Follesdal and Dietlind Stolle (eds) 2004. *Politics, products, and markets: exploring political consumerism past and present*. New Brunswick, NJ: Transaction Publishers.

Miller, Daniel 1998. *A theory of shopping*. Cambridge: Polity Press.

——— 2001*a*. *The dialectics of shopping*. Chicago: University of Chicago Press.

——— 2001*b*. The poverty of morality. *Journal of Consumer Studies* 1: 225–43.

Mingione, Enzo 1988. Work and informal activities in urban southern Italy. In *On work: historical, comparative and theoretical approaches* (ed) Raymond E. Pahl, pp. 548–78. Oxford: Basil Blackwell.

Padrut, Franco 2007. Continuità e mutamenti nel voto di Palermo. *Segno* XXXIII (285–6, May–June): 7–14.

Polanyi, Karl 1957. The economy as instituted process. In *Trade and market in the early empires: economies in history and theory* (eds) K. Polanyi, Conrad M. Arensberg and Harry W. Pearson, pp. 243–70. New York: The Free Press.

——— 2001 [1944]. *The great transformation: the political and economic origins of our time*. Boston: Beacon Press.

Rajak, Dinah 2009. 'I am the conscience of the company': responsibility and the gift in a transnational mining corporation. In *Economics and morality* (eds) Katherine E. Brown and B. Lynne Milgram, pp. 211–33. Lanham: AltaMira Press.

Raynolds, Laura T. 2000. Re-embedding global agriculture: the international organic and fair trade movements. *Agriculture and Human Values* 17: 297–309.

Renard, Marie-Christine 1999. The interstices of globalization: the example of fairtrade coffee. *Sociologia Ruralis* 39: 484–500.

Sayer, Andrew 2000. Moral economy and political economy. *Studies in Political Economy* 61: 79–103.

Schneider, Jane, and Peter Schneider 1975. *Culture and political economy in western Sicily*. New York: Academic Press.

——— 2003. *Reversible destiny: mafia, antimafia and the struggle for Palermo*. Los Angeles: University of California Press.

Shukaitis, Stevphen and David Graeber (with Erika Biddle) (eds) 2007. *Constituent imagination: militant investigations, collective theorization*. Oakland: AK Press.

Simmonds, Peter 1995. Green consumerism: blurring the boundary between public and private. In *Debating the future of the public sphere: transforming the public and private domains in free market societies* (eds) Stephen Edgell, Sandra Walklate and Gareth Williams, pp. 147–61. Aldershot: Avebury.

Tallontire, Anne 2006. The development of alternative and fair trade: moving into the mainstream. In *Ethical sourcing in the global food system: challenges and opportunity to fair trade and the environment* (eds) Stephanie Barrientos and Catherine Dolan, pp. 35–48. London: Earthscan.

Trigilia, Carlo 1992. *Sviluppo senza autonomia: effetti perversi delle politiche nel Mezzogiorno*. Bologna: Il Mulino.

Valera, Lorenzo 2005. *GAS: gruppi di acquisto solidale*. Milano: Terre di Mezzo.

Chapter 7

ON THE CHALLENGES OF SIGNALLING
ETHICS WITHOUT THE STUFF:
TALES OF CONSPICUOUS GREEN ANTI-CONSUMPTION

Cindy Isenhour

Intimately embedded in the global economy and bound up with ideologies of growth, consumer culture is a powerful force.[1] Humans are consuming more per capita each year, more products, more energy, more resources. In many ways our identities have become inextricably linked to consumption, and alternatives to consumer-based ways of life are difficult for many to imagine in a world seemingly dependent on growing consumer demand.

Many scholars have set out to explain why consumption has become so central to contemporary societies. Some draw on social theories of consumption, connecting the importance of material culture to a heightened need for communication in increasingly complex, postmodern, global and mobile societies (Crew 2003; Holt and Schor 2000; Leach 1993). As more people become alienated from productive resources and move into urban centres and wage work, they find themselves without home towns, relatives or the products of their labour to anchor their identities. Many, thus, have little choice but to build their identities around symbolic objects that strangers can easily understand, their possessions. Anthropologists have long studied material goods as tools for communication, a way that we signal our social status, our membership in a group and our understanding of shared norms and values. Mary Douglas (2004: 145) wrote: 'a consumer knows that he is expected to play some part or he will not get any income. Everything that he chooses to do or to buy is part of a project to choose other people'; and she continues: 'the forms of consumption which he prefers are those that maintain the kind of collectivity he likes to be in'.

If this theory is correct, then it seems that Swedes have become much more expressive in recent decades. According to the Göteborg Center for Consumer Science (2008), Sweden has experienced significant growth in several sectors of household consumption over the last twenty years, including expenditures on leisure, household goods and clothing. In Sweden, where a culture of conformity (described below) is apparent to ethnographers and citizens alike, there is a strong pressure to consume to these heightened levels. Yet, if we view consumption as a means of constructing and communicating identity, then these significant increases in consumption are not inherently irrational, as some have suggested, but are functional in an increasingly complex society such as Sweden's.

Meanwhile, the past several decades have also seen growing anti-consumption sentiment. Certainly critiques of high consumerism have long been present in Sweden and elsewhere, as Peter Collins's discussion of Quaker consumption reminds us (this volume). In the nineteenth century Veblen (1899) condemned the conspicuous consumption of the leisure class, while Thoreau (1854) advocated a return to the simple life and de Tocqueville (1835–40) warned that excessive materialism threatened to weaken social networks and make working toward common social goals more difficult. In Sweden, people have long criticised the *slit-och-slang* (wear and throw away) culture typically associated with the United States (O'Dell 1997) and have relied on the core concept of *lagom* (roughly 'just enough') to moderate needs (Erickson 1997). Yet in recent decades, those criticisms have gained force as people increasingly link high consumption and environmental problems.

These environmental concerns are particularly salient in Swedish society, which is characterised by an overriding environmentalism and what has been described as an almost religious connection to the land (Frykman and Löfgren 1987; Gullestad 1989). As such, Swedish consumers have been particularly attracted to forms of 'green' consumption when compared to the citizens of other nations (Ferrer and Fraile 2006; Michelleti 2003; Micheletti and Stolle 2004), such as recycled or second-hand goods and items that are 'eco-labelled', marked as indicating that the manufacturer conforms to voluntary environmental standards higher than those required by law. At the same time, many Swedish consumers are actively trying to consume less. They argue, along with a growing number of scholars (e.g., Carolan 2004; Schor 1999; Wilhite 2005), that shopping for environmentally responsible products will not be enough to ensure sustainability if the efficiencies gained with greener products continue to be outpaced by significant increases in per capita consumption. These consumers point to the irony of trying to solve problems associated with over-consumption with even more consumption, regardless of how green and efficient production processes become (Isenhour 2010). For these individuals, ethical consumption means consuming less, not just consuming green. As Richard Wilk (2004: 27) argues, it is not necessarily about 'reducing consumption' per se, but about making sure that the 'goods and services people buy, use and throw away' consume fewer resources. For these individuals, ethical consumption means consuming fewer resources, not just buying green.

So, it seems that there are two opposing trends in Sweden. On the one hand, people there are heavily embedded in a consumer culture, one dependent on things as symbols of cultural capital, relationships, social status and personal values. Because Swedish culture is highly conformist, most feel pressure to consume at socially approved levels in order to remain comfortably within the mainstream. Yet these levels have increased significantly over the last twenty to thirty years. If we subscribe to social theories of consumption, this growth may reflect increased social complexity and thus a heightened role for material culture as a tool for communication. Yet, on the other hand, there is a pervasive environmentalism in Sweden and a small but growing number of people who are trying to focus on buying less, buying second-hand, reusing and repairing. This chapter is concerned with a specific question: if material culture has become increasingly instrumental in Sweden over the past several decades, then how are those consumers, who are trying to be more ethical by buying less, able to communicate without all the stuff?

In the pages to come, I utilise several case studies to examine how environmentally concerned families negotiate these tensions. The case studies illustrate that Swedes who are trying to consume less rarely do so at the expense of their cultural capital and markers of class status. Class-based theories are therefore an essential compliment to social theories of consumption, particularly in Scandinavia, where an egalitarian ethic contrasts sharply with the reality of increasing class inequality. Before addressing this question and outlining these arguments, however, it is necessary to provide a brief description of the research project.

(Re)Searching Sustainability

The research presented here is part of a larger project that seeks to contextualise alternative consumer movements in post-industrial consumer cultures. As such, the project focuses on Swedes who have changed their lives and consumption patterns in response to perceived environmental risks. Yet rather than starting from an individualist assumption that these people operate from an alternative and independent set of values, preferences or ethics, the research explores the articulation of individual consumer motivation with political-economic structures and shared discourses on the economy and the environment in order to better understand the meanings that individuals accept or contest as part of the habitus (Bourdieu 1977, 1990). The project is thus designed to take theories of practice and structuration seriously, bringing to light the tensions these consumers face as they attempt to do what is a central part of ethical consumption, insert their ethical concerns and social values into the economic realm (Introduction, this volume).

The research started with 28 interviews with representatives of organisations working to encourage more environmentalist consumer behaviour. These interviews helped to contextualise the sustainability movement in Sweden, providing insight into the assumptions upon which sustainability discourse and practice are built. However, the primary focus of the research was directed toward individuals who had modified their lives and consumption in response to perceived environmental risks. During fourteen months of field work, 58 individuals sampled from five different environmental organisations participated in semi-structured interviews. These lasted approximately one to four hours each, and covered views on things like nature, sociability, sustainability and ecological risk. Twelve of these participants and fourteen of their family members also participated in more in-depth research, which included consumption histories and inventories, a series of informal household interviews and accompanying them on some of their shopping trips. In total, 44 men and 56 women, aged from 26 to 91 years, participated in the research.

Like the Hungarian ethical consumers that Tamas Dombos (this volume) describes, these people were highly educated (91 per cent had vocational, university or post-graduate qualifications), and the bulk of them were located securely within Sweden's middle class. With only a few exceptions, they identified themselves as Swedish in nationality and thus were representative of the country's dominant social groups. The demographic make-up of the sample is consistent with survey-based studies of green consumers in Sweden and elsewhere (Anderson and Tobiasson 2004; Center for a New American Dream 2004; Micheletti and Stolle 2004). The research thus speaks not only to ethical consumption in Sweden, with all its particularities, but also has the potential to help explain a larger movement toward green consumerism among well-educated, urban, middle-class citizens in other post-industrial countries.

Despite the commonalities shared by members of the sample, the actions these individuals and their families took to live more sustainably varied considerably. While most bought organic and eco-labelled goods whenever possible (88 per cent) others went much further, by, for example, attempting to buy less (66 per cent), reusing and repairing goods (22 per cent), becoming more politically active (28 per cent) or working (and hence earning and spending) less (9 per cent) (see Table 7.1). Many of the participants, particularly those most committed to building more sustainable societies, did not confine their actions to the realm of consumption. These people insisted that while their roles as consumers were important for demanding change in the market, their actions as citizens were equally, if not more, important. These respondents refused to draw what they saw as a false distinction between their roles as citizens and consumers. Echoing the organic farmers that Audrey Vankeerberghen (this volume) describes, they argued that it was not enough just to buy green, it was also necessary to live green.

This chapter looks specifically at a subset of the sample, those people who are concerned not only with consuming ecologically sound products, but also with consuming significantly less. Their actions raise, once again, the central question I have posed. If contemporary consumption is functional, providing people with a means of producing identity, maintaining boundaries and sending social signals in modern society, how, then, do these educated, middle-class and fairly conformist Swedes communicate without all the stuff?

Table 7.1. Action categories

Food (buy organic, local, less meat, sustainable fish, free range)	88%
Travel (fly less, drive less, use public transport, walk, bike)	86%
Buy less (cut back total consumption, less stuff)	66%
Improve home efficiency (short showers, full wash loads, lights/bulbs)	60%
Reduce waste (less packaging, recycle, compost)	47%
Cooperate (cooperative living, borrow, trade services)	47%
Use alternative technologies (efficient appliances, cars, green energy)	45%
Educate yourself (do research, read newspapers, attend conferences)	45%
Change values (prioritise in life, think about what is important)	38%
Advocacy (educate children, talk to friends, blog, etc.)	33%
Citizenship (vote, demonstrate, communicate with elected officials)	28%
Membership (support, join, get active)	28%
Do it yourself (grow/cook your own food, make things)	28%
Avoid chemicals (fewer cleaners/lawn chemicals, eco-labelled products)	22%
Reuse/repair (make things last longer, use what you have, get creative)	22%
Buy used, second hand, hand-me-downs	21%
Buy quality (longer life, high price, replaces infrequently, fair labour)	17%
Demand alternatives (talk to retailers, producers, customer service)	10%
Work less (work fewer hours, less money, more time with family/friends)	9%
Invest green (invest money in environmentally responsible businesses)	2%

Note: These categories were generated by asking people to list all the things that they do and others could do to live a more sustainable life.

In order to answer this question, I focus here on the home as a vehicle of identity performance. As Rita Erickson (1997), Marianne Gullestad (1989), Orvar Löfgren (1995), Tom O'Dell (1997) and others point out, social norms surrounding the home are very important to people in Scandinavia. Many Swedes, even those concerned about the environment, do not question the use of energy or environmentally irresponsible products when it comes to meeting culturally mandated standards of housekeeping, appearance and hospitality (Erickson 1997). With the advent of home remodelling and redecorating shows on television, many Swedes are redoing their homes more frequently. Indeed, many of my friends and research participants living in the Stockholm area relayed stories of acquaintances who redecorate on a seasonal or yearly basis in order to keep up with the latest designs in textiles, furniture and lighting.

Certainly those who are trying to consume less are not oblivious to the shared meanings and cultural values placed on the home in Scandinavia. Yet for these individuals and families, the purchase of a new couch or curtains can be a stressful endeavour, as they strive to reconcile their desire to cause less ecological harm with their desire to create a home that meets culturally defined notions of stylishness, cleanliness and comfort (see Shove 2004). In what follows, I present several case studies to illustrate the strategies that families use to reconcile these tensions. It is important to note, however, that I am presenting these cases as ideal types. In reality, these strategies often blend together, overlap and sometimes oppose one another within complex and dynamic households.[2]

Strategy One: Conspicuous Green Consumption

Rather than dealing with the tension between the desire to consume less and the need to communicate via consumption, many attempt to circumvent it by purchasing goods that have a smaller environmental impact and are explicitly branded 'green'. These consumer-citizens make great efforts to research and locate products that are better for the environment. In their eyes, it is important not only to support alternative markets and drive demand for products that are less harmful to the environment, but it is also important to signal to others that alternative forms of consumption are possible and do not require significant sacrifices.

Gustav and Erika's family[3] provides a good example of what might be called conspicuous green consumption. Gustav is self-employed and works at home, while Erika works in middle-management for one of Sweden's largest communications corporations. In their late 40s, they live with their two children in an affluent suburb of Stockholm. While the family members are aware of the energy and resources embodied in things, they focus primarily on the consumption of less environmentally intensive goods and services. Their flooring, for example, is made of sustainably harvested bamboo, all of their lighting systems and household appliances have been replaced with the most energy-efficient models on the market, they heat their home with a combination of solar and geothermal power and they drive a hybrid car. Gustav and Erika are proud of these green possessions and are quick to point them out. Walking through their house it is not difficult to infer that the family is working to build an explicitly green identity. From their environmentally labelled dish soap and kitchen composter (which sit proudly on the counter rather than below the sink) to their hemp-upholstered couch, there are signs of green living everywhere. Gustav and Erika are in a unique position to live green lives. Their combined annual income after tax exceeds Skr 2 million (at the time, about €214,000, or $317,000), so they can afford many of these expensive alternative products, a luxury that most, no matter how ethical or ecologically minded, can not.

The research participants who follow this strategy tend to be those who have only recently come to identify with environmentalist concerns, typically engaging for the first time with questions of global climate change. These individuals and families are generally not as aware of the energy and resources embodied in products, and thus focus on reducing their energy use by turning off lights and replacing light bulbs or by purchasing eco-labelled products. Instead of buying less, they are trying to buy better and more efficiently; at least in theory and in the long run. They believe that sustainability can be reached without significant changes in the way they live, as long as technologies continue to improve. Their efforts do not take them outside the realm of mainstream consumerism as they are, in many ways, consuming more in the short term to build upon their desires for a green life. Their consumption habits signal membership in an emerging group of upper-middle-class people who can afford ethical goods targeted toward those willing to pay more for a greener lifestyle.

By working within the confines of the market and the social structures that define mainstream needs and values, consumers like Gustav and Erika are responding both to their own desire to have a smaller impact on the environment and to normative constraints on their consumption decisions. This delicate balance is well illustrated by the concept of 'moral selving' (Barnett et al. 2005), which points to the ways that sustainable consumers are motivated not only by the desire to do the right thing, but also by the promise that sustainable goods will help them to construct a moral identity consistent with their values and beliefs. Through the purchase of 'moral products' consumers are able to demonstrate their ability to care across both spatial and temporal distance (Bryant and Goodman 2004). In a process that resembles what Giovanni Orlando (this volume) says of critical consumers in Palermo, Barnett and his colleagues argue that conspicuously ethical goods displayed in the home or given as gifts are intimately bound in a process through which consumers attempt to inform and educate their family and friends about the virtues of a more responsible form of consumption and serve to communicate the consumer's values and what they call the consumer's 'ethical credentials' (Barnett et al. 2005). Ironically, however, many of these people end up consuming more, particularly in the short term, in an effort to create their green identities, replacing functional items with newer, greener and more ethical goods.

Strategy Two: Retro Chic

Another strategy for dealing with these tensions is illustrated by a young professional couple living in downtown Stockholm. Karin and Thomas both work for organisations concerned with sustainability: Thomas for a governmental agency linked to environmental issues, and Karin for a non-governmental organisation involved in international relief. They extend their concern for sustainability into their personal lives and are extremely committed to reducing their environmental impact. In addition to activities such as buying organic, fair-trade, local and seasonal foods, significantly reducing their meat consumption, using a bicycle or public transportation and refraining from flying, they also try to buy as much as they possibly can from second-hand shops.

Three of the four walls in Thomas and Karin's living room are lined with bookshelves from the 1950s. Designed by Nils Strinning, a central figure in Scandinavian Modern design, the bookshelves are extremely fashionable and in high demand. Thomas and Karin had to be extremely patient to gather all the modules needed to line their walls. In fact, they invested a significant amount of their time over several months searching second-hand stores throughout the city to decorate their apartment with furniture and lighting from this period. But they do not stop with second-hand retailers. Karin and Thomas also go 'dumpster diving' (searching for something desirable in people's trash) on occasion to look for discarded mid-century furniture. Interestingly enough, they have been quite lucky, finding, among other things, a bedside table that perfectly matched one they already owned.

Yet Thomas and Karin do not do these things out of economic necessity. They have a comfortable household budget for a couple their age, with a combined annual income after tax of approximately Skr 690,000 (about €74,000; $110,000). While many people continue to associate second-hand shopping or dumpster diving with economic disadvantage, many of the vintage pieces that Karin and Thomas own are significantly more expensive than new furnishings. Further, Thomas and Karin think that their second-hand consumption, even if less economical at times, is more ethical than new, mass-produced furniture, which, while inexpensive, is often made far from Sweden, in places where environmental and labour standards are weak, and where significant resources must be used to transport these goods to Sweden.

By focusing on one time period to decorate their home, perhaps the heyday of Scandinavian Modern design, Karin and Thomas have insulated themselves from the whims of contemporary fashion. At the same time, they are able to communicate their membership in Stockholm's highly educated class of cultural creatives who value design: these sorts of objects are quite fashionable among Swedes in their late 20s to early 40s. Further, Karin and Thomas are able to consume less in a way that does not signal that they are living in poverty or that they do not share middle-class values and tastes. This was a concern for Thomas. When speaking about the challenges of consuming less, he said:

> Sometimes people that don't know you very well don't understand if you're not buying anything new. They think that you are poor or that you're not well educated, that you don't have nice taste or that you are not successful. It is not that I really care what people think about me, I am secure. … I know what I like, and I have always been interested in Swedish design.

Karin and Thomas are clearly green, since they rely on second-hand furnishings and décor that were produced many years ago and thus require no new resource inputs. Yet at the same time, their home does not explicitly communicate environmental concerns. The style is fashionable regardless of its environmental merits and those who create such homes do not sacrifice their mainstream status. Rather, they enhance it, while living in a manner consistent with their values.

Strategy Three: Prestige Posh

A third and related strategy is what we might call 'prestige posh', illustrated by Charlotte and Lars, another young couple. They live in central Stockholm with their infant son. Both have advanced degrees from one of Sweden's best universities, and their combined annual income after tax is Skr 780,000 (about €83,000; $124,000). Like Thomas and Karin, Charlotte and Lars also work very hard to live a more sustainable lifestyle. They try to buy local and organic products whenever possible and focus on buying less via second-hand consumption. Charlotte and Lars have furnished and decorated their highly fashionable home with goods passed down from family members or purchased second hand. In this case, however, I want to emphasise a slightly different strategy, the possession of prestigious, expensive items of high quality. In this apartment, which is relatively small for a family of three but in a very desirable location on the water, the family places special emphasis on the purchase of high-quality products that represent the latest in technological advancement when they need something that does not lend itself to second-hand purchase.

During my last visit with Charlotte and Lars, they showed me that they had recently purchased a top-of-the-line standing mixer. Lars was currently at home on paternity leave with their son, had started making most of their own bread and wanted the mixer for baking. The couple also has a state-of-the-art video projection system in their living room for watching television and films and a pair of the most advanced mobile phones on the market. While these high-quality and expensive items were all purchased new, Lars and Charlotte argue that if they are going to buy new items, it is more important for them to buy a few high-quality items that will last a long time than it is to buy a lot of cheap items that might have been produced with poor labour or environmental standards, or that might not last very long and would thus need to be replaced in a few years. However, another participant whose family practices the 'prestige posh' strategy did seem to question the rationale behind this approach to sustainable living. Consider, for example, the following discussion with Erik about cutting back on consumerism:

> Erik: I don't want to have a lot of things but they should be of really good quality.
> Cindy: Because they last longer or why?
> Erik: Yes, that is part of my rationale but I don't know if it is true because people that have expensive, good electronic things, they are also the ones who buy a lot and change them a lot.
> Cindy: They upgrade them often?
> Erik: Yeah, exactly.

Strategy Four: Beyond the Mainstream

While some attempt to negotiate the tensions that arise when trying to consume less, others have learned to embrace those tensions. These individuals and families are more comfortable stepping outside the mainstream. While it is difficult to generalise about the people who practice this strategy, they tend to be those who have been involved with the environmental movement for quite some time, many since the 1960s and 1970s, or are highly engaged and passionate young people who do not yet have families.

To illustrate this strategy I use Olle and Emma, both pensioners in their early 70s. Emma had long been active in the environmental movement, becoming engaged in the 1970s when debates about nuclear power and proliferation were at their peak in Sweden. She was also active in the creation of Sweden's Green Party and in the establishment of non-governmental organisations focused on social and environmental sustainability.

Today Emma and Olle share a simple life on their small farm a few hours north of Stockholm. Olle sails most of the summer and spends his free time the rest of the year repairing or, as Emma says, fiddling with, machines and tools. Emma focuses on caring for the garden, the orchard and the sheep. She acknowledges that she and Olle try to represent the simplicity of their life in their home. Most of their possessions are older, many historical, and it does not appear that they seek to communicate social status with the possession of rare or valuable things. However, they prominently display books throughout their home, signalling their cultural capital and high levels of education. Emma and Olle are quite comfortable in their social position as simple, environmentally concerned pensioners. She notes that most of their friends and family understand them as such. Further, she has become comfortable with the idea that those who do not share or understand these values are not her ideal friends.

Emma and Olle, and other people like them, are much more concerned with consuming less than are conspicuous green consumers like Gustav and Erika. They place much more emphasis on reusing, repairing and doing without. Most people who do this have spent significant time considering their impact on the environment and associating with like-minded people. For them, reduced consumption may compromise their relations with people who do not share their concern for the environment. However, and echoing the situation of Quakers that Collins (this volume) describes, this reduced level of consumption is also essential for their membership in groups of people who place value on the environment, simplicity and asceticism. At the same time, most such people are highly educated, well travelled and typically have urban, upper-middle-class backgrounds. As such, their definitions of good taste reflect those backgrounds, and very few of them compromise their ability to communicate their cultural capital, whether through the display of books, artwork and travel souvenirs or through their mastery in the kitchen or garden.

When the Tension is Too Much: Confronting Barriers

Many of those who care deeply about the environment face barriers that make it difficult to create and maintain a life that meets their ideals. Some of the barriers are rather obvious, for example those associated with the amount of time it takes to identify alternative products, their availability and their price. Other barriers are, perhaps, not so obvious. For many who try to consume less overall, the social tensions created by living in a manner that is different than the mainstream prove insurmountable, as modest consumption was for some of the dynastic Quakers that Collins describes. One research participant, Ebba, recounted the difficulties associated with living in a fashion-conscious city. While she buys most of her clothing second hand, she acknowledges that it is difficult to find fashionable clothes without spending a lot of time shopping. Because she does not enjoy shopping, it is tempting for her to go to the cheap, mass retailers where the latest fashions are inexpensive and easy to find.

Others noted that they feel pressured to create a tasteful home that will not compromise their ability to entertain friends. One participant, Felicia, noted:

> You see a lot of commercials all around you, television, newspapers all over town and TV programmes, it is really big now to refurnish your house, and you get reminded all the time that everything has to be so nice and new and fresh. And it's cheap. Ten years ago maybe people wouldn't refurnish their house so often. But now it is like, okay it's spring and now I need new curtains.

Yet others experience significant stress as their lives diverge from their friends'. Johan recalls that, as he became more interested in sustainable living, he suddenly found he had less in common with his childhood friends. Many of them could not understand why he began shopping at second-hand stores or why he seemed aloof when they spoke about the latest electronic equipment. Nor did Johan's friends understand his decision to cut back on his work hours. He suspects many of them thought that he was being lazy and a bit 'weird'. They did not understand that he intentionally took a cut in pay so that he could focus on buying less and spending more time with his family. As a result, Johan felt ostracised and found himself searching for alternative social networks, new friends to whom he could relate and with whom he could communicate.

These examples certainly seem to support social theories of consumption, illustrating that it is difficult for even the most interested and committed individuals to consume less and simultaneously maintain their social relationships. Indeed, we have long known that people choose goods that help them to signal their belonging in groups that share their values and interests. From this perspective, consumption is indeed productive, helping to form and maintain social relations (Crew 2000, 2003; Miller 2001). It certainly is not true that it is hard to communicate with fewer things: quite the contrary. In consumer-based societies, older and unfashionable furnishings and decor are frequently read as a sign of poverty or lack of taste rather than as a choice. For these well-educated, middle-class people with high levels of cultural capital, then, the trick is not one of communicating without a lot of stuff. Rather, it is communicating their social position in a society that sees high levels of consumption as a symbol of elevated social status and power.

Conclusion: Subtle Class Conflict in a 'Classless' Society

The significant rise in consumption over the past twenty years in Sweden might be explained, in part, by factors that have increased social complexity and thus the need to use material culture to communicate. However, as the case studies illustrate, there is no simple relationship between the volume of consumption and the ability to communicate. Indeed, even individuals who have very little communicate quite a lot. Increases in consumption are, therefore, not just tied to a heightened need to communicate in complex societies; they are tied to a heightened need to communicate particular social boundaries and class differences. The case studies thus reflect a different source of increased social complexity in Sweden over the past few decades, growing differences between classes. During that time, many countries have experienced a widening income gap and witnessed the sharper definition of class boundaries, but these changes are particularly salient in Sweden, a nation long focused on ensuring class equality.

For many years the Swedish government, dominated by the Social Democrats, emphasised national solidarity and equality, in the form of policies designed to reduce income inequalities and create a strong middle class. Many have argued, however, that the legacy of social democracy meant also that the remaining class differences were played down (Bihagen 2000; Gullestad 1984; Löfgren 1987; Rowe and Fudge 2003). Over time, this legacy resulted in an 'egalitarian ethos' within which class dissimilarities were 'muted' (Löfgren 1987) and 'undercommunicated' (Gullestad 1984). Moreover, as Norman Ginsburg (2005) points out, recent changes have drastically altered the class landscape in Sweden. With growing unemployment and debates about liberalisation in the 1990s, the policies of the Social Democrats began to lose support. Meanwhile, members of the upper-middle class began to demand tax cuts, privatisation and reduced public spending. There has since been a growing tension between the middle class and the upper-middle class that has become increasingly important in Swedish politics. However, the egalitarian ethos remains, making explicit discussions about class differences taboo.

In *Deconstructing Swedishness*, Löfgren (1987: 81) argues that the ideology of classlessness in Sweden has resulted in subtle yet powerful class conflicts: 'The ideology of classlessness can be contrasted with an everyday obsession with rituals of social distinction and boundary markers. In the age of consumerism, taste and tastelessness became a new cultural arena of muted class conflict'.

Löfgren's argument suggests that the exacerbation of class differences, based in economic realities but projected through cultural capital, can help to explain the continued rise of consumerism in Sweden. This may particularly be true with the 'democratization of desire' (Leach 1993), when a strong focus on equality, a culture of conformity and cheap mass-produced items all combined to encourage all Swedes to consume at the same, gradually increasing level. It may also help to explain the social pressures that can make it so difficult for middle-class people who are concerned about the environment to consume less.

While many theories have been proposed to explain the growth of ethical consumption, here I want to explore class-based theories that see such consumption among the middle class as one of the ways that its members seek to maintain social boundaries and class advantage through the accumulation of cultural capital via 'ethical', 'moral' and 'sustainable' consumption. Such an approach builds on the work of those, most notably Bourdieu (1984), who have suggested that consumption is intricately related to social status, relations of privilege and social control in hierarchical capitalist societies (e.g., Appadurai 1986; Bryant and Goodman 2004; Carrier and Heyman 1997).

Douglas Holt (2000) draws on Bourdieu's concept of class to argue that to be cultured is a potent social advantage for the individual. Yet strangely enough, because the powerful discipline of economics treats tastes simply as individual preferences, this fact is rarely acknowledged. Holt argues against the popular assumption that there is a direct, linear relationship between income and consumption, at least in the United States. He found that consumers with the highest levels of cultural capital are more interested in distinguishing themselves by way of aesthetic consumption that is 'socially scarce' (Holt 2000: 218). Echoing what Bourdieu said in *Distinction*, Holt (2000: 247) argues that when there is pervasive materialism, the only way for cultural elites to differentiate themselves is, 'structurally speaking, … to develop a set of tastes in opposition to materialism: consuming which emphasizes the metaphysical over the material. Thus unreflexive materialism is associated with "showy," "ostentatious," "gaudy" or "unrefined" [tastes].'

Marianne Gullestad's (1984) classic ethnography of working-class mothers in Norway illustrates this opposition well. She describes the scorn that cultural elites direct towards the working class and their consumption patterns. While liberal, educated members of the middle class in Norway place great emphasis on recycling and buying second-hand goods, they condemn the consumption practices of the working-class mothers who equate value and economic success with new home furnishings, regardless of quality. Similarly, Löfgren's analysis of consumption histories among Sweden's educated middle class, those with accumulations of cultural capital, reveals an 'obsession with distinction and taste' and 'a recurrent need to distance oneself from other consumers, to stress one's role as a critical observer of the consumption habits of the others' (Löfgren 1994: 55), which is echoed in the distinctiveness of Kornélia, described by Dombos (this volume).

These arguments are interesting in the context of contemporary alternative consumerism. Löfgren's argument that taste and tastelessness, as well as morality and immorality, constitute grounds for muted class conflicts in the age of consumerism implies that sustainable consumers in Sweden utilise their ethical consumption not only as a means to identify with like-minded people, but also as a means of excluding others who do not share their middle-class values concerning nature.

Alternative consumerism in Sweden is a middle-class movement set in opposition to both the lower and upper classes. The movement is embedded in a hierarchical system, but one which, as I said, tends to downplay class differences. Thus, class-based explanations of sustainable consumerism certainly seem to have merit, reflecting the contradictions between Sweden's egalitarian ethic and hierarchical, capitalist economy. At the same time, class-based arguments risk over-simplifying consumer motivation and can fail to consider the creative and social capacity of human actors. Ultimately, to understand movements toward both increasing consumption and decreasing consumption, we must understand both the powerful reproductive structures of capitalist society and the reflexive, creative capacity of individual consumers.

Certainly consumers, both rich and poor, are constrained in their economic choices by their position in capitalist political economy and by more localised social structures that shape understandings of what is socially acceptable or even conceivable. We must continue to remind ourselves of the power that existing structures have over individuals. As social beings, deeply embedded in social networks and normative structures that identify what is desirable, what is necessary and what is superfluous, many people are not willing to abandon their current levels of consumption, to withdraw from the capitalist system and adopt simpler lives.

However, many consumers actively interpret the ideologies and social structures of the capitalist system to arrive at their own meanings and values. They often display complex and contradictory consumption imperatives based on values that both contradict and reflect conformity to social structures and the expression of individuality (Crew 2000). These people may resist the imperatives and expectations that they confront in ways that are subtle and perhaps not very effective. However, those ways are not nearly as costly as total rejection, at least in terms of people's desire to live reasonable lives. Because of the costs of substantial rejection of consumerism and its social and cultural underpinnings, significant reductions in consumption are unlikely unless the economic, political and social structures that drive consumption change.

However, as Bourdieu and Wacquant (1992: 14) once wrote: 'if we grant that symbolic systems are social products that contribute to making the world, that they do not simply mirror social relations but help constitute them, then one can, within limits, transform the world by transforming its representation'. So while middle-class ethical consumers may have more cultural capital with which to define 'sustainability' and the 'unsustainable' actions of others, we must also consider the possibility that these middle-class and typically well-educated Swedish ethical consumers are, within limits, altering both the social structure and the capitalist system, redefining the relationship between the economy and society in a manner consistent with their ideals of an ethical, fair and just society. All of the research participants spoke of their efforts in terms of responsibility, rights, morality and ethics. These people are making efforts to live in a way that does not impinge upon the rights of others in the Third World or in the future, often with great effort and commitment.

Notes

1. In using the singular here I do not mean to imply a single consumer culture. There are many different forms of consumer culture, but here I refer to a spreading global phenomenon of increased consumption (see Sklair 1995).
2. Although I do not have the space to address the issue properly here, it should be noted that household members often take radically different views on sustainable practice and, thus, often several are used within one household.
3. Research participants have been given pseudonyms and some details of their lives have been changed to ensure confidentiality.

Bibliography

Anderson, Jorgen Goul and Mette Tobiasen 2004. Who are these consumers anyway? Survey evidence from Denmark. In *Politics, products and markets: exploring political consumerism past and present* (eds) Michele Micheletti, Andreas Follesdal and Dietlind Stolle, pp. 203–22. New Brunswick, NJ: Transaction Books.
Appadurai, Arjun 1986. *The social life of things*. Cambridge: Cambridge University Press.
Barnett, Clive, Paul Cloke, Nick Clarke and Alice Malpass 2005. Consuming ethics: articulating the subjects and spaces of ethical consumption. *Antipode* 37: 23–45.
Bihagen, Erik 2000. The significance of class: studies of class inequalities, consumption and social circulation in contemporary Sweden. Doctoral thesis, Department of Sociology, Umeå University. Umeå, Sweden: Umeå universitets tryckeriet.
Bourdieu, Pierre 1977. *Outline of a theory of practice*. Cambridge: Cambridge University Press.
——— 1984. *Distinction: a social critique of the judgement of taste*. London: Routledge & Kegan Paul.
——— 1990. *The logic of practice*. Cambridge: Polity.
Bourdieu, Pierre and Loic J.D. Wacquant 1992. *An invitation to reflexive sociology*. Chicago: University of Chicago Press.
Bryant, Raymond L. and Michael K. Goodman 2004. Consuming narratives: the political ecology of alternative consumption. *Transcripts of the Institute for British Geographers* 29: 344–66.

Carolan, Michael S. 2004. Ecological modernization theory: what about consumption? *Society and Natural Resources* 17: 247–60.

Carrier, James G. and Josiah Heyman 1997. Consumption and political economy. *Journal of the Royal Anthropological Institute* (NS) 3: 355–73.

Center for a New American Dream 2005. *Americans want more of what matters.* (New American Dream Survey Report September 2004). Takoma Park, Md: Center for a New American Dream. www.newdream.org/about/pdfs/Finalpollreport.pdf

Crew, Louise 2000. Geographies of retailing and consumption. *Progress in Human Geography* 24: 275–90.

——— 2003. Geographies of retailing and consumption: markets in motion. *Progress in Human Geography* 27: 352–62.

Douglas, Mary 2004. Consumers revolt. In *The consumption reader* (eds) David B. Clarke, Marcus A. Doel and Kate M.L. Housiaux, pp. 144–49. New York: Routledge.

Erickson, Rita J. 1997. *Paper or plastic: energy, environment and consumerism in Sweden and America.* Westport, Conn.: Praeger.

Ferrer, Mariona and Marta Fraile 2006. Exploring the social determinants of political consumerism in Western Europe. (Working Papers Online Series 57/2006). Department of Political Science and International Relations, Universitad Autonoma de Madrid. Madrid: Universitad Autonoma de Madrid. portal.uam.es/portal/page/portal/UAM_ORGANIZATIVO/Departamentos/CienciaPoliticaRelacionesInternacionales/publicaciones%20en%20red/working_papers/archivos/Working-paper-UAM-2006.%20Marta%20fraile.pdf

Frykman, Jonas and Orvar Löfgren 1987. *Culture builders: a historical anthropology of middle class life.* New Brunswick, NJ: Rutgers University Press.

Ginsburg, Norman 2005. Review of: *The politics of the welfare state: Canada, Sweden and the United States. British Journal of Sociology* 56: 316.

Göteborg Center for Consumer Science 2008. *Konsumptionsrapporten 2008.* Gothenburg, Sweden: Handelshögskolan vid Göteborg Universitet.

Gullestad, Marianne 1984. *Kitchen-table society: a case study of the family life and friendships of young working-class mothers in urban Norway.* Oslo: Universitetsforlaget.

——— 1989. Nature and everyday life in Scandinavia. *Folk* 31: 171–81.

Holt, Douglas B. 2000. Does cultural capital structure American consumption? In *The consumer society reader* (eds) D.B. Holt and Juliet B. Schor, pp. 212–52. New York: New Press.

Holt, Douglas B. and Juliet B. Schor 2000. Introduction: do Americans consume too much? In *The consumer society reader* (eds) J.B. Schor and D.B. Holt, pp. vii–xxiii. New York: New Press.

Isenhour, Cindy 2010. Sustainable consumerism in Sweden: ecological risk perception and response in the age of high consumption. Doctoral dissertation. Department of Anthropology, University of Kentucky. Lexington: University of Kentucky.

Leach, William 1993. *Land of desire: merchants, power and the rise of a new American culture.* New York: Pantheon.

Löfgren, Orvar 1987. Our friends in nature: class and animal symbolism. *Ethnos* 3–4: 184–213.

——— 1994. Consuming interests. In *Consumption and identity* (ed) Jonathan Friedman, pp. 47–70. Amsterdam: Harwood Academic.

———— 1995. Being a good Swede: national identity as a cultural battleground. In *Articulating hidden histories* (eds) Rayna Rapp and Jane Schneider, pp. 262–74. Berkeley: University of California Press.

Micheletti, Michele 2003. *Political virtue and shopping: individuals, consumerism, and collective action*. New York: Palgrave Macmillan.

Micheletti, Michele and Dietlind Stolle 2004. Swedish political consumers: who they are and why they use the market as an arena for politics. In *Political consumerism: its motivations, power and conditions in the Nordic countries and elsewhere* (Proceedings from the Second International Seminar on Political Consumerism, Oslo, 26–29 August) (TemaNord 2005: 517) (eds) Magnus Boström, Andreas Føllesdal, Mikael Klintman, Michele Micheletti and Mads P. Sørensen, pp. 145–64. Copenhagen: Nordisk Ministerråd. norden.org/pub/velfaerd/konsument/sk/TN2005517.pdf

Miller, Daniel 2001. *The dialectics of shopping*. Chicago: University of Chicago Press.

O'Dell, Tom 1997. *Culture unbound: Americanization and everyday life in Sweden*. Lund: Nordic Academic Press.

Rowe, Janet and Colin Fudge 2003. Linking national sustainable development strategy and local implementation: a case study in Sweden. *Local Environment* 8: 120–48.

Schor, Juliet B. 1999. *The overspent American: why we want what we don't need*. New York: HarperPerennial.

Shove, Elizabeth 2004. *Comfort, cleanliness and convenience: the social organization of normality*. Oxford: Berg.

Sklair, Leslie 1995. *The sociology of the global system* (Second edition). Baltimore: Johns Hopkins University Press.

Thoreau, Henry David 1854. *Walden; or, life in the woods*. Boston: Ticknor and Fields.

de Tocqueville, Alexis 1835–40. *Democracy in America*. London: Saunders and Otley.

Veblen, Thorstein 1899. *The theory of the leisure class*. New York: The Macmillan Company.

Wilhite, Harold 2005. Why energy needs anthropology. *Anthropology Today* 21(3): 1–3.

Wilk, Richard 2004. Questionable assumptions about sustainable consumption. In *The ecological economics of consumption* (eds) Lucia Reisch and Inge Røpke, pp. 17–31. Cheltenham: Edward Elgar.

Chapter 8

ETHICAL CONSUMPTION AS RELIGIOUS TESTIMONY: THE QUAKER CASE

Peter Collins

One of the purposes of this volume is to place ethical consumption in its context, and the Introduction considers a number of such contexts. This chapter is concerned with a particular context, the sets of people within which ethical consumption takes place. The set that is the focus of this chapter is the Religious Society of Friends (Quakers) in Britain. My primary concern is with the ways in which the norms of that set of people come to determine, to a significant extent, the pattern of consumption of individual members.

The Introduction to this volume says that decisions made by ethical consumers are substantially shaped by their understanding of the moral nature of the commodities they confront. It goes on to say that this moral nature 'could, in principle, spring from almost anywhere; in contemporary ethical consumption it resides in the objects' social, economic, environmental and political contexts'. In light of this definition, it would appear that Quakers are ethical consumers, as their decision either to buy or refrain from buying this or that item is informed by their moral judgement.

However, if we consider the historical trajectory of Quaker consumption we can identify a principle, *plaining*, that suggests that Quaker consumption does not so readily fit the image of the typical ethical consumer, motivated by his or her individual moral calculus and the object's social, economic, environmental and political contexts. As we shall see, the focus on individual and object that is part of the presentation of ethical consumption as a consumer practice in a market system needs to be supplemented by the social contexts of ethical consumers.

During the first hundred years of the movement, roughly 1650 to 1750, Quakers adopted a system of discipline in which there were committees at various organisational levels, ranging from the local to the national. Those committees imposed upon the membership a strict regime of prescriptions and proscriptions concerning what we, but not necessarily they, would call consumption. These increasingly precise lists of do's and don'ts were justified by reference to Biblical text and concerned with just about every aspect of life. Quakers were told what they should eat and drink, how they should spend their leisure time, the kind of work they should and should not do; they were instructed how to bring children into the world, how they should marry and even how they should manage their funerals. Many, if not most, of these rules had a direct bearing on the kinds of things Quakers could and could not buy. I use the word 'could' rather than 'should' here because transgressors would, after a number of warnings, be 'disowned', that is, expelled from the group. To be a Quaker was to uphold the discipline, and the discipline demanded plain living: the conscious and careful disavowal of unnecessary purchase.

At first glance, then, Quakers looked like contemporary ethical consumers because their purchasing decisions reflected an assessment of the moral nature of objects on offer. However, their motivation and the bases of their assessments were rather different from those of present-day ethical consumers. Friends in the seventeenth and eighteenth centuries accepted the discipline imposed upon them primarily because they believed it was sanctioned by God, and that was enough. This appears to set these Quakers apart from present-day ethical consumers, free individuals assessing the moral nature of the individual objects that confront them. Instead, Quakers in previous centuries were compelled, in accepting Quaker discipline, to adopt particular patterns of consumption.

During the following two centuries, up to around 1950, the Religious Society of Friends changed in significant ways. The group became less embattled, less inward-looking. Individual Quakers began to move with increasing freedom among those who were not Friends, 'the world'. There were several reasons for this development, but I will briefly describe three.

Firstly, the old regime was viewed increasingly as unnecessarily repressive, emphasising relatively trivial aspects of life. These 'peculiarities' were seen increasingly as burdensome and hard to justify and they were removed during the 1850s, a time when the membership of British Quakers had reached a very low ebb (around 13,000).

Secondly, the state, which always found it difficult to tolerate a group that was so energetically critical of both state and state church, excluded Quakers from the universities, the church and from government; as pacifists, Quakers excluded themselves from the military. As Weber (2001 [1905]) argues, the Protestant work ethic drove Quakers into business, industry, commerce and banking. The result was the establishment of numerous Quaker dynasties, immensely wealthy families that had the resources to buy anything they liked. However, they were more or less committed to a religious faith and practice that constrained them markedly. This put them in a quandary, with the result that the majority of wealthy family members ceased to be Quaker, often becoming either Methodist or, more commonly, Anglican.

Thirdly, Friends abandoned the rule of endogamy that, up to the 1850s, had ensured that they married within the group. Theologically, the justification was that this practice ensured that members were not married by priests, whom the

Quakers, once again claiming Scriptural authority, abhorred as 'the hireling ministry'. The more liberal Friends said that the rapid decline in numbers during the first half of the nineteenth century was primarily a result of this marriage rule. With the abandoning of religious endogamy, Quakers could marry whomever they pleased, and this weakened Quakers' ability to socialise their children into the religion.

Together, these factors generated a number of awkward tensions both within the group and for individuals themselves. In the case of 'dynastic Quakers', and of many others who aspired to join the middle classes, the costs of constraint outweighed the benefits (including economic benefits). As a result, Quaker numbers may have stopped declining, but they failed to grow. To reach, after much toil and hardship, 'a certain social standing' and then to be prevented from enjoying its many pleasures (music and dancing, the theatre, hunting, literature), as well as the social relationships which that enjoyment facilitated, was too great a price to pay for a place in the Quaker Meeting, especially in a society whose ambient world view was increasingly secular.

But on top of this lies the continuing narrative of Quaker faith and practice, which is sustained in multifarious ways, but especially in and around the meeting house. It is this narrative that facilitates a conceptual and practical continuity between the present and the past. Friends are, nowadays, less restrained and constrained in their purchases by the minutiae of rules and regulations. Instead, they are more likely to make purchases based on what can be thought of as informed choice. It is important to note, though, that even though individual Quakers are not subject to the intrusive scrutiny of the past, the information on which choices are made remains in keeping with traditional Quaker faith and practice.

That traditional faith and practice continues to be driven both by Biblical injunction and, especially, by the simple belief that there is 'something of God in everyone' and that this belief should ground all of one's actions, even the most quotidian and certainly including the purchases one makes. The quasi-canonical text *Quaker faith and practice* (a handy and frequently up-dated repository of key Quaker writing) remains the group's most significant text, and provides a constant reminder of the continuity of faith and practice from 1650 to the present.

To the extent that Quakers voluntarily submit to, even welcome, group discipline and are willing to sustain the economic and social costs of that discipline, they are not free to determine their patterns of consumption in the way that the majority of ethical consumers are seen to do. To understand the effects of this, moreover, it is important to understand not just Quaker ethics, but two further things. One is the Quaker institutions and practices that have shaped and disseminated those ethics. The other is the broader social and historical events that have affected the context of those ethics and the composition of the body of Quakers who adhered to them.

Quaker Plain and Plaining

During the first fifty years of the movement, from about 1650 to 1700, influential committees of the Religious Society of Friends sent down hundreds of minutes to all members of the group that they should avoid purchasing clothing of a particular type, including the following (Minutes):

> – upon a query that was offered at our last Quarterly Meeting concerning f[riends]s buying, selling, making or wearing stript Cloth, Stuffs, Silks or any sort of flowered, or figured thing of different colours – It's the judgement of this meeting that f[riends]s stand clear of all such things, & that it be recommended to the mo. meetings.

> – that cross pockets before in men's coats, side sleeves, overfull skirted coats, & broad hems on cravats are not allowed by friends.

> – that f[riend]s enquire in their particular meetings that none be in the use of unnecessary & extravagant Perriwigs [later this is amended and Friends were merely required to ask their meeting's permission before their wore periwigs; 'full wigs' remained anathema].

Broadly speaking, the minute proscribes the wearing of, and therefore purchase of, apparel that is either *à la mode* or less than plain.[1] I present these minutes in order to give some idea of the precision with which these sets of rules (of which there were many) were formulated. Less than fifty years later the same committee proscribed the use of the umbrella and identified the acceptable design of gravestones: they should be small and semi-rounded, inscribed only with the name of the person deceased and the years of that person's birth and death. These rules were codified with increasing efficiency during the early eighteenth century (Collins 2002*b*). By 1850 the Society was in the vanguard of the abstinence movement and members were prevented from purchasing alcohol. By the 1990s, we find Friends meetings purchasing only 'long-life' electric bulbs. In this chapter I shall attempt to shed further light on these various happenstances, but first let us consider the origins and early development of Quakerism.

The shape of the religious landscape had been changing more or less continuously since the time of the Reformation in the sixteenth century. The hold on public and private life sustained by Roman Catholicism for more than five hundred years was broken down. Henry VIII established the Church of England, which owed allegiance to the monarch and not the pope. The Church of England was itself soon under attack from a growing number of sects, some of which came to be seen by the established church and the state as a serious threat to national stability. One such group was the Quakers (only later to become formalised as the Religious Society of Friends).

Quakerism emerged in England as a radical religious sect during the 1650s, a period of considerable social, political and religious turmoil (on the part played by Quakers during the English Civil War, see Reay 1985). Charles I was executed in 1649 and until the Restoration of the monarchy twelve years later,

England was ruled by the republican government of the Commonwealth, established by Oliver Cromwell. This was a time during which, it has been said, 'the world was turned upside down'. The aristocracy, so long the largely unchallenged bastion of power in England, was under sustained attack and, although the final outcome of this upheaval might not meet the criteria for revolution, the degree of change brought about by these events was considerable and long-lasting.

The origins of the movement are ambiguous, but in the tidied-up history of Quaker scholarship the founder is generally taken to be George Fox, a Leicestershire artisan. Fox began preaching what would become identifiable as 'the Quaker message' late in the 1640s, drawing on ideas already extant among small amorphous tendencies such as The Children of the Light and Seekers (Braithwaite 1955 [1912]; Moore 2000). These groups themselves shared segments of their very loosely constituted theology with continental movements such as Zwinglism, which itself drew in various ways on the faith and practice of earlier heretical groups such as the Cathars (Lambert 2002). Although these various faith-based social constellations were different in many ways, they have one important thing in common: an overt allegiance to 'the simple life' or, as I would prefer to say, *the plain* (Coleman and Collins 2000; Collins 1996, 2008*a*).

Since Ancient Greece, the plain is a tendency (for want of a better term) which is in a state of perpetual tension with its opposite: *the elaborated*. For the Greeks, and for the Romans after them, this tension was played out in the public sphere primarily by orators. There was a professional class of rhetoricians who plied their trade among those whose ambition it was to win arguments, legal arguments for the most part. The rhetoricians were regarded with considerable distaste by those who believed that language should remain pure, free of the various tropes employed in the art of rhetoric. So, here we have a clear distinction between the good (pure speech, the use of which was to discover the truth) and the bad (rhetoric, as embellished or elaborated speech, used to gain the ascendancy not only in argument but also in life) (Auksi 1995).

This plain–elaborated tension can be tracked easily through the centuries in various aspects of life, such as the separation of institutional Catholicism from the ascetic, and later monastic, traditions in Western Europe, even to the Catholic Reformers such as Fisher, More and Erasmus. And so we arrive, better prepared to understand the intellectual circumstances of the Reformation, commencing with Luther's nailing of his ninety-five theses to the door of the castle church in Wittenberg in 1517. Although this was an extremely complex social and political, as well as religious, transformation, the Protestant Reformation can be seen as a culmination of the plain–elaborate opposition. Catholicism had come to be perceived by many to have drifted very far from the simple message preached by Jesus in the New Testament. Its theology had become labyrinthine, its liturgy increasingly theatrical and its institutional organisation gargantuan. Luther, as well as other leading Reformation theologians such as Calvin and Zwingli, pared down Catholicism in their writings in an attempt to bring it back (as it were) to a simpler, more transparent New Testament Christianity. Luther argued that Catholicism had become rotten, exemplified by such abominations as indulgences.

During the next two hundred years, the Reformed Church replaced Catholicism in much of Northern Europe. Under Henry VIII (and later Elizabeth I) Anglicanism swept through England, forcing major changes on theology, liturgy and church government. Eamon Duffy (2005) describes this process in his *The stripping of the altars*, and it certainly involved a removal of much that underpinned the wealth and therefore the authority of the Catholic Church, including the monasteries. However, within a century of Luther's nintey-five theses, Anglicanism was under attack in England, first from a revitalised Catholicism during the Counter-Reformation and then by groups that developed outside the established church. These groups were loosely knit but increasingly determined to bring the process of Reformation to its conclusion, which they believed was religious toleration. The belief and practice of these groups varied considerably, but a number of them felt that the simplification of faith and practice had not gone nearly far enough. The degree of elaboration reached by Catholicism was obnoxious to the members of these groups, but they were disappointed that Anglicanism had not developed far enough and believed that the simplification of religion they desired could not be attained except from without. We come, then, to the upheavals in England in the middle of the seventeenth century.

The Canonic Foundations of the Quaker Testimony to the Plain

Early Quakers stood out against the practices of the established church. Indeed it might be said that Quakerism played the *vis-à-vis* with it, standing in all things as its opposite (Boon 1982; Collins 1996). Friends denied the authority of priests trained at the universities, saying that such qualification was no guarantee that one's words derived from God. They regularly interrupted the sermons of priests and were involved in lengthy, convoluted and public pamphlet-wars with clerics and divines. They refused to pay tithes and all other church dues. Indeed, the majority of Friends suffered for this, mostly through distraint of property, imprisonment or, in many cases, both (Braithwaite 1921, 1955 [1912]). They denied absolutely the validity of the sacraments, arguing that outward signs of inward grace were entirely unnecessary and a means only of confusing ordinary people who only had to look within themselves to find God. They did not, therefore, celebrate the Eucharist, did not baptise ('dip') infants, married themselves (without recourse to a priest) and conducted their own burials. Should a Quaker fail to follow these practises then he or she would, in most cases, have been disowned. Indeed, by the middle of the nineteenth century the number of disownments resulting from 'marrying with a priest' almost brought an end to the Society.

Apart from their radical anti-establishment views and actions, the first generation of Quakers established themselves as plain people. Although they developed no creed, there was a shared belief among them that God was immanent in everyone. The entire emphasis in their theology was on the Inward Light, and outer manifestations of 'the religious' were of little interest. Paradoxically, however, they could not avoid exemplifying their emphasis on the inner through outward manifestations. For example, they adopted a simple liturgy, which some theologians might argue is hardly a liturgy at all. Quakers met for worship in a convenient place, sometimes in the home of one of their number and at others in the open air. Their meetings, or conventicles as they were defined by the state, were illegal from the outset. When a Meeting's adult participants were carted off to gaol, their children would continue to meet. No sooner were those imprisoned released than they returned to their meetings.

Apart from their steadfastness, it was the simplicity of their liturgy that enabled them to continue to meet despite sustained and often brutal attacks, imprisonment and heavy fines. Friends were further united in their sufferings. Friends met together and waited for God to speak through one of their number. If so moved, the man or woman would rise and offer ministry, then sit down. This practice of 'waiting in the Light' proved impossible for the authorities to suppress. They adopted plain dress, as indicated at the beginning of this chapter, and plain language. Plain language was achieved in a number of ways. For instance, Quakers did not distinguish between higher and lower status, through the use of 'thee' or 'thou'. It was customary at the time to address one of a higher social status as 'you', and Quakers disrupted the status quo by addressing everyone as 'thee' and 'thou'. Whether intentional or not, this usage was seen as dangerously levelling, as was their absolute refusal to use titles. In greeting, Quakers eschewed the usual bowing and scraping and refused to raise their hat in any circumstance, causing them further problems with those in authority. Drawing overtly on Biblical text, they refused in every case to swear, which caused them particular difficulty when facing charges in court. Such behaviour was taken as radical indeed, in a society whose stability depended to a large extent on maintaining social distinction (Bauman 1983).

In the second paragraph of Proposition 15, Barclay (1678) sums up the main social testimonies as practised by Friends at the time of writing (the 1660s and 1670s):

1) That it is not lawful to give to men such flattering titles as, 'Your Holiness', 'Your Majesty', 'Your Eminency', 'Your Excellency' 'Your Grace', 'Your Lordship', 'Your Honor', &c., nor use those flattering words commonly called 'compliments'.

2) That it is not lawful for Christians to kneel or prostrate themselves to any man, or to bow the body, or to uncover the head to them.

3) That it is not lawful for a Christian to use superfluities in apparel, as are of no use save for ornament and vanity.

4) That it is not lawful to use games, sports, plays, nor, among other things, comedies among Christians, under the notion of recreations, which do not agree with Christian silence, gravity, and sobriety: for laughing, sporting, gaming, mocking, jesting, talking &c., is not Christian liberty, nor harmless mirth.

5) That it is not lawful for Christians to swear at all under the Gospel, not only not vainly, and in their common discourse, which was also forbidden under the Mosaical law, but even not in judgment before the magistrate.

6) That it is not lawful for Christians to resist evil, or to war or fight in any case.

Many of these rules were not as clear as they might have been. In terms of dress, for instance, it was not enough to know that 'it is not lawful for a Christian to use superfluities in apparel, as are of no use save for ornament and vanity', because this injunction does not make clear what is to be counted as a 'superfluity'. Friends needed to have spelled out to them just what counted as plain dress, which led to the torrent of minutes containing the requisite information that Friends had to act upon. Barclay's justification of such proscriptions (proposition 15, Paragraph 7), as follows, is long but merits quoting in full:

> the Scripture severely reproves such practices, both commending and commanding the contrary, as Isa. 3. How severely doth the prophet reprove the daughters of Israel for their tinkling ornaments, their cauls, and their round tiars, their chains and bracelets, &c., and yet is it not strange to see Christians allow themselves in these things, from whom a more strict and exemplary conversation is required? Christ desires us not to be anxious about our clothing (Matt. 6:25), and to show the vanity of such as glory in the splendor of their clothing, tells them, that even Solomon in all his glory was not to be compared to the lily of the field, which today is, and tomorrow is cast into the oven. But surely they make small reckoning of Christ's words and doctrine, that are so curious in their clothing, and so industrious to deck themselves, and so earnest to justify it, and so mad when they are reproved for it. The apostle Paul is very positive in this respect (1 Tim. 2:8–10): 'I will therefore in like manner also, that women adorn themselves in modest apparel, with shamefacedness and sobriety, not with broidered hair, or gold, or pearls, or costly array: But (which becometh women, professing godliness) with good works.' To the same purpose saith Peter (1 Pet. 3:3–4): 'Whose adorning, let it not be that outward adorning, of plaiting the hair, and wearing of gold, or of putting on of apparel. But let it be the hidden man of the heart, in that which is not corruptible, even the ornament of a meek and quiet spirit,' &c. Here, both the apostles do very positively and expressly assert two things: First, that the adorning of Christian women (of whom it is particularly spoken, I judge, because this sex is most naturally inclined to that vanity, and that it seems that Christian men in those days, deserved not in this respect so much to be reproved) ought not to be outward, nor to consist in the apparel. Secondly, that they ought not to use the plaiting of the hair, or ornaments, &c., which was at that time the custom of the nations. But is it not strange, that such as make the Scripture their rule, and pretend they are guided by it, should not only be so frequently and ordinarily in the use of these things, which the Scripture so plainly condemns, but also should allow themselves in so doing? For the apostles not only commend the forbearance of these

things, as an attainment commendable in Christians, but condemn the use of them as unlawful, and yet may it not seem more strange, that in contradiction to the apostles' doctrine, as if they had resolved to slight their testimony, they should condemn those that, out of conscience, apply themselves seriously to follow it, as if, in so doing, they were singular, proud, or superstitious? This certainly betokens a sad apostasy in those that will be accounted Christians, that they are so offended with those who love to follow Christ and his apostles, in denying of, and departing from, the lying vanities of this perishing world, and so doth much evidence their affinity with such as hate to be reproved, and neither will enter themselves nor suffer those that would.

The use of Scripture is typical not only of Barclay but of all Quaker writers defending their faith and practice at this time. The testimony to the plain was supported primarily by Biblical text and was less a matter of economy or society and more a matter of theology, more precisely: faith. A simpler statement was issued by the Yearly Meeting of 1691:

> It is our tender and Christian advice that Friends take care to keep to truth and plainness, in language, habit, deportment and behaviour; that the simplicity of truth in these things may not wear out nor be lost in our days, nor in our posterity's; and to avoid pride and immodesty in apparel, and all vain and superfluous fashions of the world (Quaker Faith and Practice 1995: para 20.28).

This short paragraph is important for at least two reasons. First, the text clearly indicates that one should consume only what one needs. Second, the text has not only survived to the present but is included in *Quaker faith and practice* (the latest edition of the *Book of discipline*), the materialisation of the Quaker canon, thereby demonstrating the continuity of this key testimony.

The Significance of Discipline

Quaker discipline, justified Biblically, was strictly maintained from the outset (Collins 2008b). How was this achieved? There were several reasons, but two are of particular significance. First of all, George Fox was not only a charismatic preacher, he was also blessed with a genius for organisation. Fox established a simple though effective structure that was more or less complete by 1690 (Fox died in 1691) and that has remained mostly intact until the present day (see Figure 8.1).

Major decisions, such as the introduction of formal membership in the middle of the eighteenth century, were taken at Yearly Meeting (YM), which was then generally held in London during the spring. YM sent minutes 'down' to Quarterly Meetings (QM; which, unsurprisingly, met four times a year), which sent minutes 'down' to Monthly Meetings (MM; which usually met once a month), which sent minutes 'down' to local congregations or Preparative Meetings. And there was simultaneous movement in the opposite direction. 'Concerns' (such as the state of slaves) developed at

Preparative (local) Meetings (PM)

↑ ↓

Monthly (county) Meetings (MM)

Quarterly (regional) Meetings (QM)

Yearly (national) Meeting (YM)

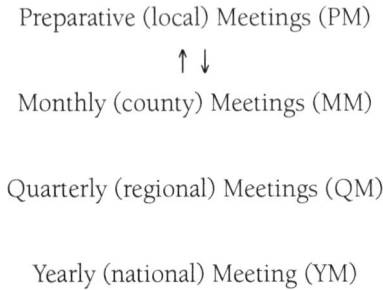

Figure 8.1. The structure of Quaker meetings (the arrows represent minutes which were sent up and down the organisational ladder)

Preparative Meetings (PM) would be sent 'up' to MM, and so on. Indeed, the PM was so-called because its major role was to 'prepare' business for MM. Fox placed MM at the centre of this structure. Meetings which comprised MM would, in most cases, be near enough for Friends to travel to them. MM was, therefore, not only a time for transacting church business but also a major social occasion. Given that the Society remained endogamous until 1860, such occasions provided an opportunity for future marriage partners to meet and mingle. It was to MM that an individual applied for membership and it was MM which was responsible for marriages and funerals. Senior members of the Society, Elders and Overseers (and until 1926, Recorded Ministers), were appointed by MM.

Together with the proscription against 'marrying out', the tight organisation led, from 1700, to the construction of a tightly knit and extremely well-disciplined group. Elders and Overseers were expected to police their meetings and bring those who were thought to be 'walking disorderly' to book. The various prescriptions and proscriptions multiplied enormously after 1660 (the Restoration of the Monarchy in England) and were circulated freely throughout the Society. The process became increasingly formalised after 1700, when meetings were expected to respond to a list of queries, often as Minutes sent down to local meetings, that sought to discover the extent to which a meeting was 'abiding in the Light'. At the same time, of course, members policed one another. Surveillance was, then, intense. For the most part, Quakers did indeed abide by the rules. After all, they would have been familiar with the central testimonies (against tithes and the military, for instance) and indeed would have been drawn into the group largely because they subscribed to these beliefs and practices. Friends, in addition to being unusually well organised, were literate (Peters 2005). This enabled leading Friends to communicate by letter to newly forming Meetings all over England. Fox himself was a prolific writer and communicator sending out thousands of epistles, many of which offer advice, for the most part Biblically grounded, on how to live the Quaker life. The theology of the group was worked out in a more or less ad hoc way, often during skirmishes with priests, both in print and in public debate.

Robert Barclay wrote the only systematic Quaker theology. His *Apology* was published first in Latin (1676) and later in English (1678). It is difficult to say how many Friends were familiar with the details of Barclay's arguments, but most would have been familiar with them in broad terms. Barclay's defence of Quakerism is a piece very much of its time. He assimilated the various attacks on Quaker faith and practice and responded systematically to each with infinite care and with constant reference to Biblical text. He presented fifteen propositions dealing with key theological or doctrinal issues (*The True Foundation of Knowledge*, *Immediate Revelation*, *The Scriptures*) liturgy (*The Ministry*, *Worship*, *Baptism*, *The Communion*), and what we might call practical religion (*The Power of the Civil Magistrate in Matters purely Religious and pertaining to the Conscience*, *Salutations and Recreations*). Barclay's fervently Christian text has never been revised and nowadays is seldom referred to in Quaker discourse.

In Bourdieu's (1977) terms, the Religious Society of Friends generated a particular habitus. The group was well organised, inward-looking and steadfast in it faith and practice. Friends met at home, at meeting and, in many cases, at work. Children growing up in Quaker families were socialised into the Society from birth, developed friendships among Quakers, often went to school together and often were apprenticed into businesses owned and managed by Quakers. By 1750 the Society of Friends comprised a web of kinship networks: the community was tightly knit and one's life was perpetually exposed to the critical eye of one's peers within the group. Social control ensured that discipline was strictly maintained. Miscreants would find themselves, after a sometimes lengthy period of interviews, cast out from the group, and thereby deprived of the benefits accruing to members, including financial aid in difficult times.

Quaker discipline, increasingly formalised after 1700, touched on every aspect of an individual's life, from the moment of birth to the point of death and beyond. At this point, the majority of Friends were indeed people of the 'middling sort', artisans, shop-keepers, husbandmen. They strove to lead what they, and others, regarded as simple lives. Their discipline embraced the plain and encouraged the active and ongoing definition of consumables as more or less plain. I have called this activity, which appears to have been more or less conscious, 'plaining'. The vast number of rules that Quakers were expected to assimilate gave them the ability to distinguish what was and what was not plain, and so they developed a plaining gaze. What would now be called peer-group pressure, ever-present given the closed nature of the Society, functioned as a means of checking the quotidian decision making of individuals. Consumer items that were new on the market, as were umbrellas in the mid-eighteenth century, were routinely proscribed: a hat was considered plain, but not an umbrella. One who lived the simple life was necessarily closer to God, and that belief, simple in itself, provided a sufficiently strong moral and theological foundation on which to construct a way of life. Plaining was fluid, however, and at some point after they were fashionably new, Quakers joined the mass of the population in their consumption of umbrellas.

The plain should not be confused with the cheap. The characteristic dress of Quakers in the eighteenth century was cut from a grey cloth that was heavy and relatively expensive. Well-off members might have furnished their homes plainly (in the aesthetic sense) but not inexpensively. In this case it was not the quality of cloth that underwent plaining, but the cut and the colour and pattern. 'Gay' colours and patterns, including stripes and checks, were listed as proscribed in several minutes sent down before and after 1700. The discipline implied (always) that to pay too much attention to the outward (and especially regarding gestures and dress, one's public front) was to pay too little attention to one's inward state, to that place where God was located.

As well as being consumers, Quakers were obviously producers. Indeed, male Quakers were more or less forced into trade and industry on account of their legal exclusion from the gentlemanly occupations. Their discipline ensured that they traded fairly, and in many cases (as we will see later on) they prospered because of it. Quaker retailers and traders were among the first and the most consistent in their use of standard weights and measures. They also gained a good reputation for maintaining the purity of their products, for they tended not to dilute liquids or mix chalk dust with flour. 'Fair trading' was, then, a part of Quaker ideology at least from 1700 onwards.

The Paradox of Worldly Success

While there were many benefits in belonging to the Religious Society of Friends in the eighteenth and nineteenth centuries, there were several major disadvantages. In the first place, as I have noted, the armed services, the church and the universities were closed to them. By 1860, the Society had undergone major changes. There is an oft-repeated anecdote about Elisabeth Fry who was a 'gay Friend', that is one who trod a narrow line between membership and expulsion on account of her (relatively) flamboyant dress. Many of those families who had been of the middling sort a century before were now wealthy bankers, manufacturers and industrialists.[2] For dynastic families such as the Lloyds, Gurneys, Cadburys, Frys, Rowntrees, Huntleys and Palmers, living the plain life became a serious challenge, what Walvin (1997: Chap. 3) calls the challenge between 'plainness and plenty' (see also Raistrick 1968).

Let us take Henry Wood and his family as an example (Boyson 1970). Henry was of sound Lancashire yeomanry stock. His grandparents and parents began to shift their interests from agriculture to trading and manufacture, and eventually into the manufacture of cotton. Henry's father had become a Quaker in 1793; his mother Isabel was born into a Quaker family of considerable standing. Henry and Isabel sent all their children to Quaker boarding schools, and as adults they married Quakers and were dependable members, regularly attending business meetings. The Ashworth children had assimilated the Quaker habitus long before they grew into adulthood (Collins 2002*a*).

Henry, the eldest child, came to play a leading role in the financial and administrative life of Bolton Meeting. He married Letitia Binns in 1823 and soon set up a twelve-bedroom mansion on his 102-acre estate overlooking his factory just outside Bolton: clearly 'the simple life' was a relative concept. Boyson suggests that Henry was a pragmatist both in business and in his Quakerism. Henry remained a weighty member of the Society throughout his life, but by middle age he was hunting and shooting, smoking cigars and drinking port. The fortunes of the Wood family climaxed after Henry found himself in the heartland of cotton manufacture. In the early 1850s he rented various shooting lodges, eventually renting the 14,500-acre Rottall Lodge in north Forfarshire at £500 a year. Boyson (1970: 254) adds: 'Henry Ashworth did not look or act like a typical Quaker … he dressed extremely well and at the age of eighty-four bought a black beaver waistcoat and a black beaver swinging coat with silk linings from a Savile Row tailor.'

Furthermore, although Quakers by birth and all educated in Quaker public schools, few of his eleven children remained Quakers. His older sons, by the time they had entered their majority, began to behave in ways that disturbed even their father's relatively liberal feelings. They were disciplined by Bolton and eventually 'married out' and into Anglicanism. This was not uncommon for the sons of Quaker manufacturers: such men were inheriting large amounts of capital and are unlikely to have felt comfortable with the restrictions imposed by Quaker discipline. They may have begun moving in Quaker circles, but soon found themselves mixing and mingling with the families of other manufacturers, regardless of their denomination. Indeed, it was the haemorrhaging of members in the first half of the nineteenth century (membership reached a low of 13,859 in 1861) that led to the implementation of far-reaching changes to Quaker discipline, including the ending of endogamy and the rescinding of the welter of rules relating to dress, language use and so forth (Isichei 1970: 111–43; Kennedy 2001: 12–46).

Plaining represents the Quaker form of ethical consumption, a form that differs from typical contemporary ethical consumption. When present-day consumers buy good-quality Fairtrade tea, which costs about the same as good-quality regular tea, they get a decent cup of tea and achieve their aims. It is, thus, reasonable to represent this sort of consumption as relatively free of cost. Plaining, on the other hand, is achieved at a price. The Ashworths, like the majority of members of the Religious Society of Friends, remained members so long as benefits were perceived to outweigh costs, and membership had significant spiritual, sociocultural and economic benefits. What emerges very clearly from the account of the Ashworth family is that the cost of membership, and of plaining in particular, could be high: it is this, perhaps above all else, that sets the Quaker case apart from contemporary practices of ethical consumption. For Quakers, particularly Victorian Quakers, there has always been a very real price to pay for adhering to Quaker faith and practice. The Ashworths were typical of wealthy middle-class families who accepted, voluntarily, the challenges posed by accepting Quaker discipline. However, such families were also aware, and painfully so, of the costs of that discipline, including the extent to which sociocultural, political and economic networks were closed to them. These costs were diffuse and often difficult to assess, but they were real all the same. In many cases, it seems, wealthy Quakers came to believe that the costs outweighed the benefits and left the Society as a result.

Conclusions

Since the earliest years of the movement, Quakers have maintained a testimony to the simple, the plain. Rather than focus on their behaviour at the point of purchase, which would reflect the stress on market decisions that exists in ethical consumption, we have found it more profitable to concentrate on why they eschew consumption in the ways they do. The first generation of Friends preached this message in public and in their own meetings for worship, they wrote epistles to each other and to the general population, they published pamphlets and debated with clergy in the streets and churches. The testimony is emphasised in the quasi-canonic *Book of discipline*, which was first published in the eighteenth century and has passed through many editions since then, the most recent appearing in 1994. The plain is a vital component of Quaker faith and practice, of its ideology, if you like. Unlike the majority of cases presented in this collection, it is an ideology that is less concerned to defend the social sphere against the onslaught of the economic and far more concerned with the significance for this life and the next of 'God's Kingdom', that is, of the religious sphere.

What marks Quakerism as different from other contemporary religious groups is that their view of ethical consumption remains a part of a broader worldview which has a historical trajectory reaching back to the 1650s: the plaining tendency. The testimony to plain living implies that, during the course of the last 350 years, Quakers pursued a form of consumption that fits the fundamental dimension of 'ethical' laid out in the Introduction (the volume). That is not to say that each and every individual Quaker has, in every purchase, abided by the discipline that the testimony imposes upon them. What I argue, however, is that the principle is certain to have coloured the kinds of choices that Quakers have made and, as I have shown elsewhere, have continued to make (Coleman and Collins 2000; Collins 1996, 2001). This is bound to be the case, in that those who flouted the testimony will either have been disowned by the group or would have chosen to leave of their own accord. This is the position in which the sons and daughters of many wealthy Victorian Quakers found themselves, as the example of the Ashworth family indicates. The circle of potential spouses simply became too narrow.

The Quaker case, then, illustrates points that are pertinent for this volume. Firstly, and as noted in the Introduction, that case shows the risk of treating as ethical consumption all the sorts of market behaviour that superficially resemble it. Quakers certainly are ethical consumers in the broad sense, but their motivations and orientations differ markedly from the contemporary body of ethical consumers. Secondly, what I have presented here shows the importance of broadening our attention beyond the market transaction, the shopper standing in the supermarket aisle, that is so important in ethical consumption.

One such broadening involves placing the consumer in his or her social setting, in the way that Bourdieu (1984) did when he presented taste and distinction as creatures of social structures and relations. In this regard, Quakers show the pressures that can face those who seek to live modest and ethical lives, the sort of pressures that affect many of the Swedes that Cindy Isenhour (this volume) describes. As the dynastic families of the nineteenth century show, the desire for social status in a materialistic society, especially among those who are reasonably wealthy, can induce individuals to change their lives away from their previous values and practices, and instead to become fairly conformist members of the upper ranks of society.

A second broadening is related to the previous one, for it too locates ethical consumption in a social setting. Here, though, the setting is the practices and mechanisms that shape ethical consumption and that have consequences for what ethical consumers do and think. Among the Italian ethical consumers described by Grasseni (this volume), those practices and mechanisms shape the presentation of objects as more or less local, and hence ethical, and they constrain the ability of Italian ethical consumers to locate suppliers, make purchases, acquire and consume in an ethical way. Among the Quakers that I have described, these practices and mechanisms shape Quakers' values and lives, and so shape their decisions about what to purchase and consume and also, in the longer term, whether to continue to adhere to Quaker faith and practice.

During the last century there have been many attempts to describe and account for the relationship between society (religion) and economy (consumption) but there is an inherent weakness in much of this scholarship, and it is a weakness found even in Weber: the tendency to treat the religious motivation of those involved in economic practices as epiphenomenal. What I hope to have shown in this chapter is the ways in which the *disciplinary* nature of the religious life partially drives the economy. I have focused in this instance on processes of consumption, but the same argument can be shown to hold for production. That, however, is a different paper.

Notes

1. As implied in this volume's Introduction, there is an aesthetic as well as an ethic involved here. I have written about this issue in some depth elsewhere (Collins 2001).
2. . Although eighteenth-century Quakers were not as central to Weber's thesis in *The Protestant ethic and the spirit of capitalism* as were Calvinists, they do warrant at least a brief mention. Commenting on Barclay's *Apology* (with particular reference to Puritan asceticism) Weber correctly maintains that 'The campaign against the temptations of the flesh, and the dependence on external things, was, as besides the Puritans the great Quaker apologist Barclay expressly says, not a struggle against the rational acquisition, but against the irrational use of wealth.' (Weber 2001 [1905]: 171)

Bibliography

Archival Material

Minutes. Report from Representatives to Quarterly Meeting from Marsden Monthly Meeting 12th Month 1704. Minutes (Mens) of Marsden Monthly Meeting (1678–1918). FRM 1/3. Lancashire Records Office, Preston.

Published Material

Auksi, Peter 1995. *Christian plain style: the evolution of a spiritual ideal*. Montreal: McGill-Queen's University Press.
Barclay, Robert 1678. *An apology for the true Christian divinity*.
Bauman, Richard 1983. *Let your words be few: symbolism and silence among seventeenth-century Quakers*. Cambridge: Cambridge University Press.
Boon, James 1982. *Other tribes, other scribes: symbolic anthropology in the comparative study of cultures, histories, religions, and texts*. Cambridge: Cambridge University Press.
Bourdieu, Pierre 1977. *Outline of a theory of practice*. Cambridge: Cambridge University Press.
——— 1984. *Distinction: a social critique of the judgement of taste*. London: Routledge & Kegan Paul.
Boyson, Rhodes 1970. *The Ashworth cotton enterprise: the rise and fall of a family firm, 1818–1880*. Oxford: Clarendon Press.
Braithwaite, William C. 1921. *The second period of Quakerism*. London: Macmillan.
——— 1955 [1912]. *The beginnings of Quakerism*. Cambridge: Cambridge University Press.
Coleman, Simon and Peter Collins 2000. The plain and the positive: ritual, experience and aesthetics in Quakerism and charismatic Christianity. *Journal of Contemporary Religion* 15: 317–29.
Collins, Peter 1996. 'Plaining': the social and cognitive practice of symbolization in the Religious Society of Friends. *Journal of Contemporary Religion* 11: 277–88.
——— 2001. Quaker plaining as critical aesthetic. *Quaker Studies* 5: 121–39.
——— 2002a. Habitus and the storied self: religious faith and practice as a dynamic means of consolidating identities. *Culture and Religion* 3: 147–61.

———— 2002*b*. Discipline: the codification of Quakerism as orthopraxy, 1650–1738. *History and Anthropology* 13(2): 17–32.

———— 2008*a*. The problem of Quaker identity. In *The Quaker condition: the sociology of a liberal tradition* (eds) Pink Dandelion and P. Collins, pp. 39–53. Newcastle: Cambridge Scholars Publishing.

———— 2008*b*. The practice of discipline and the discipline of practice. In *Exploring regimes of discipline: the dynamics of restraint* (ed) Noel Dyke, pp. 135–55. Oxford: Berghahn.

Duffy, Eamon 2005. *The stripping of the altars: traditional religion in England 1400–1580.* New Haven: Yale University Press.

Isichei, Elizabeth 1970. *Victorian Quakers.* Oxford: Oxford University Press.

Kennedy, Thomas 2001. *British Quakerism 1860–1920.* Oxford: Oxford University Press.

Lambert, Malcolm 2002. *Medieval heresy.* Oxford: Blackwell.

Lippe, Toinette 2002. *Nothing left over: a plain and simple life.* New York: J.P. Tarcher.

Moore, Rosemary 2000. *The light in their consciences.* University Park: Pennsylvania State University Press.

Peters, Kate 2005. *Print culture and the early Quakers.* Cambridge: Cambridge University Press.

Quaker Faith and Practice 1995. *Quaker faith and practice.* London: Yearly Meeting of the Religious Society of Friends (Quakers) in Britain.

Raistrick, Arthur 1968. *Quakers in science and industry: being an account of the Quaker contributions to science and industry during the 17th and 18th centuries.* Newton Abbot: David and Charles.

Reay, Barry 1985. *The Quakers and the English Revolution.* London: Temple Smith.

Walvin, James 1997. *The Quakers: money and morals.* London: John Murray.

Weber, Max 2001 [1905]. *The Protestant ethic and the spirit of capitalism.* London: Routledge.

Chapter 9

RE-INVENTING FOOD:
THE ETHICS OF DEVELOPING LOCAL FOOD

Cristina Grasseni

The title of this chapter recalls the phenomenon of the 're-invention of food' (Grasseni 2007*a*), a way of rediscovering and revaluing food as patrimony, as cultural heritage and as a catalyst of new forms of relationships and ways of life. This process is diverse and often entails a transformation of the production, perception, representation and consumption of food. In this chapter I will approach this process and these transformations, and the entanglements that they entail, through a consideration of contemporary forms of the production and distribution of food in Italy. The production I describe is the certification of varieties of local cheese, while the distribution hinges on voluntary groups for alternative provisioning practices.

Both cheese certification and alternative distribution touch on issues that are central to ethical consumption more generally, for both seek to move away from the anonymous commodities and impersonal relations of large-scale agriculture and food distribution that have generated social and political critique (Petrini 2005; Shiva 2007). In Italy, but also in other countries, one sign of that critique is the emergence of self-organised networks, for instance *gruppi di acquisto solidale* (GAS, solidarity purchasing groups; Saroldi 2001). A second sign of the critique is the increasing influence of international movements like Slow Food. In addition, local agricultural associations, and some local development projects based on what Italians call 'typical' (*tipico*) products, focus increasingly on values other than the commercial. These networks, movements and associations are part of an effort to create a food system that allows and even expresses the sorts of concerns that characterise much ethical consumption.

Food is a highly constructed object. Different social actors, politics and practices coalesce around it, so that it carries a complex sedimentation of meanings (e.g., Camporesi 1993; Lévi-Strauss 1964; Montanari 2004). Here, I shall present only two such social actors, related to different but at times overlapping forms of 'authentic' consumption: traditional producers striving for official recognition and 'critical consumers' (as ethical consumers are commonly called in Italy; see Orlando, this volume). Both are concerned with the revitalisation of locality and tradition, with the critical and problematic role played by technological innovation, and with processes of standardisation in 'typical' and 'traditional' food production.

In this chapter, I shall present examples of two kinds of things that can happen to local food when it becomes re-invented. The first of these is its transformation into 'typical products'. In considering this, I focus on the local conflicts that can ensue from the transformation of marginal rural areas into locations for the production of typical foods, commonly through systems of certification such as that described by Audrey Vankeerberghen's chapter (this volume) on organic farming in Belgium. The second of these is the cultivation of direct relationships between producers and consumers, as in the case of the GAS. In considering this, I provide a brief overview of some increasingly popular strategies of alternative consumption, which attract increasing scholarly attention (see Forno and Ceccarini 2006; Forno and Gunnarson 2009; Roos, Terragni and Torjusen 2007; Sassatelli 2007).

I wish to note at the outset that my focus is not on how authentic food is or can become, nor is it on how ethical critical consumers are or could be. Rather, it is on what happens to local food when it enters new circuits of exchange and resignification, a process that entails its reassessment in terms of authenticity. I approach this in terms of two questions: What happens to local food in the process of trying to prove its authenticity or to consume it ethically? What happens to those who produce it and consume it?

What I say in my attempts to answer these questions will echo some of what Peter Collins (this volume) says about Quakers and their ethical consumption. That is, while ethical consumption may be presented and imagined in terms of individuals making assessments of the objects that they confront, this is in fact an area of collective and associative behaviour, which is much more complex than an individualistic model of consumer choice. Social processes and relations shape and frame the nature of such choice, the ways that people assess the objects they confront and their motives for and practices of consuming ethically.

The Ethics of Developing Local Foods

When we face the problem of the authentic-in-practice, 'typical products' reveal themselves for what they are: oxymorons (Papa 2002). They are specialist foods with a mass-market success that testifies to the widespread search for tasteful consumption as a sign of distinction (Bourdieu 1987). Because this taste for the local is a global phenomenon, we would expect it to increase standardisation. However, one can witness several 'glocal' strategies (Bauman 1998) aimed at regaining local diversities that can also be appreciated in market terms.[1]

Strategies of food rediscovery imply a novel reading of local histories and the re-evaluation of local resources as patrimony, often associated with formal systems of certification and sale to distant consumers. At least in Italy and Europe, local policy makers, entrepreneurs and producers are the agents of this latter kind of innovation, with effects at the microscopic level as well as the global. In the case of mountain cheese, for instance, the reorganisation of its artisanal production (and the resulting changes in the competencies of the producers and in their social roles) are reflected and reinforced in the dynamic of offer and demand, as well as in the variable strategies of logistics and marketing. It becomes important for niche producers to have dedicated customers as well as reliable and trustworthy merchants (the specialist cheese-shop owner, the restaurant cook, the president of a cooperative of consumers or the coordinator of a collective purchasing group), as access to large distribution chains is expensive and extremely competitive. The effects, including the risks, are often hard to foresee. These include an increase in local conflicts because of heightened competition, a loss of local knowledge and skills and the increasing dependence of regional economies on world markets. Also, the practices and discourse, as well as the gestures, routines and environments, of work change.

Especially in the case of food, it is difficult to determine what lies inside or outside of a global technoscientific process of innovation, and hence what counts as valid or harmful local practice and what counts as traditional or artificial production. The bitterness of the current arguments for and against the re-introduction of raw milk in farmers' markets, or the heated controversies that have arisen about what is gained and what is lost when using ferments in cheese (see Paxson 2008), are controversies not just over plain technical facts, but also are over local histories of skilled practice and the associated cultural assumptions and values.

It is useful, then, to focus on 'boundary objects' (Leigh Star and Griesemer 1989). Precisely because they lie at the intersection of different discourses and practices, they often occasion controversy. Apt examples are the milk ferments used in making cheese that 'contaminate' local cheese with industrially selected bacteria in order to assure faultless maturation and predictable taste; the protocols of production that codify local practice and report it to national and international institutions; or the extra nutrients that are routinely added to the ration of an industrially bred cow. Boundary objects remind us of the specific materiality of the contexts of transformation of food production and consumption, and such objects (manure, for instance) are systematically absent from the collective imaginary about food consumption.

To focus on the very agents of food calibration means posing not only the problem of innovation but also that of the standardisation of expert practice and tacit knowledge (Polanyi 1966). The technical culture of standards (of taste, of packaging shapes, of the procedures of self-monitoring and of protocols of production) is also and especially a scientific culture that permeates social culture (Strathern 2000) and thus enforces a 'global hierarchy of value' (Herzfeld 2004).[2]

At the same time, there is a symbolic aspect of the process of food re-invention, which refers to questions of identity and territorial belonging, to marking boundaries and retracing lineages and memory as part of an 'invention of tradition' (Hobsbawm and Ranger 1992). I have elaborated elsewhere (Grasseni 2007*a*) on the transformation of traditional mountain cheese in the Italian Alps as a result of the lengthy processes leading to the official assignment of a European, certified denomination such as a Protected Designation of Origin (*Denominazione di Origine Protetta*, DOP) or a Protected Geographical Indication (*Indicazione Geografica Protetta*).[3] Here, I wish to approach this re-invention specifically in relation to ethical consumption.

An instance of this is a local product such as alpage cheese. In Southern Europe, particularly Italy and France, this is made in the mountains during the summer season, when transhumant herders take their stock to graze pastures at high altitudes (higher than one thousand meters), which are not available during the winter. Because of the difficulty of conserving and transporting the milk, when goats and cattle are milked in the high pastures the milk is immediately transformed into cheese. Necessarily, these are small producers, but they are linked by diverse traditions of cooperation and labour division.

An historical and ethnographic cartography of the cultural heritage of dairy production, in the Italian Alps at least, sketches a complex and dynamic map. For instance, a traditional distinction holds in Vallée d'Aoste between two alpine dairy practices. One, '*à grande montagne*', produces fat *fontina* cheese for the market and is based on collective practices of alpage and cheese-making in common premises. The other, '*à petite montagne*', produces skimmed cheese (*tome*) and butter for domestic consumption on the basis of family pastures and cattle. Anthropologists have debated whether this distinction was due to a cultural diversity in associative practices between the ethnically diverse valleys of Romance (Latin) or Walser (Germanic) descent, each characterised by distinct systems of land inheritance. While the former would be keener on associative practices (also due to land dispersal through inheritance), the latter would be characterised by individualism and the maintenance of one single homestead through the generations. In fact, long periods of continuity are followed by sudden diversifications in production practices, and the distinction between these types is not strictly determined either by ethnicity or by the quality of pasturage ('rich' vs 'meagre') (see Bodo, Musso and Viazzo 2002).

Here, I shall compare the commercial success and the degree of transformation of two types of alpage cheese, Bitto and Strachìtunt, produced in two localities about 80 km apart in Lombardy, in northern Italy. Both are celebrated mountain, peasant cheese whose re-evaluation has changed their production processes and location. In the case of Bitto cheese, made of mixed goat's and cow's milk, growing consumer demand led to changes in its formulation and in the areas where it was produced. In the case of Strachìtunt, the struggle to have it recognised as a protected cheese made only in Valtaleggio has sparked a set of local conflicts which has so far prevented it from becoming the pivot of successful projects for sustainable development and eco-tourism.

The politics, the poetics and the irony of the re-invention of a traditional food such as alpage cheese, currently rediscovered to promote marginal alpine areas, lie in its complexity, nuances and ambiguities. Firstly, the peasant is meant as the protagonist of local development, and tasteful food consumption becomes an aesthetic and ethical value that is directly linked with the knowledgeable practice of such protagonists. This entails acknowledging 'low' foods in *haute cuisine*, 'contaminating' elite tastes, food styles and networks of distribution (typically expensive restaurants, gourmet food shops and the like). Low, peasant foods are re-evaluated by wealthy, niche consumers, both because they epitomise healthier and more ethical lifestyles and because they are seen as better nutritionally than *haute cuisine*. Networks of connoisseurs, restaurant guides and retail chains contribute to turning typical and local products into new types of luxury commodities. The mastery of tasting skills, recipes and knowledge about the origins of foodstuffs becomes, therefore, proof of a higher quality of life as well as of knowledge of one's territory. Local food itself, then, is celebrated as an element of cultural heritage.

The irony in this process is the associated proliferation of new technical, social and political actors around the producers, often with ambivalent outcomes. In one case, the rising fame of, and demand for, Bitto cheese from Valtellina has brought about a progressive expansion of the certified *terroir* producing DOP Bitto. In the attempt to have the whole province gain from the increased interest in a 'local' product, the process of expansion was continuous since certification in 1995. Also, the proportion of goat's milk required by the Bitto trademark consortium was progressively reduced because of the increasing pressure from local cow dairies, which wanted a new market for their milk (a detailed, though partisan, history of Bitto cheese is in Corti 2006). Milk producers in the lower valley tend to use cows rather than goats, while goat herding and mixed herding is more typical in the higher valley. Thus the pressure to allow a higher proportion of cow's milk reflected the shift from the traditional practice of high-pasture dairies to a more industrial mode of production in the lower valley. Finally, a number of traditional producers reacted against this trend and organised themselves in an association which obtained the status of a Slow Food Presidium in 2003, justified on the basis of their usage of traditional recipes, tools and nutritional standards for their cows and goats.[4]

These producers were so successful with their 'real Bitto' cheese that customers order it before it is actually produced (Grasseni 2006). Since October, 2005, this *Associazione produttori Valli del Bitto – Slow Food* have made a public stand by withdrawing from the consortium producing DOP Bitto cheese. The paradoxical situation, then, is that those who claim to produce the most authentic Bitto cheese sell it successfully *against* the European DOP certification, which they have refused by leaving the consortium. They claim that the consortium's geographical spread and protocol of production are not sufficiently restrictive, that the consortium is indifferent to the specificities of the mountain pastures where stock should graze and that too much has been conceded to industrial technology (e.g., the use of ferments) and to an intensive, lowland dairy model (e.g., feeding cows with fodder and supplements).

Here the problem of the authentic-in-practice displays its many facets and contradictions. In order to protect authentic Bitto cheese, a DOP was defined. However, the process and political negotiations it entailed resulted in an enlargement of the area in which the cheese was made and a transformation of the product. The point is that the 'historical' producers have not dropped out of the DOP consortium because it is too demanding, but because they think it is too easy. They achieve a commercial advantage from this; their claimed superiority over mainstream production justifies charging higher prices. However, they also believe that continuing to produce authentically is an ethical issue, for it allows continuity with tradition, sustainability and transparency to the discerning customer.

In this case, the Slow Food support of the association of producers from the Valli del Bitto was important, because it granted them visibility and negotiating power in the name of authenticity and locality. Most importantly, it provided a supporting network of contacts and customers, as well as the authority of Slow Food, to a group of producers who had effectively relinquished the right to call their cheese 'Bitto'. At the time of writing, after years of polemics and increasing quarrels, the regional administration is reported as trying to mediate a compromise.[5] This will succeed only if the DOP protocol recognises different zones of production and differences between the standard DOP practice and a 'traditional' production (including the use of raw milk straight after milking, no use of fodder other than hay or grass, no ferments).

When they come to the media's attention, the political nature of these distinctions appears clearer. The natural–artificial boundary is not, after all, simply a fact, but neither is it reducible to a matter of cultural variability or of semiotic construction. Consider 'traditional' mountain cheese that is 'stabilised' with industrial ferments or made with pasteurised milk. To maintain that ferments and pasteurisation are mere technical interventions would mask a real transformation of the cultural identity of food. On the contrary, innovation inevitably involves political decision making, social practice and debate, as shown in several cases in the social studies of science (see European Commission 2007; Fondazione Giannino Bassetti 2008). The use of new production techniques, in fact, involves strategic operations of calibration of the routines, tacit knowledge, skills and shared representations of its own objects. This case shows the intense activity of boundary construction that accompanies the process of the re-invention of food, changing it from an everyday, family affair to a 'typical' commodity, acknowledged by trademarks and certificates of authenticity.

The case of Strachitunt cheese of Valtaleggio, in the Bergamasque Alps (see Grasseni 2007*a*, 2007*b*), shows the same thing. Not too far from the Valli del Bitto, the cooperative of cow breeders of Valtaleggio, together with a few well-organised cheese traders in the valley, requested a DOP for the valley's Strachitunt cheese in 2004. This is a Gorgonzola-type cheese, made by compounding the curd from two consecutive days (typically, from the evening milking of the first day and the morning milking of the second day) in such a way that, during maturation, the cheese develops natural moulds. In other words, this is a type of natural blue cheese from unpasteurised milk that develops a sharp combination of hot and sweet flavours, thanks to highly diversified bacteria.

Making this cheese requires some skill in working the curd and perforating the cheese before it matures, in order to allow contact with the air. The skill had been almost lost before it was re-established through the intervention of a local cheese merchant and connoisseur. A commercial cheese producer invested in a publicity campaign and led an initiative to build an association of producers. In the context of dwindling mountain agriculture, supporters hope for a successful but strictly local product, the demand for which would increase the demand for milk from the valley's dairy cooperative.

Some of the traders in Strachitunt outside of the valley, though, claim that they have known the recipe for this kind of cheese and kept it alive when it had virtually died out within Valtaleggio, and hence have retained the right to hand down and change the recipe. In other words, they claim justification by lineage rather than by geographical origin. Those within the valley reject this. They say that now that Strachitunt has gained notoriety and has risen in price thanks to the political activism and publicity of the valley's consortium, outsider producers rediscover it, make it according to the recipe they want and sell it as their own, precisely because the absence of certification makes the market open to fraud.

In the case of Bitto cheese, the philosophy of the regional administration seems to be that of cultivating diversity in unity. There would be different kinds of Bitto, more or less real and in greater or lesser quantity, allowing a wide range of producers, from small-scale operations to large dairies in the area, to target more or less discriminating consumers. In the case of Strachitunt, though, the lower negotiating power of the 'traditional' producers (who have failed, for instance, to secure a Slow Food Presidium in the valley), coupled with the small amount of cheese they actually produce, has left them more exposed to what they see as unfair competition.

These two cases of re-invention of mountain cheeses, resulting in heightened local competition, tell us how there is much more to bringing alpage cheese to the consumer than milking cows in the Alps. The strategies involved in the construction and defence of typicality can be positive for local producers, especially if they are associated in strong consortia, but also destructive for a more diffuse and less organised body of smallholders (Grasseni 2007*b*).

Moreover, translating alpage cheese from a subsistence product into a marketable commodity requires a host of activities: commissioning historical and laboratory studies to certify traditional origin, nutritional contents, taste, colour, texture, aroma and so forth; standardising tools, routines and curdling agents; establishing production protocols and the boundaries of areas of certified denomination; being aware of legal tools to defend those boundaries, and being able to use them; promoting the product through appropriate branding and so forth. These combine to displace *alpage* cheese from its local contexts, to recontextualise it within Herzfeld's 'global hierarchy of value'.

In sum, the re-invention of food in terms of 'typical production' or 'food heritage' brings particular kinds of pressure to bear on specific local systems, especially in their relationship with the market, with social structure and with local politics, and that pressure has important effects. In Italy, and in Europe more generally, debate around the preservation of local and traditional foods is heated, whether it focuses on authenticity or economic viability, and the two aspects are often intertwined. Concerns for the strength of regional economies, and the interests lying behind the rediscovery of traditional recipes, provide a useful frame for evaluating the many possible combinations of environmental sustainability, community building, social sustainability (or social conservation), cultural sustainability (rediscovery of tradition) or new conflicts (and new boundaries).

Understanding food, then, involves recognising the technoscientific knowledge that influences its production, as well as the different epistemological, political and economic criteria that shape the generation and application of that knowledge (Lang and Heasman 2004; Wilk 1996, 2006). These different logics and criteria include the survival of large, powerful companies versus the promotion of diffused and diverse contexts of production; the use of intensive animal husbandry in the face of soil and water pollution due to over-manuring; the standardisation of the protocols of production of certified denominations versus the preservation of the diversity of tastes and recipes.

In the face of these differences, ethical consumers want to regain their say and rebuild the conditions for a direct relationship with the producer. As I have explained (Grasseni 2003), the very same alpage cheese, made in a mountain retreat, can be 'cheese for customers' or 'cheese for friends'. As cheese for customers, it may be retained, sold at a later date or for a higher price and is subject only to the impersonal law of economics. As cheese for friends, it can be a gift, a signifier of a personal relationship, and it is given freely (though maybe in the expectation of a counter-gift, which can include trust, appreciation of the product, publicity to potential or returning customers).[6]

I turn now from the complexities of production to those of critical and responsible consumption (Centro Nuovo Modello di Sviluppo 2003; Gesualdi 2002) in Italy. This is a growing phenomenon. The spontaneous association of people, searching for more sustainable livelihoods and for strategies of self-organisation, contrasts with the anonymous strategies and unaccountable decisions of the globalised market, from the bottom, up. This also echoes the point that Collins (this volume) makes: their ethical consumption is not a matter of personal value in any simple way. Rather, it is a creature of social networks and relations that both enable and constrain ethical consumers.

Consuming Critically: Food for Thought

In Italy, a whole constellation of different actors is currently at play in the re-invention of food as a critical way of performing consumption, ranging from Slow Food Presidia and the network of Terra Madre, to 'bottom-up' movements such as the GAS. Those movements are only one of a range of initiatives aimed at re-inventing patterns of distribution and informed consumption, with the objective of influencing production by way of redirecting the choices and lifestyles of self-conscious consumers.

In this regard, it is pertinent that GAS are not simply cooperative purchasing groups. Rather, they are solidary. The purchasing group:

> chooses the products and producers on the basis of respect for the environment and the solidarity between the members of the group, the traders and the producers. Specifically, these guidelines lead to the choice of local products (in order to minimise the environmental impact of the transport), fair-trade goods (in order to respect disadvantaged producers by promoting their human rights, in particular women's, children's and indigenous people's) and reusable or eco-compatible goods (to promote a sustainable lifestyle). (Rete Nazionale di Collegamento dei G.A.S. n.d.)

A recent estimate reports about 507 GAS, but the figure is conservative, both because new groups are constantly created and because the estimate only includes those groups that formally register with provincial networks (Baiocchi 2009). For instance, in a recent meeting of the GAS network in the province of Bergamo, 37 groups were identified as being active in the province, of which only 29 were formally part of the network.

These and other similar movements, which often arise out of associations and initiatives related to the first fair-trade and ethical-finance movements of the 1980s, now focus on strategies and models of self-development and aim to be motors of wide-ranging social, political and economic transformation. Such movements are in the process of establishing more robust and long-lasting networks that could, in turn, negotiate with small farmers and producers, encouraging them to take up more responsible and sustainable practices, thus effectively building new solidarity-based economies (Biolghini 2007; Saroldi 2003).[7] The objective is to reach the critical mass necessary to achieve transformation of the economic system, tilting the balance towards forms of alternative consumption.

An example of such groups is the movement *Bilanci di Giustizia* (Family Budgets for Justice; see Valer 1999). Their mission is to go:

against the grain of contemporary society, by consuming less and better we gain in quality of life and we re-appropriate our own time, we enjoy the pleasures of own-production, we rediscover traditions and new cultures. This is the Budget of Justice: monitoring our own consumption to change the economy starting from small things, from everyday gestures. (Bilanci di Giustizia n.d.)

Born in Verona in 1993, this movement is the initiative of the association 'Blessed be the peace-makers', which is engaged in spreading a new 'culture of sobriety' against thoughtless consumption (and thus resembles somewhat the Quakers described by Collins, this volume). Participants keep a detailed record of all expenses, monthly and then yearly, and analyse them critically with the aim of shifting expenses that entail unhealthy, unsustainable or unjust practices towards fair-trade and organic produce, and towards a general reduction of consumption and waste. Various forms of self-production are preferred, as are alternative and solidary forms of conviviality, tourism and self-training (Riva et al. 2006: 59–62).

This movement is particularly active in the rediscovery of practical know-how in cooking, gardening, toy making and the like. For instance, at a recent *Bilanci di Giustizia* presentation a representative explained home baking as a strategy that allows the re-appropriation of time and skills for one's family. Thus, baking bread becomes a way of better treasuring one's family relationships. This allows one to appreciate the moral, philosophical and possibly religious self-consciousness that accompanies these kinds of choices, and their difference from the preference for specialist recipes and tastes that is becoming the norm even within mass consumption. Those who bake bread at home need not be critical or ethical consumers: making bread can be just another way of enjoying one's everyday food, part of a thoroughly consumerist striving for product diversification, or it can be based on health needs and preferences. However, this particular movement does not treat home baking as a mere technique, but as a self-conscious process of own-production aimed at simplifying food consumption, whilst being acutely aware of all that is entailed (such as one's time, the planet's natural resources and human relationships).

Movements like *Bilanci di Giustizia* do not propose only strategies for family accounting or social ways of making ends meet. In addition, their members study, test and disseminate specific models of practice and relationship. These include distributed leadership and non-violence, as well as social and environmental sustainability attained by way of 'self-reduction'. That is reduced consumption aimed at lessening one's impact on environmental resources, capitalising on relationships and networks, and enjoying one's time as producers (similar to 'degrowth'; see Latouche 2004, 2006). They often choose part-time work, cultivate gardens and prefer public and 'softer' means of transport (e.g., rail rather than air). Their radical approach to consumption as a problem, both in ecological and in ethical terms, has earned them the description of 'new fundamentalists' (Guadagnucci 2007: 17; on the social strain that this can entail, see Isenhour, this volume). In fact, though a lay movement, their source of moral inspiration is visionary Catholic priests such as Gianni Fazzini and Alex Zanotelli, and no more than a thousand families are actively involved in the campaign.

Although this and similar groups are small, they have a significant effect on pertinent scholarship and critical thinking, and their members often participate in various philosophical, sociological and critical movements, such as ecosophy or deep ecology, non-violence and various forms of environmentalism. In the case of the followers of Father Zanotelli, then, references to the Catholic Social Doctrine, especially in its Liberation Theology inflection, are explicit, though the practices and networks of critical and responsible consumption linked to these specific Catholic priests are mostly secular and political.

They rediscover food through a relational apparatus, rather than a technological one (and can therefore be defined as communities of practice, or as 'communities of research'; Manara 2004), rethinking issues such as the alienation of work in the light of their subversive, bottom-up practices. Their members often cultivate not only scholarly learning in various fields, but also practical solutions, good knowledge of their territory, local social and political networks and educational models. Through all of these, they elaborate capacities for social planning and change, while re-appropriating skills as knowledgeable forms of making and sharing.

The Italian panorama of movements and groups that are currently active in redefining consumption is vast and only partially mapped (see Biolghini 2007; Guadagnucci 2007; see also Orlando, this volume). These range from well-rooted, long-time cooperatives engaged in fair trade, to GAS groups and networks, time banks, local self-help funding associations, a nationwide Ethical Bank and much more, with each group having its own history, often intertwined with others as spin-offs or splinter groups or networks of local groups. The people in these movements that I have met are active rethinkers of the urban–rural relationship, of environmental rights and of the rights of peasants (as experts on sustainable development, educational advisers, food scholars, etc.). They are interested in translating sophisticated, critical theory from philosophy, sociology and the hard sciences, with which they have been conversant for years, into practical social action. They are, therefore, interested in experiments in community building and active citizenship, supporting and monitoring regional or local experiments involving short production and distribution chains that take food miles into account and involving local knowledge and skills, and they encourage comprehensive analyses of the environmental impact of intensive agriculture.

It is reasonable, then, for them to try to build *reti di economia solidale* (RES, networks of solidarity-based economy). These are defined according to their national charter (Reti di Economia Solidale 2007) as 'an experiment to build *another kind of* economy, building on the numerous experiences of solidarity-based economy existing in Italy', through 'economic networks that are mutually supportive towards the objective of collective welfare'. Local networks are called *distretti di economia solidale* (DES, districts of solidarity-based economy) after the idea of industrial districts. Their long-term objective is not to use the existing economic system to signal ethical preferences (see Introduction this volume), but to question and change that system by, for instance, linking up with organic producers and affecting regional strategies of local agricultural production.

In addition to their policies and goals, these organisations entail a number of more menial, everyday aspects of engagement that put food, once again, at the forefront, with its own logistics and seasonality, and that point to the material and cultural fabric of economic and relational networks. These can test the will and commitment of the members involved (cf. Collins, this volume). Firstly, these tend to be time-consuming, particularly for those who act as volunteers in the day-to-day management of mailing lists, websites, budgets, logistics and the like. So, for instance, the first comparative analysis of two sample DES, in Rome and Lombardy, stressed the high degree of voluntary work involved, and saw it as hindering these voluntary associations in their efforts to achieve stability and strength and to create actual jobs.[8]

Secondly, local groups need the support of larger networks in order to achieve the competence required to identify local producers and monitor them for their adherence to GAS eligibility criteria (these favoured local products, small producers, organic produce and no exploitation of labour). Small groups of activists do not always have the expertise, contacts and time needed to carry out all the necessary checks on producers, ranging from questionnaires to site visits. Such groups are even less equipped to investigate more complex chains of production and distribution, such as those of energy or water supply.

Thirdly, wider networks are necessary in order to acquire reasonable knowledge of the territory and of available contacts. Such knowledge can help avoid problems like groups of ethical consumer who wish to buy organic but can not find local sources, with the ironic result that too many buy, say, oranges from the same source, which then quickly runs out of stock, or the problem of local farmers who are reluctant to switch to organic methods without adequate funding or trusted contacts who want to buy their produce. Preventing such problems calls for a higher-order coordination among local ethical-finance representatives, stable networks of GAS providing a fairly guaranteed demand, and local agricultural operators. A celebrated instance of that sort of coordination was the rescue of an organic cheese factory, Tomasoni, in the province of Brescia. It was saved from bankruptcy by a network of 200 GAS, already customers of the firm, which provided €140,000, partly in anticipation of future orders and partly through the support of a local ethical-finance cooperative, Mag 2, itself one of the founding members of the nationwide Banca Etica.[9]

The issue of logistics, then, arises even when we consider only basic foodstuffs. Switching from shopping in a supermarket to buying directly from an organic farmer seems not only ethical, but convenient and fun.

Nevertheless, one should keep in mind what it means for people with jobs and families to find the time, storage space, transportation and the like needed to manage orders for large quantities of foodstuff from producers, to collect the orders and pay for them, and to manage the collection of individual members' payments and the distribution of what they ordered. For instance, dealing with rice orders for a group of twenty families twice a year means collecting their orders, driving a car or rented van to the producer, bringing back tens or even hundreds of kilos of rice and either finding the space to store it until members collect it or delivering the rice to them. Managing meat orders entails supervising the butchering, sometimes early in the morning, and organising the packaging of freezer-ready portions of at least 25 kilos for each customer.

Often, those who participate in these groups have extra motivation or specific expertise deriving from special needs. Families with coeliac children, for instance, are used to selecting their rice carefully to avoid contamination with other grains, and they are used to storing large quantities of food. While some members may have special skills and motivations, it is important that groups assure a fair distribution of work among members. Otherwise, tensions may arise between the small set of members who manage orders, logistics, mailing lists and contacts with the producers, and the others, who 'just buy'.

Moreover, relying on seasonal produce means negotiating the difference between the produce actually available on the one hand and, on the other, expectations based on global supply, negotiation that requires some planning and a few renunciations. As opposed to day-by-day shopping according to needs and buying produce that have become fairly uniform all year round, GAS aim to be strictly seasonal. In a meeting I attended we reasoned that, otherwise, the GAS would not distinguish itself from, say, buying fair-trade products such as tea, coffee or chocolate, or from cooperatives that abide by trade-union rules and regulations and sometimes specialise in organic produce but that ship produce in by air. Others, nevertheless, protested that 'one cannot live all winter on cabbage'.

Aside from a sense of consuming ethically and of being an active citizen and consumer, what one seems to gain from being involved in such organisations is a facility at cooperation: the same group of people who share GAS tasks can decide, for instance, to set up a time bank and exchange services on a non-monetary basis, which is easier if people are used to dealing with each other. Networking amongst different kinds of groups engaged with solidarity-based economy is then easier, and this can alleviate some of the problems these groups may face. For instance, a group might choose the nearest fair-trade shop as the place where fresh produce is delivered weekly for members to collect, and so solve the logistical problems presented by this type of food. As well, encouraging members to buy at least one fair-trade product when they collect their orders makes the arrangement more agreeable to the shop.

In sum, while criteria for selection of products and producers and practices are easily theorised and disseminated, the actual practices of critical, responsible or solidarity-based consumption are rooted in specific material contexts, characterised by their own logistics and seasonal issues, by the social history of the group involved and the relationships that develop within it. Engagement relies upon of a vast amount of motivation and dedication from individual members, and each group develops its own alliances, strategies and adjustments.

In the process, what happens to the authenticity and locality that are part of ethical consumption? The real difficulties that self-organised groups such as GAS encounter indicate how deep the hiatus is between production and consumption in contemporary capitalist society. Beyond the will to 'get personal' about food, activists fight to overcome a common lack of skills, contacts and knowledge of their local territory. It is not surprising, then, that in cases such as the Bitto cheese mentioned previously, niche producers more often seek elite customers who are prepared to pay the price for quality, rather than critical consumers who are prepared to pay the price for solidarity.

In the previous section I argued that, in the process of trying to prove its authenticity, local food often gets entangled in technical, political and territorial issues, about fodder for cows, chemically treated milk or administrative, historical and geographical boundaries. Those who produce 'local' food may well find themselves battling for its name or for the defining characteristics matching that name. In this section I have argued that those who strive to consume local food have to overcome logistical, cultural and economic difficulties in order to achieve their goal. If I argued in the previous section, then, that 'local food' is a slippery and disputed concept, in this section I have argued that such food is difficult to find and acquire, well beyond the anonymous laws of demand and offer. Together, these indicate the way that ethical consumption is much more than just the individualist image of the shopper in the supermarket aisle, assessing the value of the products on the shelves.

Conclusion

We have seen how, for both producers and consumers, efforts to re-invent local food in order to make it or name it in more authentic ways are entangled with many different difficulties, not all of which are relevant only locally. In fact, most of these difficulties are significant for a higher-level understanding of issues that are of general importance. The re-invention of food thus includes the symbolic construction of food as an identity strategy; the consequent social positioning of various actors; the perception of technoscience, especially in relation to food hazards; a social representation and construction of 'typical' foods; as well as including the specificities of the contexts of the production and transformation of foodstuffs (including more or less felicitous inputs of technical expertise) and the evolution of the cultural and social contexts of consumption.

It is fairly obvious, then, that typical foods are not always authentically local and that being a critical consumer is much more complex than it may appear at first sight. Beyond that simple conclusion, I have tried to show, however briefly, that there are many possible links, including ambivalent ones, between the patrimonialisation of local food as a form of territorial heritage and its rediscovery as a strategy of sustainable development and cultural critique. There are many facets of, and potential conflicts amongst, the competing strategies of rediscovering food, which include the promotion of typical products as an economic strategy; the convergence of sustainable consumption on local products; the re-evaluation of food as a catalyst for communities of practice that search for and define critical and responsible modes of consumption (Centro Nuovo Modello di Sviluppo 2003; Gesualdi 2002).

Critical consumers could be the ideal customers for local producers who embrace the Slow Food logic of what is 'good, clean and just': indeed, a convergence between Slow Food Presidia and GAS networks is already happening in places. This convergence is significant also for all those who would be left out, including EU and other certification schemes and their corresponding consortia, which often uphold the good of the locality but seem to have been less successful in validating and sustaining the authenticity of geographical origins, recipes and existing patterns of production. The Bitto consortium, for instance, would accuse the historical producers of the Valli del Bitto of elitism, arguing that their limited production and high price means that they want only to cater to a niche clientele. Allowing a larger *terroir* to be trademarked as Bitto, or a higher percentage of cow's milk to be used, would mean benefiting the average local producer, though the result would be a more conventional cheese. Local representatives of the farmers' trade union have argued that introducing changes to traditional products in a way that benefits local producers over a wide area is ethical and democratic, since it contributes to local development. However, others, and especially the traditional producers, would retort that such changes are intended simply to solidify support for the trade union among farmers, and that they would make the cheese more ordinary and so eliminate the market advantage that traditional producers can claim.

These conflicts of interest, and the negotiations and adjustments that they continually entail, are often not perceived by the customer, who may well think that a certification would somehow define a status quo and preserve it. Analogously, the large number of choices, adjustments and negotiations that solidarity-based consumer groups have to make in practice (for instance, having members who do not want to live on cabbage for six months) and the substantial effort involved in maintaining and servicing the network, seem not to be encompassed in the ethical description of values and principles on the one hand, and on the other in the objectives and goals of ethical, critical or responsible consumption.

Granted this combination of contingent complexity and judicious pragmatism, there does not seem to exist an all-encompassing recipe: the destinies of local cultures of consumption will depend on creative, ad hoc solutions to the problem of the contamination of solidarity by calculative reason.

There are many possible politics of food, including the possibility that people seek to have the contexts of local production meet the contexts of local consumption. For instance, Slow Food activists could meet GAS representatives and draw up plans to strengthen the farming basis of local provisioning. This would mean a major innovation in food provisioning, reaching beyond local resonance, though it must be remembered that no innovation is immune to political reasoning and free of conflicts of interest.

The capacity to re-invent themselves as custodians of biocultural diversity, for instance, could become a new form of expertise for small, traditional producers who currently can embrace the big distribution chains by presenting themselves as modern and well-informed entrepreneurs of local commodities, or can stress the sustainable and intangible patrimony of local histories, tacit knowledge and living skills. Both options are laborious. Interesting experiments are emerging in food consumption, inspired by sustainability and co-responsibility, such as the GAS network I described that effectively sponsored their dedicated cheese producer. What will be of interest for the future is to map and identify different possible forms of co-responsible innovation involving both production and consumption, and to monitor their reciprocal adjustments.

Notes

All translations are by the author.

This essay owes a lot to many conversations. Many thanks in particular to Keith Hart, Mao Mollona, Jonathan Parry and all participants in the ESRC *Rethinking economies* seminar, at Bologna in 2006; to Michele Corti and Jeff Pratt for their correspondence; to the participants in the panel and post-panel discussion on ethical consumption convened by James Carrier and Peter Luetchford, in Ljubljana in 2008. Special thanks to the network *Cittadinanza Sostenibile*, created by my colleague Francesca Forno, at Bergamo University; to Andrea Borella and to the GAS 'Time bank' in Bergamo. I have elaborated my 'state of the art' on the re-invention of food in a research project formulated with several other colleagues, in particular Letizia Bindi, Fulvio Manara, Federico Neresini, Elisabetta Moro, Cristina Paganoni and Mario Salomone.

1. I have explained elsewhere (Grasseni 2003) how the transformation of mountain cheese from simply 'local' to 'typical' can be described in terms of Richard Wilk's (1995: 118) concept of 'structures of common difference'.
2. In his work on the transformation of Cretan artisan workshops and products, Michael Herzfeld (2004: 2–3) defines the global hierarchy of value as an 'increasingly homogeneous language of culture and ethics' that 'is everywhere present but nowhere clearly definable'. 'Its very vagueness constitutes one source of its authority … while it often appears as a demand for transparency and accountability'. The aspect that is most interesting with regard to my own work is that it applies to artisanal products, work and workers in such a way that 'even "diversity" can become a homogeneous product. So, too, can tradition and heritage: the particular is itself universalized' (2004: 2).
3. These are intended to safeguard regional foods from fraud or unfair competition. The European legislation came into force in 1992 and is modelled on the French *Appellation* and the Italian *Denominazione di Origine Controllata*.
4. Slow Food Presidia are projects for the conservation of 'endangered' foods and of the breeds involved in their production. Conserving and valuing traditional systems of production, recipes and nutritional standards for local animals is a substantial part of the effort of Slow

Food Presidia. According to the Slow Food Foundation for Biodiversity (n.d.), there exist about 200 such presidia in Italy and another 120 worldwide.

5. With this, the 'historical producers' would accept external controls and DOP certification of their produce, but they would not re-enter the consortium as partners (*Newsletter Ruralpina* 2009). As well, 'traditional' producers who operate in the 'historical' area of Bitto production (which includes a few valleys outside of the Slow Food Presidium) could join the association in order to obtain Slow Food certification.

6. Obviously, the place to start for a reflection on the reciprocity of the gift is Mauss (1990 [1925]). Marco Aime (2002) projects the significance of gift economy on to ethical consumption, the economy of self-reduction (Latouche 2004, 2006) and anti-utilitarianism.

7. According to the working group on 'Other Economy' (AltraEconomia, Rome), an economy based on solidarity is best seen as 'a network, or a network of networks, of economic operators (but also political and cultural operators), whose functioning behaviour is based on ethical and solidarity principles that focus on the communal and collective good' (Biolghini 2007: 11).

8. *Nuovi Stili di Vita* (new lifestyles) was a project running from 2005 to 2008 in the EQUAL framework (favouring opportunities of work in weak social sectors), funded by the European Union. Its aim was to map and promote conditions to set up and support existing RES. The groups in Lombardy were engaged in fair trade, GAS, ethical finance, responsible tourism, time banks, *Bilanci di Giustizia*, biological agriculture (see Vankeerberghen, this volume) and social cooperatives, and 86 per cent of the staff worked on a voluntary basis (Biolghini 2007: 50–56).

9. This is only the latest step in what has been celebrated as a successful process of degrowth, which has brought the firm from a gross product of €2.5 M to about €300,000 per year, specialising in organic Grana Padano (a mature cheese similar to Parmesan) for GAS custom. (Venturelli 2009; thanks to Francesca Forno and Davide Biolghini for providing this information at their seminar 'Sustainable Citizenship', 2009).

Bibliography

Aime, Marco 2002. Introduzione. In Marcel Mauss, *Saggio sul dono*, pp. i–xxviii. Torino: Einaudi.

Baiocchi, Paola 2009. Un'altra economia esiste in rete dal basso. *Valori: Rivista di Economia Sociale, Finanza Etica e Sostenibilità* 67 (March): 19.

Bauman, Zygmunt 1998. On glocalization: or globalization for some, localization for some others. *Thesis Eleven* 54(1): 37–49.

Bilanci di Giustizia n.d. [Opening message, untitled]. Venezia: Bilanci di Giustizia. www.bilancidigiustizia.it

Biolghini, Davide 2007. *Il popolo dell'economia solidale: alla ricerca di un'altra economia.* Bologna: Editrice Missionaria Italiana.

Bodo, Mariangela, Michele Musso and Pierpaolo Viazzo 2002. Dalla Toma alla Fontina: trasformazioni della produzione casearia nella Valle del Lys. In *Formaggi e mercati: economie d'alpeggio in Valle d'Aosta e Haute-Savoie* (eds) S. Woolf and P. Paulo Viazzo, pp. 135–68. Aosta: Le Chateau.

Bourdieu, Pierre 1987. *Distinction: a social critique of the judgement of taste.* Cambridge, Mass: Harvard University Press.

Camporesi, Piero 1993. *Le vie del latte: dalla Padania alla steppa.* Milano: Garzanti.

Centro Nuovo Modello di Sviluppo 2003. *Guida al consumo critico.* Bologna: Editrice Missionaria Italiana.

Corti, Michele 2006. Bitto: una storia esemplare, una questione aperta. *Caseus* 11(3): 20–39.

European Commission 2007. *Taking European knowledge society seriously*. Luxembourg: Office for Official Publications of the European Communities. http://ec.europa.eu/ research/science-society/document_library/pdf_06/european-knowledge-society_ en.pdf

Fondazione Giannino Bassetti 2008. *Science and governance: the report for the European Commission presented at the Bassetti Foundation*. Milano: Fondazione Giannino Bassetti. www.fondazionebassetti.org/en/events/2008/03/science_and_governance_ the_rep.html

Forno, Francesca and Luigi Ceccarini 2006. From the street to the shops: the rise of new forms of political action in Italy. *South European Society & Politics* 11: 197–222.

Forno, Francesca and Carina Gunnarson 2009. Everyday shopping to fight the Italian Mafia. In *Creative participation: responsibility-taking in the political world* (eds) Michele Micheletti and Andrew McFarland, pp. 101–24. London: Paradigm Publishers.

Gesualdi, Francesco 2002. *Manuale per un consumo responsabile, dal boicottaggio al commercio equo e solidale*. Milano: Feltrinelli.

Grasseni, Cristina 2003. Packaging skills: calibrating Italian cheese to the global market. In *Commodifying everything: relationships of the market* (ed) Susan Strasser, pp. 341–81. New York: Routledge.

———— 2006. Slow Food, fast genes: timescapes of authenticity and innovation in the anthropology of food. *Cambridge Anthropology* 25: 79–94.

———— 2007a. *La reinvenzione del cibo: culture del gusto fra tradizione e globalizzazione ai piedi delle Alpi*. Verona: Qui Edit.

———— 2007b. Conservation, development and self-commodification: doing ethnography in the Italian Alps. *Journal of Modern Italian Studies* 12: 440–49.

Guadagnucci, Lorenzo 2007. *Il nuovo mutualismo: sobrietà, stili di vita ed esperienze di un'altra società*. Milano: Feltrinelli.

Herzfeld, Michael 2004. *The body impolitic: artisans and artifice in the global hierarchy of value*. Chicago: University of Chicago Press.

Hobsbawm, Eric and Terence Ranger (eds) 1992. *The invention of tradition*. Cambridge: Cambridge University Press.

Lang, Tim and Michael Heasman 2004. *Food wars: the battle for mouths, minds and markets*. London: Earthscan.

Latouche, Serge 2004. Degrowth economics: why less should be so much more. *Le Monde Diplomatique* (November). http://mondediplo.com/2004/11/14latouche

———— 2006. *Le pari de la décroissance*. Paris: Fayard.

Leigh Star, Susan and James Griesemer 1989. Institutional ecology, 'translations' and boundary objects: amateurs and professionals in 1907–1939. *Social Studies of Science* 19: 387–420.

Lévi Strauss, Claude 1964. *Mythologiques I: Le cru et le cuit*. Paris: Plon.

Manara, Fulvio Cesare 2004. *Comunità di ricerca e iniziazione al filosofare: appunti per una nuova didattica della filosofia*. Milano: Lampi di Stampa.

Mauss, Marcel 1990 [1925]. *The gift*. London: Routledge.

Montanari, Massimo 2004. *Il cibo come cultura*. Bari: Laterza.

Newsletter Ruralpina 2009. Al tavolo convocato dall'assessore ferrazzi passi avanti per la soluzione dei problemi del Bitto. *Newsletter Ruralpina* 9 (April). www.ruralpini. it/Inforegioni4.4.htm

Papa, Cristina 2002. Il prodotto tipico come ossimoro: il caso dell'olio extravergine di oliva umbro. In *Frammenti di economie: ricerche di antropologia economica in Italia* (ed) Valeria Siniscalchi, pp. 150–89. Cosenza: Luigi Pellegrini Editore.

Paxson, Heather 2008. Post-Pasteurian cultures: the microbiopolitics of raw milk cheese in the US. *Cultural Anthropology* 23: 15–47.

Petrini, Carlo 2005. *Buono, pulito e giusto: principi di nuova gastronomia.* Torino: Einaudi.

Polanyi, Michael 1966. *The tacit dimension.* Garden City, NY: Doubleday.

Rete Nazionale di Collegamento dei G.A.S. n.d. What's a G.A.S.? Rete nazionale di collegamento dei G.A.S. www.retegas.org/index.php?module=pagesetter&func=vie wpub&tid=2&pid=10

Reti di Economia Solidale 2007. Carta per la Rete Italiana di Economia Solidale. (Revised 2007.) Reti di Economia Solidale. www.retecosol.org/docs/CartaRes0703. pdf

Riva, Sara, Matteo Zanibelli, Francesco Belotti, Milena Gamba and Sara Omacini 2006. *Un mondo più giusto facendo la spesa insieme: la scelta dei GAS – gruppi di acquisto solidale.* Bergamo: Associazioni Cristiane Lavoratori Italiani.

Roos, Gun, Laura Terragni and Hanne Torjusen 2007. The local in the global – creating ethical relations between producers and consumers. *Anthropology of Food* S2. http://aof.revues.org/sommaire402.html

Saroldi, Andrea 2001. *Gruppi di acquisto solidali: guida al consumo locale.* Bologna: Editrice Missionaria Italiana.

———— 2003. *Costruire economie solidali.* Bologna: Editrice Missionaria Italiana.

Sassatelli, Roberta 2007. *Consumer culture: history, theory, politics.* London: Sage.

Shiva, Vandana (ed) 2007. *Manifestos on the future of food and seed.* Cambridge, Mass: South End Press.

Slow Food Foundation for Biodiversity n.d. *Presìdi Slow Food.* Bra, Italy: Slow Food Foundation for Biodiversity. www.presidislowfood.it/welcome.lasso

Strathern, Marilyn (ed) 2000. *Audit cultures.* London: Routledge.

Valer, Antonella 1999. *Bilanci di giustizia: famiglie in rete per consumi leggeri.* Bologna: Editrice Missionaria Italiana.

Venturelli, Luigina 2009. Le banche tagliano il credito: il caseificio salvato dai clienti. *L'Unità* (27 February). http://archivio.unita.it/archivio/navigatore.php?page=33&dd =27&mm=02&yy=2009&ed=&url=http://82.85.28.102/cgi-bin/showfile. pl?file=edizioni/20090227/pdf/NAZ/pages/20090227_33_27ECO33A.pdf

Wilk, Richard 1995. Learning to be local in Belize: global systems of common difference. In *Worlds apart: modernity through the prism of the local* (ed) Daniel Miller, pp. 110–33. London: Routledge.

———— 1996. Sustainable development: practical, ethical, and social issues in technology transfer. In *Traditional technology for environmental conservation and sustainable development in the Asian-Pacific region* (eds) Kozo Ishizuka, Shigeru Hasajima and Darryl Macer, pp. 206–18. Tsukuba, Japan: University Of Tsukuba.

———— 2006. *Slow food/fast food: the cultural economy of the global food system.* Lanham, Md: AltaMira Press.

Woolf, Stuart 2002. Introduzione. In *Formaggi e mercati: economie d'alpeggio in Valle d'Aosta e Haute-Savoie* (eds) S. Woolf and P. Paulo Viazzo, pp. 7–15. Aosta: Le Chateau.

Conclusion

James G. Carrier and Richard Wilk

People in Europe and North America are presented with a host of messages about problems in the world. Rainforests and polar ice are shrinking, farmers in the Third World are suffering, workers in the foreign factories that make what we buy are exploited, our food is laced with chemicals, our resources are being used up, the climate is warming. Some of these problems are distant, some affect us more closely, but all are problems that many people would like to address.

Given the importance of consumption in those people's lives, it is reasonable that they would accept the idea that they can address those problems through what they buy and use. That idea is manifest in a set of institutions, social movements and practices that encourage people to think about their purchases in terms of the values that they hold, whether about Third World farmers, the environment or Third World workers. The result is ethical consumption, the topic of this volume.

Understanding ethical consumption requires more, however, than looking only at its most visible forms, things like concern for trade justice and the Fairtrade mark, for environmental sustainability and the marks of the Soil Association and the Forest Stewardship Council, for global warming and the EnergyStar and fuel efficiency. These are important. However, if we take the phrase 'ethical consumption' seriously, it is apparent that they are just a part, albeit the most visible part, of something more basic. As laid out in the Introduction to this volume, that is the attempt to protect and advance social values that appear to be threatened by the activities and institutions that are part of the market realm. In the more visible, modern ethical consumption mentioned above, those attempts take a particular form: people are urged to convert their moral values into money terms, and reward some companies and business practices through their market transactions, while punishing others. However, approaching ethical consumption in terms of its basic aspects allows us to see that such attempts can take other forms.

This broader approach allows us to place visible forms of ethical consumption in a comparative frame along with other kinds of consumption, and other kinds of ethical behaviour. Within that frame, as described in the Introduction, we can see other movements and practices in the present and the past that also seek to protect social values threatened by the logic of the marketplace in the economic realm. People may espouse different social values and goals, perceive different threats from the economic realm and employ different means to deal with those threats, but they still are dealing with the same fundamental conflict. Recognising this allows us in turn to think critically about those modern, visible forms of ethical consumption. Why these particular goals and values rather than others; why these means and agents rather than others; what does the choice of goals, means and agents tell us?

These values and goals spring from a concern with social relations and processes that are linked to durable entities and states of being. These are seen as distinct from the relations and processes of the economic realm, which are understood to be linked to transient interests, entities and tasks. As indicated in the Introduction, this difference can be summarised in different ways. For David Schneider (1980 [1968]: 46) it is the distinction between home, the realm of love and sociality, and work, the realm of money and impersonal calculation. For Steve Barnett and Martin Silverman (1979: 51) it is the distinction between people's fundamental attributes, important in the social realm, and their superficial attributes, important in the economic realm. It is summarised as well, albeit in another way, in the distinction that Maurice Bloch and Jonathan Parry (1989) make between transactions oriented toward long-term social goals and values, and transactions oriented toward short-term individual calculation and profit.

Drawing on the Introduction, we have mentioned some of the ways that writers have cast this distinction. However, it is worth remembering that it is an old one in Western thought and that it takes many forms. In anthropology it is perhaps best known as the distinction between gift exchange and commodity exchange, the former oriented toward durable social relations and the latter toward individual, calculative transactions (see Mauss 1990 [1925]; see also Carrier 1995; Gregory 1982). And as Stephen Gudeman (Gudeman and Rivera 1991) reminds us, it extends back to Ancient Greece and outward to Colombian peasants. Indeed, one of us has suggested that the distinction is something like a basic feature of human thought, as people consider their actions in terms of a shorter or longer time frame and a narrower or broader social frame: the short and narrow look like economistic rational calculation; the long and broad look like moral sociability (Wilk 1996: 147–53).

When we approach ethical consumption in terms of the distinction between these realms, and especially in terms of efforts to protect the social from the incursions of the economic, it is apparent that the goals of trade justice, the environment and food safety that drive the visible forms of ethical consumption are only some of the goals that can motivate people who fit our broader definition of ethical consumers. Some of the chapters in this volume describe the less visible forms. One of the most striking instances is described by Tamás Dombos, the woman who selects among objects on offer in terms of how well they express and further her extreme Hungarian nationalism. Examples that are less striking, but equally revealing, are found in the two chapters concerned with Italy. In one of these, Giovanni Orlando describes people in Palermo whose consumption decisions are guided by their dismay at the state of the city and their disgust at the alliance between the Christian Democrats and the Mafia that, they say, brought that state about. In the other, Cristina Grasseni describes sets of people in the north of the country who see in their consumption a vehicle that can bring about a radical reorganisation of commercial and even social life, associated with new systems of producing and supplying food, new collaborative forms of social organisation and new forms of banking.

Unless we restrict the meaning of ethical consumption only to the most visible contemporary forms, the people that Dombos, Orlando and Grasseni describe have to be seen as ethical consumers. However, their sorts of ethical consumption, like the sorts of goals and values that guide them, are relatively invisible. They rarely make it into newspaper articles or television programmes. Dombos points to this matter of visibility in his chapter, when he presents what he calls the 'official discourse' of ethical consumption, and while he is describing a discourse that is presented in Hungary, its main features closely resemble the common presentation of ethical consumption and ethical consumers in many parts of Europe and North America. What he has to say raises an intriguing question: why is the official discourse so limited? A thorough answer to that question is beyond our knowledge and wit. However, it is reasonable to suppose that it springs to a significant degree from the preferred means of the visible forms of ethical consumption.

It is fairly obvious that those preferred means revolve around market transactions. It should be equally obvious, however, that saying this does not tell us very much. After all, Keynesian economic policies, the cooperative movement and even the Luddite movement revolved around transactions in markets. It is more rewarding to say that the official discourse that Dombos describes revolves around a particular sort of market transaction and, more profoundly, a particular sort of market transactor, the agent in that discourse. These transactions and transactors are those associated with an ideology that is often seen to be fairly recent and is given the name 'neoliberalism'. It is probably more realistic to see them as important aspects of what Marx, a very long time ago, had to say about bourgeois individualism, elements of the ideology of the free market (see Carrier 1997).

The sort of market that the official discourse invokes is one in which autonomous transactors dispassionately consider the attributes of the objects on offer. Like the Homo Economicus of neoclassical economics (see Nelson 1998), they assess these objects in light of the purchaser's utility function, but unlike most of the common representations of Homo Economicus, their utility function includes the social and environmental dimensions of what is for sale. The choice is made, the sale is completed and the transactors walk away. Of course the transaction has consequences, as the notion of the market signal reminds us. However, those consequences flow from the instant of the transaction, not from any subsequent activity of the ethical consumer.

The autonomous, calculating consumers of official discourse also are independent in roles beyond those of buying and selling. That is, they appear to be independent of pretty much all social ties of any substance, as well as independent of all social groups. With this independence, they embody a particularly pure form of freedom, which, as we describe below, is a complex notion that many people value highly. Our ethical consumer of the official discourse may well have a family and responsibilities towards it. However, this is a vague and abstract family. It resembles something like the idea of familiness, the sort of general notion of the family described by Schneider (1980 [1968]: 45) and discussed in the Introduction. In other words, this is an idealised realm of familial affection rather than a real family with a real past and full of real people that could constrain or even define our ethical consumer.

In being idealised, this ethical consumer's family resembles the producers that, it appears, many ethical consumers want to assist. The ethical coffee in the bag on a supermarket shelf has a past full of the people who grew, processed and shipped it. However, as Peter Luetchford describes in his chapter in this volume, the information the purchaser has concerning them is vague to the point of being generic. They represent the idea of Third-World coffee growers. They are not real people who have a significance, or even an existence, that is beyond the consumer's control. Moreover, as Audrey Vankeerberghen's chapter on organic agriculture in Belgium indicates, many people appear happy to abandon the real producers in favour of the images.

In addition, in the official discourse that Dombos describes those consumers may be concerned with their neighbourhood or locality. Again, however, these are vague and abstract, and they appear to come into being only because of their relationship with the ethical consumer. The neighbourhood of this discourse is where the consumer happens to live, and if he or she moves house, it will cease to exist and a new one will take its place. Unlike this abstraction, real localities and groups are rather different. Like the nation of Hungary and the city of Palermo, they exist independently of the ethical consumer and they constrain and even define that consumer in ways that belie the image of the asocial individual judging objects in the marketplace according to their utility.

In sum, then, in their preferred means, the most visible forms of ethical consumption imagine preferred agents, who are egocentric, asocial market transactors who live in a world of no social groups or institutions that have a constraining force, or even an existence, independent of the market actor's will. These imagined transactors are free of the socio-moral structures of religion, the sort of beliefs and institutions that Peter Collins describes in his chapter in this volume, just as they are free of the sorts of social pressures that Isenhour describes in hers. Moreover, while these people may be concerned with family and neighbourhood, these are idealised in a way that strips them of independent existence and force.

In implying such a market, such transactors and such a world, the official discourse presents an image that resonates with powerful beliefs about what it means to be a modern person. Those beliefs have a power that is likely to make the image attractive, and also make attractive the forms of ethical consumption that accord with it. However, they exclude many things from view. Most obviously, to reinforce a point made in the Introduction, in portraying an imagined maker and consumer who meet in a market transaction, they exclude everyone who stands between these two, imaginary people. There are many such people, they impose many costs and they carry many costs.

More importantly for the argument we are making here is that the market, transactors and world portrayed in the official discourse exclude the sorts of ethical consumption that spring from people's understanding of themselves as being part of social groups and rooted in particular locations, rather than independent beings, as they exclude from view the ways that these groups can react to, and so shape, people's ethical consumption. In this, the official discourse creates and ignores a contradiction (see Moberg and Lyon 2010). The world that it imagines and projects appears to lack the durable relationships and long-term values that ethical consumption often is supposed to express.

Unless, of course, the values and relationships associated with these forms of ethical consumption are themselves like the family and neighbourhood of the official discourse and the Third-World coffee growers portrayed on the bag of coffee. Unless, that is, they are not things that are part of people, but instead are abstracted, idealised representations of such things. Considering this possibility can cast a somewhat different light on the distinction that Daniel Miller (2001) makes, between moral and ethical consumption. Like the official discourse, that distinction is considered especially in the chapter by Dombos, but it appears also at various other points in this volume. For Miller, remember, moral consumption centres on the household in which the consumer exists. On the other hand, ethical consumption centres on distant others.[1] If what we have argued here is correct, then Miller's moral and ethical realms may not be centred in the way that they may appear at first glance, on the household and on what goes on outside of it.

Rather than being centred on the household, the moral realm looks like a realm of social entities of which the consumer is a member, and that define and constrain that person in a way that is, or perhaps only is perceived to be, independent of that person's will. That realm is likely to include the household, for regardless of the image of Homo Economicus, we are defined and constrained by the others in our households independently of our will. However, it seems that the moral realm can include as well Hungary and its history, for these appear to define and constrain Dombos's extreme nationalist independently of her will, as it seems that it can include Palermo and its history, for these appear to define and constrain Giovanni's ethical consumers independently of their will.

Miller's ethical realm, on the other hand, is one of abstract entities and relationships that, in their abstraction, are very different. The coffee growers portrayed on the package may well be real and may in fact have grown what it is in the bag. However, when they are portrayed they are abstractions, growers idealised and made legible as part of a market transaction, nothing like the complex sets of producers Grasseni describes in her chapter, with their legitimate but conflicting moral claims. These idealised growers on the bag may endow the coffee with an ersatz personality that people find appealing (Carrier 1995: Chap. 6). They do not, however, embody a social entity that defines and constrains us. We have no dealings with these people, we have only the images, which intrude only if we let them. If we ignore the images, those people do not exist for us. Less obviously, this realm of distant others may include people in our neighbourhood, or even in our own household if we have an au pair or a servant. While we may be attracted by abstract representations of the ideas of community and neighbourhood, our lives may be so ordered that we have no noticeable social relationships with those who live on our street. In this regard, it is interesting that Miller (2008) himself has recently argued that people's link to their neighbourhood is very different from the ideal.

Miller's moral realm, then, is likely to include those in our household. However, it can include as well people and things at a distance. Equally, the distant others of his ethical realm may be very close to us indeed.

We have pointed to the same tension between the goals, means and agents of the most visible forms of modern ethical consumption that others have noted. That tension is likely to have consequences that are unfortunate, for it may well reduce the chance that ethical consumers can act in ways that will bring about the world that they seek. However, it may also be difficult to resolve this tension, at least in some areas of the world. Those are the areas where the notion of the autonomous individual is entrenched strongly, a notion that often carries with it a concern for, or at least a rhetoric of, freedom. This is another of the contextual factors considered in this volume that affect the practices of ethical consumption. We want to look at how this is so in one such place, North America.

In this, we draw on the work of George Lakoff, especially his discussion of the metaphors of North American conceptions of freedom. They include a whole strange, loose agglomeration of different things, like property rights, political speech, wealth, justice and shopping. These are brought together not by any kind of natural order or logic, but by their common role in constructing the metaphor of freedom in its modern, and particularly North American, cultural form.

Lakoff's concern with metaphor reflects his earlier work, with Mark Johnson (esp. Lakoff and Johnson 1980). In that work, Lakoff and Johnson argued that much human thought is not reducible to logic in its formal sense. Rather, it reflects fundamental metaphors that people live by. These metaphors are embodied, in the sense that they reflect and assign significance to physical experience. They shape thought and judgement by being the core of 'fuzzy sets', made up of events or ideas that more or less resemble the core metaphor that defines the set.

For Lakoff, the centre of what he sees as the core North American form of freedom is what he (2006: 25–6) calls 'simple freedom', which is based on an embodied experience, non-metaphorical and uncontested:

> Freedom is being able to do what you want to do, that is, being able to choose a goal, have access to that goal, pursue that goal without anyone purposely preventing you. … Political freedom is about the state and how well a state can maximize freedom for all its citizens. … A free society is one in which such 'basic freedoms' are guaranteed by the state.

Freedom of this sort is visceral because it is metaphorically connected to the experience of being restrained, confined or threatened. Freedom is experienced bodily, as the movement entailed in escaping confinement or reaching a destination, acquiring a desired object or performing a desired action. The metaphors of simple freedom connect desire, the physical experience of wanting something, with autonomous action to satisfy that desire. This, in turn, connects quite well with some common views of consumption, an activity in which desire is satisfied. It also helps explain why, in places like North America, the free market is valued as an ideal: that is the realm in which people are free, for they act autonomously to satisfy their desires.

Lakoff goes on to dissect the North American folk model of how freedom works, through the action of a homunculus-like agent residing in people's heads called the 'will'. North Americans believe that this will motivates action, that it can be strong or weak, and that true freedom comes when the will prevails over internal weakness, emotions and passions, and over external obstacles and temptations. From there he goes on to show how this simple, embodied form of freedom underpins American folk theories of rights, justice, property, security, law and the role of the state.

In this worldview, there are only two situations where the free will can legitimately be thwarted or limited. One is by nature, which imposes limits. We may disagree about what is natural but, as Lakoff (2006: 53) observes, everyone agrees that when an earthquake strikes, or we are struck down by an injury, this is not an abridgement of freedom. The other legitimate way freedom is limited is through competition for scarce resources. Freedom to compete is accepted, as long as the rules of competition are seen as 'fair'. As Lakoff (2006: 57) says, 'If you are free to enter the competition, there is no abridgement of freedom. If you lose or are eliminated on the basis of rules, there is no abridgement of freedom.'

This notion of fairness under competitive rules leads into contested territory, because it turns out that there are a wide variety of different principles that can be used to decide what is fair (see Lakoff 1996). This is important, because it underlies ideas about equity of distribution and rights to use and own things, and it may underlie our consistent failure to understand the values and processes used by people when making choices in the marketplace.[2]

Lakoff (2006: 50–1) identifies different kinds of fairness, some of which are important for certain forms of ethical consumption. As is apparent, some are mutually compatible, while some can not coexist with others. However, all should be familiar to us from childhood arguments and family negotiations.

> Equality of distribution (one child, one cookie)
> Equality of opportunity (one person, one raffle ticket)
> Procedural distribution (playing by the rules determines what you get)
> Equal distribution of power (one person, one vote)
> Equal distribution of responsibility (we share the burden equally)
> Scalar distribution of responsibility (greater abilities, greater responsibilities)
> Scalar distribution of rewards (the more you work, the more you get)
> Rights-based fairness (you get what you have a right to)
> Need-based fairness (you get what you need)
> Contractual distribution (you get what you agree to)

It is not hard to see that many of the debates about globalising trade and about trade justice, for instance, are founded in conflicting definitions of fairness.

One thing that should be clear from what Lakoff says is that people in North America are prone to take a highly sceptical view of government regulations, even if those regulations are intended to bring about the goals that ethical consumers espouse. That is because such regulations would threaten the practical efficacy of people's freedom to choose, by restricting their ability to achieve their goals through wilful purchases. This sceptical view was illustrated during the recent debate in the US Senate about increasing standards for automobile fuel economy, when Tom Coburn, Senator from Oklahoma, said: 'What if you want to drive a gas hog? You don't have the right any longer in this country to spend your money to drive a gas hog?' (in Mirsky 2009) Similarly, during that same week one of us overheard an angry couple at a sushi bar complaining that 'soon the FDA [US Food and Drug Administration] is going to be telling us what we can and can not order in a restaurant!'

A different implication of what Lakoff says may be less clear. That is that the everyday notion of freedom that he describes is likely to lead to sterile debates that oppose freedom to regulation, as if these two formed a single linear scale. As we see from Lakoff's analysis, that notion of freedom is not formally logical, however much people try to persuade each other that it is so. Rather, it is a name for a fuzzy set that is centred on a bodily sense of unfettered ability to reach a goal or obtain a desired substance. The logic that binds law, rights, political action and the marketplace is metaphorical, not formal, and there are many alternative alignments.

Lakoff's analysis helps unpack, and so shed light on, the freedom that many people value and that they claim in their market transactions. However, there is more light to be shed. The freedom that Lakoff describes is valued as a good.

However, his analysis indicates that it is a good because it serves a purpose: it allows the will to act to achieve its goals. Freedom is a virtue, then, because it facilitates the purposeful expression of the will. Equally, government regulation is an evil because it hinders that purposeful expression. This accounts for the stress on market choice and market mechanisms in the more visible forms of modern ethical consumption.[3] However, this logic seems less compelling when we recognise that the focus on choice in a free market diverts attention from mechanisms other than government regulations that constrain the ability of wilful people to achieve their goals.

Some of these mechanisms are social. This is apparent in Cindy Isenhour's chapter on Swedish ethical consumers, as well as in some of the cases that Dombos describes. What they present is some of the ways that people are constrained by the people they know and by their broader social world. These constraints can be simple: advocating ethical consumption can alienate one's friends and acquaintances. More subtly, practising ethical consumption can mean having possessions that deviate in undesirable ways from the standards of one's group, and so can bring about censure and rejection. In both circumstances, ethical consumers are not the autonomous calculators of the official discourse, but instead are constrained by the social costs entailed in their consumption.

Other chapters in this volume point to another constraint, one coming from the market itself. If freedom is to be efficacious, people need reasonably accurate knowledge of the world that they confront. Without that knowledge, the will that Lakoff describes may be able to express itself. However, the activities that express that will may be misdirected, so that the desired goal comes no closer. This constraint is as serious as government regulation. It is one result of the processes of the ethical-consumption commerce described in the Introduction, and it is illustrated in some of the chapters in this volume. In different ways, for instance, Peter Luetchford, Lill Vramo and Amanda Berlan describe how the values and assumptions of ethical consumers lead them to misperceive the nature of the objects that they confront, so that their wilful actions do relatively little to help them achieve the goals that they espouse. In Luetchford's case, those misperceptions concern the way coffee is grown, in Vramo's case they concern the values that Bangladeshi women place on wage labour, in Berlan's case they concern the operation of the cocoa market and chocolate companies.

As indicated in the discussion of ethicality in the Introduction, these misperceptions do not require acts of wilful deception for commercial purposes. Certainly such deception exists, and instances of it are described in the Introduction. However, the sheer existence of a body of ethical consumers in a market system makes it likely that those misperceptions will occur. We do not, of course, argue that wilful deception and market mechanisms are the only causes of these misperceptions: as Berlan argues in her chapter, more fundamental cultural processes can lead to them as well. However, given the stress in ethical consumption on the market, it is intriguing that the operation of the market is itself so prone to induce misperception.

These reflections about freedom, values, knowledge and practice lead us back to an important point about the nature of ethical consumption, a point made at the beginning of the Introduction. People can be guided by a variety of ethical values when they decide what to buy. However, and for reasons that we have barely begun to consider here, only some of those have become visible as present-day ethical consumption. The rest will be denied their place in Herzfeld's (2004) global hierarchy of value, and instead will be relegated to the obscurity of mere localism, like the Palermo people and the Hungarian nationalists that Orlando and Dombos describe. That visibility has an important consequence: it makes it more likely that ethical consumption reflecting these values will attract followers and the support of international organisations, and so become significant social movements of the sort that attracts scholarly attention. However, that very visibility increases the likelihood that the goals of those who practice the visible forms of ethical consumption will be incorporated in ethical consumption commerce. This in turn increases the likelihood that those people will be reduced to a specialised market that firms seek to attract with specialised products, just as it increases the likelihood that their very notion of an ethical state of affairs, ethicality, will be shaped by the impersonal commercial pressures that many of those ethical consumers appear to dislike.

Thus, the tension between social goals and market means can operate in a way that hinders ethical consumers in their efforts to address the problems that they see in the world. This, in its turn, may lead them to change what they do. It might lead them to select different means, perhaps seeing government action as more appropriate than individual market choice. However, it might lead them to quietism, to a turning inward. That is, it might induce them to abandon their desire to address problems that they see in the larger world, and instead focus on a moral private life.

Notes

1. In this, Miller is applying to purchasing decisions a distinction that has long interested anthropologists. That is the distinction between one's obligations to and dealings with those within one's group as opposed to those outside of it. A classic, extended discussion of this is by Marshall Sahlins (1974).
2. There is now a substantial literature on the failure of consumers to live up to their stated morality. In the case of environmentalist morality, see, for example, Belk, Devinney and Eckhardt (2005), Östberg (2003) and the collections edited by Bevir and Trentmann (2007) and by Boström and Klintman (2008).
3. It may also help account for why people in North America are less likely than those in many parts of Europe to pursue ethical consumption, which can easily be seen as entailing a set of constraints on consumers' choices.

Bibliography

Barnett, Steve and Martin Silverman 1979. Separations in capitalist societies: persons, things, units and relations. In *Ideology and everyday life*, S. Barnett and M. Silverman, pp. 39–81. Ann Arbor: University of Michigan Press.

Belk, Russell W., Timothy Devinney and Giana Eckhardt 2005. Consumer ethics across cultures. *Consumption, Markets and Culture* 8: 275–89.

Bevir, Mark and Frank Trentmann (eds) 2007. *Governance, consumers and citizens*. London: Palgrave Macmillan.

Bloch, Maurice and Jonathan Parry 1989. Introduction: money and the morality of exchange. In *Money and the morality of exchange* (eds) J. Parry and M. Bloch, pp. 1–32. Cambridge: Cambridge University Press.

Boström, Magnus and Mikael Klintman (eds) 2008. *Eco-standards, product labelling and green consumerism*. London: Palgrave Macmillan.

Carrier, James G. 1995. *Gifts and commodities: exchange and Western capitalism since 1700*. London: Routledge.

———— 1997. Introduction. In *Meanings of the market: the free market in Western culture* (ed) J.G. Carrier, pp. 1–67. Oxford: Berg.

Gregory, C.A. 1982. *Gifts and commodities*. London: Academic Press.

Gudeman, Stephen and Alberto Rivera 1991. *Conversations in Colombia*. New York: Cambridge University Press.

Herzfeld, Michael 2004. *The body impolitic: artisans and artifice in the global hierarchy of value*. Chicago: Chicago University Press.

Lakoff, George 1996. *Moral politics*. Chicago: University of Chicago Press.

———— 2006. *Whose freedom? The battle over America's most important idea*. New York: Farrar, Straus and Giroux.

Lakoff, George and Mark Johnson 1980. *Metaphors we live by*. Chicago: University of Chicago Press.

Mauss, Marcel 1990 [1925]. *The gift: the form and reason for exchange in archaic societies*. London: Routledge.

Miller, Daniel 2001. *The dialectics of shopping*. Chicago: University of Chicago Press.

———— 2008. *The comfort of things*. Cambridge: Polity.

Mirsky, Steve 2009. Bad mileage driving tips. *Scientific American* podcast (1 June). www.scientificamerican.com/podcast/episode.cfm?id=bad-mileage-driving-tips-09-06-01

Moberg, Mark and Sarah Lyon 2010. What's fair? The paradox of seeking justice through markets. In *Fair trade and social justice: global ethnographies* (eds) S. Lyon and M. Moberg, pp. 1–24. New York: NYU Press.

Nelson, Julie A. 1998. Abstraction, reality and the gender of 'Economic Man'. In *Virtualism: a new political economy* (eds) James G. Carrier and Daniel Miler, pp. 75–94. Oxford: Berg.

Östberg, Jacob 2003. *What's eating the eater? Perspectives on the everyday anxiety of food consumption in late modernity*. (Lund Studies in Economics and Management 75). Lund: Lund Business Press, Institute of Economic Research. www.lub.lu.se/luft/diss/soc_428/soc_428.pdf

Sahlins, Marshall 1974. On the sociology of primitive exchange. In *Stone Age economics*, M. Sahlins, pp. 185–276. London: Tavistock.

Schneider, David 1980 [1968]. *American kinship: a cultural account.* (Second edition). Chicago: University of Chicago Press.

Wilk, Richard 1996. *Economies and cultures: foundations of economic anthropology.* Boulder, Col.: Westview Press.

NOTES ON CONTRIBUTORS

Amanda Berlan is an anthropologist based at the Brooks World Poverty Institute and Sustainable Consumption Institute of the University of Manchester. She specialises in cocoa production and has carried out field work in West Africa, India and the Caribbean. Her main research interests are ethical trade, child rights and social and economic sustainability in cocoa farming. Her recent publications include 'Child labour in cocoa: whose voices prevail?' (*International Journal of Sociology and Social Policy*, 2009) and 'Making or marketing a difference? An anthropological examination of the marketing of fair trade cocoa from Ghana' (*Research in Economic Anthropology*, 2008).

James G. Carrier has taught anthropology and sociology, and carried out research, in Papua New Guinea, the United States and the United Kingdom, as well as studying environmental conservation in Jamaica. He is Hon. Research Associate at Oxford Brookes University and Adjunct Professor of Anthropology at the University of Indiana. His pertinent publications include *Gifts and commodities* (Routledge, 1995), *Meanings of the market* (ed, Berg, 1997) and *Virtualism, governance and practice* (ed, Berghahn, 2009, with P. West).

Peter Collins is Senior Lecturer in the Department of Anthropology, Durham University. His research interests include religion, ritual and symbolism, historical anthropology, space and place and narrative theory. He recently published *Quakers and Quakerism in Bolton, Lancashire 1650–1995* (Edwin Mellen, 2010), and has co-edited *The Quaker condition* (Cambridge Scholars Press, 2009, with P. Dandelion), *Locating the field* (Berg, 2006, with S. Coleman), *Texts and religious contexts* (Ashgate, 2006, with E. Arweck) and *The ethnographic self as resource* (Berghahn, 2010, with A. Gallinat). He has carried out field work among British and Kenyan Quakers, and local government employees and hospital chaplaincies in the North of England.

Tamás Dombos is a Ph.D. student at the Department of Sociology and Social Anthropology at Central European University, in Budapest, studying ethical consumption in Hungary. In addition, he is an occasional lecturer at the College for Social Theory at Corvinus University, in Budapest, is a junior research fellow at the Center for Policy Studies at Central European University and is an editor of the quarterly interdisciplinary journal *CaféBábel*.

Cristina Grasseni lectures in social and visual anthropology at the University of Bergamo. Her current research interests include the ethnography of alternative food networks and the revival of traditional foods. Among her most recent publications are *Skilled visions: between apprenticeship and standards* (ed, Berghahn, 2007) and *Developing skill, developing vision: practices of locality at the foot of the Alps* (Berghahn, 2009).

Cindy Isenhour completed her Ph.D. in the autumn of 2010 and is currently teaching anthropology and international studies at the University of Kentucky. Focused at the intersection of political ecology and economic anthropology, her research is concerned with neoliberal environmental governance and the contemporary focus on consumer responsibility in European sustainability policy. Her work has appeared in *American Ethnologist*, *The Journal of Consumer Behavior* and in several edited volumes.

Peter G. Luetchford is lecturer in anthropology at the University of Sussex, and has carried out field research in Costa Rica and Spain. He has published on ethics and the economy, including *Fair Trade and a global commodity: coffee in Costa Rica* (Pluto Press, 2008), and he is co-editor of *Hidden hands in the market: ethnographies of fair trade, ethical consumption and corporate social responsibility* (*Research in Economic Anthropology* 28, 2008). More recently he has been writing and publishing on alternative food provision in Europe and is currently working on a volume on that theme.

Giovanni Orlando recently completed his doctoral thesis in anthropology, 'New Moral Economies in Western Sicily: Fair-trade and Organic Agriculture between Change and Constraint', at Goldsmiths College, University of London. He is interested in alternative economic movements, issues of social and environmental embeddedness, and political activism. His pertinent publications include 'Sustainable food vs unsustainable politics in the city of Palermo: the case of an organic farmer's market', in a special issue of *City & Society: Sustainability as myth and practice in the global city* (2012).

Audrey Vankeerberghen is a Ph.D. student at the Université Libre de Bruxelles working on food and agriculture from a social-anthropological perspective. She is a member of the university's *Laboratoire d'anthropologie des mondes contemporains*. She is currently carrying out her doctoral research on organic farming in the southern part of Belgium.

Lill M. Vramo is an anthropologist who has carried out research in India and Bangladesh. She is a research fellow at the National Institute for Consumer

Research in Oslo, and is currently working on her Ph.D. on transnational consumption, focusing on Indian Sikhs living in Oslo. Her pertinent publications include *'Trade not aid', an anthropological analysis of fair trade between Norway and Bangladesh* (University of Oslo, 2006).

Richard Wilk is professor of anthropology and director of food studies at Indiana University. He has done research with Mayan people in the rainforest of Belize, in West African markets, and in the wilds of suburban California. His most recent books are *Home cooking in the global village* (Berg, 2006), *Off the edge: experiments in cultural analysis* (ed, Museum Tusculanum, 2006, with O. Löfgren), *Fast food/slow food* (Altamira, 2006) and *Time, consumption, and everyday Life* (ed, Berg, 2009, with E. Shove and F. Trentmann).

Index

history of corruption, 150–52
importance of public employees in, 155–56
peripheral city, 144
See also clientelism
Parry, Jonathan, 6–7
Parsons, Talcott, 4–5
Participatory Guarantee System (of organic certification), 109–11
as collective evaluation, 110
Pax World (mutual fund / unit trust company), 26–27
pieceworkers vs real work, 89
plain, the – *See* the plain; plaining
plaining (Quaker principle), 181–89, 191–92
basis in Biblical text, 189, 194
and consumption, 184
distinct from most ethical consumption, 194–95
See also the plain
Polanyi, Karl, 8–9
prestige posh, 172
producer-consumer relations
in absence of social interaction, 37, 41–42
direct, 13–14
in ethical coffee, 60–62, 64–65
in Fair Shop Ltd, 40, 92–94
in organic farming, 41
personality in, 19, 42
Product (RED), 23
Protected Designation of Origin, 201
complexities in certification, 204–05
See also certification systems
Purity and danger (by M. Douglas), 53

Q

Quaker consumption, 11, 22
Quaker discipline
Biblical basis of, 181–82, 191
dynastic Quakers, 182–83, 192–93
inculcation of habitus, 191
Minutes, 184
mutual surveillance, 190–91
organisational nature of, 181–83, 189–91, 195
reach of, 191–92
social costs of, 181, 193–95
social nature of, 183, 191
Quaker dynasties, 122, 182–83, 192–93
abandoning the faith, 193–94
Quaker faith and practice (key Quaker writing), 183, 189
Quaker meeting, 187
Quaker meeting house, 183
Quaker meetings (organisational units), 189–91
social aspects, 189–90

Quakers
early religious practices, 186–88
egalitarianism, 187–88
as merchants, 192
opposition to established church, 186, 190–91
origins of, 184–86
rules of behaviour, 187–89
social background, 191–92

R

Rainbow Alliance (certification agency), 63
re-inventing food
by consumers, 206
complexity of, 202, 211
cultural and economic aspects of, 205
effects of on local systems, 205
re-evaluation of local resources and history, 200
symbolic aspects, 201
relationship coffees, 60–61
Religious Society of Friends – *See* Quakers
Renault Twingo (automobile), 26–27
retro-chic, 170–72

S

Sahlins, Marshall, 44, 226
São Tomé cocoa plantation, 49–50
Sassatelli, Roberta, 127
Sayer, Derek, 145–46
Schneider, David, 4–5
Sewing Section, 88
association with poverty, 89
pieceworkers in, 88–89
pieceworkers' tales, 90
presentation to Fair Shop Ltd management, 90
See also Fair Shop Ltd
sharecropping – *See* coffee growers
shopping
alienation in, 62–63
and ethical consumption, 2
as intersection of economy and society, 3
signalling ethical consumption, 121, 171
conspicuous ethical consumption, 23–24, 169
difficulties, 23, 121
exclusions, 25
through taste, 24
signalling system, 5–6
Cafédirect as part of, 16
and ethical certification, 18
and ethical consumption, 26
and investors, 27
two-way flow, 52

www.ingramcontent.com/pod-product-compliance
Lightning Source LLC
Chambersburg PA
CBHW060034030426

42334CB00019B/2323